HELL AND HIGH WATER

ONE MAN'S ATTEMPT TO SWIM THE LENGTH OF BRITAIN

SEAN CONWAY

EBURY
PRESS

1 3 5 7 9 10 8 6 4 2

Ebury Press, an imprint of Ebury Publishing
20 Vauxhall Bridge Road
London SW1V 2SA

Ebury Press is part of the Penguin Random House group of companies
whose addresses can be found at global.penguinrandomhouse.com

Penguin
Random House
UK

First published by Ebury Press in 2015

www.eburypublishing.co.uk

A CIP catalogue record for this book is available from the British Library

ISBN 9780091959746

Typeset by seagulls.net

Printed in Great Britain by Clays Ltd, St Ives plc

CONTENTS

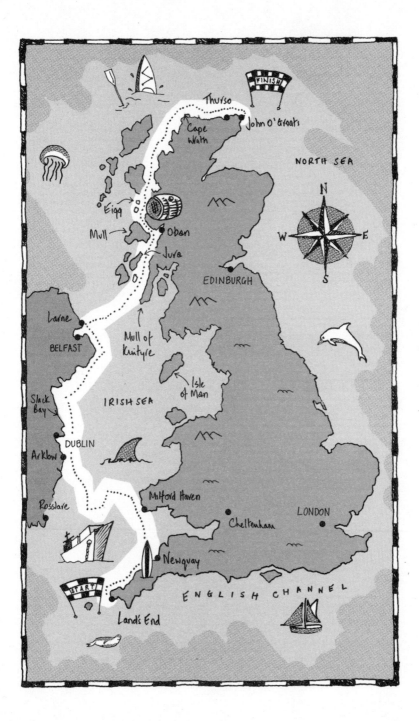

PROLOGUE

A mouthful of salt water rushed down my throat as I tried to breathe into a wave. I nearly vomited. Rain pelted down and ran into my mouth as I struggled for air. Off in the distance a horn started booming across the sea. I looked up to see where it was coming from. A lighthouse possibly? I wasn't sure. Was it a rescue siren for me? My heart started to race as I imagined being rescued on Day 2. That would be embarrassing. The horn carried on for a few minutes as a mist started to roll in, reducing my visibility to nearly nothing. Ah. A foghorn! I felt strangely relieved, but also nervous that perhaps I looked like I needed rescuing. No one in their right mind would swim in this cold, windy and foggy sea by choice.

I pushed on towards the headland where the foghorn was sounding and got caught up in a fast eddy. I pushed and pushed but no matter how hard I tried I wasn't moving. My tired arms, which had now been working for over five hours, just couldn't do it. Em, in the kayak next to me, had a look of despair.

'We're not moving!'

The tide was too strong at this time of day and I had nothing left in the tank. I tried for another 10 minutes but then had to make a decision. I told Em to go ahead to the beach and I looked for a way to get out of the water, as I started to float backwards. The rocks to my right were sharp and broken, and the waves rushed past them with daunting ferocity. I'd surely be knocked out if I got too close. The rise in water height was about one and a half metres. There was one ledge which was about the same height as the crest of each wave. If I timed it correctly, I could get beached on the top and avoid getting washed off. I waited and waited before the right wave lifted me right up to the jagged edge. I kicked hard and landed right on top of the ledge. I held on tight as the wave flowed away. I frantically tried to scramble up the rocks out of the reach of the water but nearly fell back into the sea again. I couldn't feel my feet at all. It was if they were completely separate from my body – numb bits of rubber at the end of my tired legs. Eventually I made it to the safety of the grass above and collapsed.

It was only Day 2 and I couldn't push through one eddy. I guess this was why so many people kept telling me this swim wasn't possible. I lay there for what seemed an eternity wondering if I had in fact completely misjudged the enormity of this challenge.

One thing was for sure, I'd never be able to take two months of this type of swimming.

1

GETTING TO THE START

Two months to go ...

'Sean, my boy. Would you like a cup of tea?'

I sat up and bumped my head on the ceiling. Damn it, I thought. I'm too bloody old to sleep on a bunk bed.

I climbed down the child-sized ladder, my weight nearly toppling the bed over. I'd sleep on the bottom bunk but my entire life seemed to be piled on there. I'd moved back in with my mother almost a year ago. Partly because she has been ill, but mainly to save money for my swim. So, 32 years old and living at home, on a bunk bed. It was depressing to think about it but I really needed to save as much as possible.

I left my tiny room and headed a few metres down the hall to another tiny room at the back of the flat in which I'd constructed a sort of logistical headquarters. It had no windows and the landlord had forgotten to plaster the walls. The upside was I could draw and stick various things

3

onto the wall knowing it would be covered over at some point. One of the first things I bought was a huge poster of the British Isles which I pinned right in front of me. I'd spend at least an hour staring blankly at it, wondering if it was possible to complete such a long sea swim. My heart rate always rose a little when looking at places like Cape Wrath. Yachts have come off second best there, how would a swimmer cope? So many questions to which I'd probably never get answers until I was underway. At this point everything was pure speculation.

Firstly, I had decided, I needed a support boat. I'd toyed with loads of ideas. Initially I was going to do it with just a few kayaks, but then realised we couldn't carry enough water and finding places to come ashore at the exact moment the tide changed would be impossible. The second idea was to get a motorboat, but I soon gave up on that idea when I realised the fuel bill would run into thousands of pounds. The best option was to get a yacht. I started by trawling through eBay. My budget was £4,000. Who was I kidding? I'd never find a 4-berth yacht that was ready to sail for £4,000. I had no other option though. I was planning on getting the money from credit cards, and I'd have to sell the yacht at the end to hopefully make some money back as long as I didn't trash it.

The second brainwave I had was to put a post on a yachting forum. Surely some kind-hearted gentleman who 'just didn't have the time to sail any more' would possibly lend me a yacht? It was a long shot but worth trying.

So the previous night I had posted the following:

In July 2013, I'm going to attempt to become the first person to swim the length of Britain. I'm swimming from iconic Land's End to John O'Groats up the west coast. It's going to be one of the hardest swims of all time and I am trying to raise money for War Child in Africa. I'll be swimming the equivalent of the Channel every day for two months as I battle the 1,000-mile coastal swim.

I am looking for anyone who has a 30-foot yacht that needs a bit of TLC. I'm proposing to get it cleaned up for you if you would be so kind as to lend it to me as a support boat. I'll need it from mid-June to the end of September.

Regards, Sean

There must be someone out there wanting his or her boat fixed for free?

The next morning I was delighted to see quite a few emails in my inbox. Brilliant. I excitedly opened the first one, which came only half an hour after I posted the topic. Keen, I thought. He must know someone.

It read:

'you need to do much more reserch and it will take more like 6 months'

No punctuation and bad spelling. He didn't even answer the question. Never mind. I moved on to the next email with slightly less positivity.

'Frankly I think this idea is totally daft. But you certainly didn't ask for my opinion, nor do you need anyone's permission to try.'

Well, that was helpful, I thought, but he was right on one thing. I didn't need his, or anyone's, permission. A stubborn anger started to build. Emails like that made me want to do it even more. I moved on to the next email.

'A project like this might be better supported with a RIB?'

A short answer and not exactly what I asked but at least we were getting somewhere. I moved on.

'I predict that you will have more problems trying to find a place to berth the yacht every night, 20 miles apart, than you will doing the swim. All-weather ports down the west coast are very few and far between. This will be repeated all the way down the Irish Sea and St George's Channel. A fast MOBO is the only possibility IMHO, a small yacht not an option.'

Logistical advice was great but not quite what I was asking. Also, what was a MOBO? Next.

'I don't want to be too pessimistic but Florence Chadwick who broke the England-France Channel record for both men and women after years of training, was not able to complete the Portpatrick–Donaghadee crossing: about 22 miles.'

What does that have to do with lending me a boat? Next.

'A lot of negative feedback here. If no one tries it we will never know whether it's achievable or not, best of luck with it and I will follow it with interest.'

Well someone at least feels sorry for me. Next.

There was no next. That was it. Not one person giving any useful advice. I turned my computer off and stared at the map of Britain. This swim was looking like a pipedream, but I was determined for it to become a reality. Nothing suggested it wasn't possible, but proving that the impossible is actually possible, before you even start, was proving to be near impossible. This is quite a common scenario with big adventures, I guess. If it seemed possible then it would probably have been attempted already and therefore not attract as much attention, which excites sponsors. It was a hard game to play because I needed to sound confident to potential sponsors that I'd be able to complete the swim without sounding too naïve about the task at hand. Sponsors can work out straight away if you have looked into everything or not.

Finding a company to sponsor the swim was turning out to be increasingly difficult. I always seemed to get into meetings but inevitably got the same answers: 'We love the idea but just don't think it's possible, so it's too big a risk for us. But if you want to use our kit we'd happily supply you with it.'

I didn't need kit. I needed money to pay for fuel for the support boat and food for the crew. I emailed 350 companies and most expressed no interest at all in becoming a title sponsor. A few said they'd think about it, but with less than two months to go it was looking unlikely. I never thought it would be this hard. All I was asking for was £10,000. Surely for these sorts of companies that's a small price to pay for the potential publicity? Some even said they didn't want to get involved in case I died. That's always a positive email to get.

While I struggled along to find a sponsor, I started to look for crew. I needed three crew members: someone to skipper the boat, someone to take care of press, PR, take photos, help with prepping meals and be a general deck-hand, and lastly someone to kayak next to me so that I didn't get lost. A kayak could also carry food and water so I could eat and hydrate while in the water.

I had no idea where to start so thought I'd write a blog and share it on Twitter and Facebook. I added questions like, 'Do you suffer from seasickness?' and 'Can you kayak?' Within a day I got an application from Em Bell. Em Bell? I recognised the name but didn't know why so I Googled her.

Ah, yes! She was part of the crew that supported my friend Dave Cornthwaite when he swam 1,000 miles down the Missouri River. She was 28 years old, had no commitments like a job or a husband and knew a thing or two about swimming-based adventures. On paper she sounded perfect. But I remembered that Dave had had quite a few problems with his crew so I decided to give him a quick call to see what he thought.

'Hello buddy. How's the swim prep?' Dave asked when he picked up the phone.

'Good. Just trying to find crew. Got any tips?'

Dave laughed.

'More to the point,' I said, 'Em Bell just applied. Is she any good?'

'Mate, she is incredible. Say yes to her NOW, before she finds something else to do. She was the best person in my crew and by far the hardest working person I have ever met. Honestly, you won't regret it!'

I emailed Em straight away to arrange a meeting. One crew member found, two more to go. Who knows how I was going to find a skipper. Most people who can sail a yacht probably own one and have better things to do, like run a successful business, than follow a swimmer going at two knots for two months.

Feeling a bit disheartened, I decided to do some work on the fundraising side of things to take my mind off logistics. I had chosen the charity War Child specifically to help children in the Central African Republic. Raising money for charity is an important motivator when taking on a challenge like this. I knew I would get a huge boost when people donate some money through the JustGiving page I had set up.

One month to go ...

I finally had my crew. Surprisingly, my Tweets and Facebook posts had resulted in more than 30 applications, which I'd narrowed down to five finalists. It was a hard decision as they all had pretty impressive CVs – two had even climbed Mount Everest. In the end the position of Head of Press and PR and general deck-hand went to Owain Wyn-Jones, a 35-year-old chap originally from Wales, now living in Shropshire. At first, he didn't seem the most adventurous of the applicants and even when I called him for the interview his reply was 'Really? I never expected a call from you', but he had a good eye for media, could take a great photo and said he loved fishing. My one concern was that he was married with a child but he convinced me that this wouldn't be an issue. His wife was the one who found the opportunity for him. I had a good gut feeling about Owain. This would be a big challenge for him and I knew he'd work hard at making the most of it.

I was really happy with having Em and Owain, but finding a skipper was still proving tricky. None of the blogs or forums I used came up with anything. Out of options, it was time to try my one and only lead, my good friend Jeremy. Jez was a teacher and had hinted that he'd like to come and find me during my swim for a few weeks during his holidays in August. Jez lives on a narrowboat in London and can sail, although he never formally trained. To get him for July too he'd have to get a lot of time off work right at the end of the school year. It was a long shot but I was desperate. I gave him a call.

'How's the boat?' I asked, knowing that he was busy installing a shower.

'It's coming along slowly. I've been showering at school for six months; a few more days won't kill me. How's the swim prep? Not long now, what's it, four weeks to go?'

'Just over four.' Saying it out loud gave me a slight panic attack. I had no skipper, no support boat, no kayak for Em, no RIB (Rigid Inflatable Boat), no sponsor and no food. How was I going to sort all that out in four weeks and still have time to train?

'You must be excited. Who's skippering it? Can I still come in August?' asked Jez excitedly.

'Well, that's why I am calling. I really can't find a skipper anywhere. Fancy being the skipper?'

There was a long pause.

'Interesting.'

I had no idea what he meant by that.

'When is it you start?'

'On 30 June.'

'Mmm. It's not a no, but I'd have to check with school. It could be fun!'

'Please, mate, I'll pay for you to do your VHF licence and a day skipper course if you want.'

'Well, legally I need the VHF licence and I don't need to do a day skipper course but it's always good to learn I guess. What boat have you got?'

'Yeah, um, I haven't got one yet. I was hoping a skipper might be able to help with that. I have no idea what I am doing.'

'Fair enough. Let me call you tomorrow.'

'Thank you. I am desperate.'

Jez hadn't said yes, but he hadn't said no either. I'd done my bit; it was up to him now.

*

I didn't hear from Jez for three days and I was close to giving up. Then my phone rang one morning when I was in the shower. I ran to my phone, dripping water all over the floor. It was Jez.

'Hello, mate,' I said, nervously, and slightly out of breath from my ten-metre dash from the bathroom. That was worrying, and probably reflected how little training I'd managed to fit in.

'Right, I've handed in my notice. My last day is Friday 28 June. I'm all yours from then.'

'Really? I thought you were going to ask for time off?'

'Yeah, but they said no and I didn't like the school anyway so it was a good excuse to leave.'

'Wow. This is awesome. Thank you so much. I owe you everything.'

I jumped around my bedroom, completely naked, doing a silent scream. I had a full crew now. I couldn't contain my excitement.

'I've also been thinking,' Jez continued in a calm, matter-of-fact way. 'I have a sea kayak too and I know a guy called Arthur who lives on a boat near me who has an old RIB with an outboard engine that is just sitting there. I'm sure if you service it for him he'd let you borrow it.'

'Really?!' My day was getting better. Not only had I got a skipper, who was a good mate of mine, I now had a kayak and a RIB with an engine.

'I can only ask him but he is really cool.'

'You are my hero. Thanks so much.'

'No worries at all. This is going to be fun. I'll send you

a list of things I need, like charts, etc. What do you want me to do?'

I gave Jez a long list of things he'd need to be in charge of, such as tides, route, navigation and safety, and most importantly, researching a support boat. My £4,000 budget, fuelled completely by a credit card I managed to squeeze out of Lloyds Bank, really wasn't bringing up anything suitable on eBay but I hoped Jez's knowledge might help.

I grew up in Zimbabwe, in Mana Pools National Park, where my dad was a conservation ranger. At my school swimming was compulsory and, even if you were spluttering around in the shallow end on the verge of drowning, our swim teacher, Mrs Morrison, would still shout at you to carry on. A few kids really weren't made for swimming, or wearing speedos to be fair. I wasn't a natural swimmer but I did at least learn the strokes. And I must have got reasonably good at it, as when I was 14 I took part in the Midmar Mile, a huge annual open water swimming event in South Africa.

But that was probably the last serious swimming I'd done. I was now 32 years old and apart from fetching the occasional Frisbee from the sea on Brighton beach, I hadn't actually swum for the sake of swimming for the last 14 years. So why on earth had I set myself such a huge swimming-based challenge?

Back in 2011 I was miserable and discontent, and very much just existing rather than living. I hated the life I had made for myself and was operating on autopilot. It was very much a case of, 'Get up! Do something you hate just so you can afford the flat you only sleep in and a car you need just to do the job you hate!' It was my own fault really. I'd arrived in London in 2002 with only £100 in my pocket. I did a few jobs just to get some cash, like cutting lettuces in a pre-packed salad factory in Cambridgeshire, and working six days a week developing other people's holiday photos at Snappy Snaps, before starting my own photography business. But instead of going out and chasing creative work that fuelled my imagination, I decided to chase the money and spent 99% of my time doing corporate portraits of bankers in the city, who, after the banking crisis of 2008, really didn't want to be photographed. When I wasn't photographing angry bankers it was crying babies for school portraits. Headshots in front of a white background. I was a glorified passport photographer photographing people who didn't actually want to be photographed. It was soul destroying, but it paid the bills.

I did this for almost ten years until, a few months before my thirtieth birthday, I'd had enough. I finally admitted I was miserable and walked into the office and asked my business partner, James, to buy my shares. He offered me £1. I agreed and, a month later, after helping him restructure operations so he could work on his own, I walked away. I knew what I needed now was to challenge myself to do something radically different.

Growing up on the banks of the Zambezi River meant there were some amazing opportunities to do adventurous stuff, and I have always loved getting outside. In my teens

I was really into canoeing, and competed in several river marathons including the Dusi Canoe Marathon, which takes place over three days on a 75-mile course in South Africa. I also once climbed Kilimanjaro dressed as a penguin for charity. I realised that this was the sort of stuff that made me happy.

I'd been reading a lot about round the world cyclists like Mark Beaumont, Vin Cox and Tommy Godwin. This was exactly the sort of adventure I wished I could have. Then I realised, why couldn't I do it? Honestly, I had two legs and could cycle. What was stopping me?

So that's how I came to join nine other cyclists all competing in the first ever World Cycle Race. It was the brainchild of round the world cyclist Vin Cox who, on returning home from his ride, realised his record could easily be beaten and invited people to attempt it. The idea that I might be able to break a world record was inspiring, and exactly what I needed. I worked incredibly hard training and getting ready for the challenge before setting off from Greenwich in February 2012. It was going to be one hell of a race.

A month into my ride I was way ahead of the world record, averaging 180 miles per day self-supported, when I was run over in America by a careless driver. This effectively ended my world record attempt. After a month off the bike recovering in America I carried on as I still wanted to raise money for my chosen charity, Solar Aid, but I was a lot slower and eventually limped back to London having cycled 16,000 miles in 116 days. In many ways it had still been the adventure of a lifetime, but there was one thing missing. I had failed in my attempt to break the world record for round the world cycling. I had worked so hard and really hoped to do something that no one else had.

This was the idea behind this swim. I was sure it was possible, but no one had done it. If I succeeded I would be the only one. I would really be pushing myself to my limits. Physically, as I would be battling the sea, but mentally too, as I would have to cope with being in the water for hours on end. I really wanted to make it happen to give myself the confidence back that I could do something physically and mentally on the 'extremely difficult' scale. Swimming 1,000 miles up the coast of Britain certainly ticked that box.

So, that's how it happened that ten months on from returning from my failed round the world cycle record attempt I was in the shallow end of my local pool, staring into the water. This was my first training session and I kept thinking to myself – I hope it's like riding a bicycle; you never forget.

As is turned out I had pretty much forgotten, and was so awful I had to get out after ten lengths because I felt dizzy and nauseous. I was rubbish. In between sorting out crew, logistics and finding a sponsor it was proving very difficult to fit in swim training. I was already resigned to the fact I'd have to do all my training in a pool and wouldn't be able to do any sea-training sessions; Mum lives in Cheltenham which is a good three-hour round trip from the nearest beach. It wasn't ideal, and far from the serious training sessions I did for my cycle, but I was just running out of time. I figured I would get fit along the route. If I didn't drown first.

I was told by various people who knew what they were talking about, which was almost anyone who has swum, ever, to get some coaching sessions. So, eventually, after not much progress in the pool, I decided to enlist the help of triathlon legend Mark Kleanthous who has completed more than 450 triathlons around the world. He had access to an 'endless' pool, which is a small pool that pushes a flow of water towards you. This allows you to swim in one spot while he films your technique. After my session, Mark sent me a long list of things I needed to change. He said my technique was pretty awful, but if I just changed a few little things I'd become more efficient in the water. I didn't need to be the fastest; after all, it wasn't a race. What was more important was strength – both mental and physical – as well as endurance. I would be tested to the limit and I really had no idea if I would be up to the task.

I did at least realise that getting enough fuel into my body every day would be really important, so I went to see Steve, the nutritionist I worked with before the round the world cycle. As ever, he was a fountain of useful information. He also helped me with a training program too. No one really had any idea how to eat enough calories for my body to deal with the cold water for so long, but Steve's 'eat EVERYTHING' concept seemed to be the best solution for now. There was no point in planning to eat certain food and then not being able to stomach them.

'If you can stomach it mate, then eat it,' he'd say. Seemed a good compromise for when conditions are against you.

Two weeks to go …

I still didn't have a boat or a sponsor. I decided to go down to see Jez and meet Arthur, who was lending me his RIB and outboard.

Jez lives on a canal in east London and has one of the best local pubs I've ever been to. It's called the Anchor & Hope and sits right on the towpath. It's a proper East End pub that specialises in real ale. On weekdays, there's no food except for a few packets of crisps and nuts behind the bar. Jez has his own mug which they keep especially for him. It is one of those German-type mugs with the lid you open with your thumb. He even has a special order which they have ready for him even before he reaches the bar. It's half of one ale and half of another. Most afternoons you can buy eel and fish from a chap who walks through the pub with a tray. I decided that this would be a good place to catch up with Jez and look at a few yachts I had saved to the eBay app on my phone.

Every yacht we looked at either didn't have an engine, or was missing a sail, or had no navigation equipment – all of which can be expensive to sort out after you've bought the boat. Eventually we came across an old wooden 26-foot yacht built in 1961. It was a SCOD (South Coast One Design) and was currently at a bid of £3,500, which was just in budget, and had a few days to go on the auction. Jez read the description and he was surprised how good the condition was for the price. She had good sails, was sea-worthy already, had a separate toilet that wasn't between the two front bunks as with many smaller yachts, and had all the GPS navigation and depth sounders we needed. Her name was *Friday While*, and, although 52 years old and wooden, she looked like she had character. We decided to have another ale each and carry on searching.

Two more ales later and having seen nothing remotely as good, we had another look at *Friday While*. Twenty-six foot was a little on the small side, but she had a very large keel – five foot, six inches – which would make her more stable in bigger waves. I decided to Google SCODs. They had some great reviews: steady at sea, very well engineered and lovely to sail. The only thing people said they didn't like was that they were very slow. This could become an issue in trying to fight the tides and get us to safe anchorages, but to be honest, I didn't really have a better choice. Could this be the boat for Swimming Britain?

The auction had two more days to run, but I was leaving for Jersey to do some talks at schools to earn some money as I still had no sponsor. I had no way of going down to look at her before I left and the auction would end while I was on the ferry to Jersey. It was a case of bid now on the phone or miss out. I bought another pint while I mulled it over. Several ales later, after changing my mind constantly, I decided I didn't really have much choice. I hadn't seen anything like it at all for the price. I plucked up the (Dutch) courage and, with a small amount of difficulty, I took out my phone and put a maximum bid of £4,007.51. Nervously,

I pressed BID and waited. There was a slow internet connection and the spinning wheel symbol seemed to take forever. Eventually the screen flashed green and my heart jumped. It said, 'You are the highest bidder at £3,632.'

Jez and I looked at each other. He was smiling. I was smiling too but it was more of a nervous smile. Had I just bought a yacht on the eBay app? We had a few more ales to celebrate.

I woke up the next morning with a slight headache. Had I really bid on a yacht in Jez's local? I looked at my phone. I was still the highest bidder for *Friday While*. My heart raced. Last night was all a bit hazy but I remembered Jez saying it was worth it, and I trusted him. I now needed to pack for Jersey. I'd only know when I got there whether I had won the auction or not.

The ferry crossing to the Channel Islands felt impossibly long. I was meant to be working on my talks but couldn't keep my mind off the fact that at that very moment I may or may not be the owner of a yacht. A mile offshore I got phone reception but no 3G. Then a voicemail came through. It was Jez.

'Mate, we got it. We have a boat! Final bid was £3,890 which I think is a bargain. Well done, Mr Boat Owner! Anyway, let me know when you are back, it's down on the south coast. I need to start thinking about getting it to Penzance, which will take about six days.'

An overwhelming feeling smothered me and I started to hyperventilate a little. This was it. Owning a yacht was something I never in a million years thought I'd do, and buying one the way we did probably wasn't the best idea, but nevertheless, I now had a boat and a crew. Things were looking up.

Except that I still couldn't pay for the trip.

The truth was that Swimming Britain was still a fantasy. I was acting confident and telling everyone it was happening. I'd bought a yacht and convinced three people to give up their entire summer to live on it with me. But without financial help from sponsors there was no way on earth I could afford to feed a crew and pay all the costs. If I couldn't find a sponsor I'd most certainly have to delay the swim by an entire year, or more. Apart from everything else that I'd need to start all over again with, finding another crew would be the hardest – after all, who knows where Jez, Owain and Em might be in a year. That would be so disappointing. I was excited about our team.

I knew I was probably going to need more than the £10,000 in sponsorship I was asking for, but I didn't want to scare potential sponsors off with a higher figure.

On Tuesday morning, ten days before the start of my swim, I woke up and opened my laptop to see if I'd had any luck with emails to sponsors from the day before. It was always disappointing seeing an empty inbox but this time I noticed an email from a lady called Sally at Speedo. I'd had two meetings with Speedo, and although they said they were interested nothing had been confirmed. This was probably to say they didn't want to fund it, just like the other 350 companies I'd contacted. I hesitantly opened the email.

Hi Sean

We just wanted to let you know that we're in for the full £10,000. What you're doing is remarkable and it is exactly what we believe in — normal people using swimming to explore and get fit.

Attached is a contract. You should get the funds in ten days or so!

We're really excited to be part of this.

Chat soon.

Sal

I couldn't believe it. I screamed out loud and Mum came running into my room.

'I got it Mum, I got the money!'

'Well done! So proud of you!' She hugged me.

I could feel the tension running out of my shoulders. It had been a few hard weeks of getting nowhere with anyone. Having a brand like Speedo on board was perfect because I now had funds to feed the crew properly and also they had great ideas about sharing the adventure. I couldn't have asked for a more appropriate partnership.

As if my day couldn't get any better, I then received another email from a company called Stowaways who make high-end sailing food in a bag. They wanted to provide me with 500 meals for the swim. It was exactly what I needed: good quality packet food I could just heat up and that didn't need rehydrating. That was it – pretty much everything was in place! Swimming Britain could definitely go ahead! I was brimming with excitement and nerves.

One week to go ...

My plans were finally coming together. I had been working with Jez, Owain and Em on getting most of the logistics sorted. Jez had taken *Friday While* to Penzance with the help of an amazing skipper called Lou. She and her brother Jim run a sailing school called Nomad Sailing on the south coast, and had kindly offered to donate four days of their time to give Jez a refresher course in sailing and help him get the boat down towards Land's End. I tried to go out with them on the first day but got so seasick I decided not to do the rest of the journey. This was not a good sign. I hoped I wouldn't get seasick while swimming, although I'd heard that can happen.

The last week before the start was a hive of checking things, sorting last-minute kit and making sure the crew had everything they needed. The only slight hiccup was that Speedo hadn't received my signed contract and I only realised a few days before the start when the funds hadn't arrived. I had to send another one through, and that delay meant the money would only clear a few days after the start of the swim. Normally this would be fine but I literally had no money left at all. I had borrowed everything I could from friends and family, and maxed every credit card and all overdrafts possible. It was so bad that I didn't even have enough money to fill my car with diesel to get to Land's End.

My last resort was to go grovelling to my bank manager with the email from Speedo to ask for £250. It took an hour for Robert, the bank manager, to call various people at Lloyds head office, or wherever they make decisions, before they eventually decided to give me another £250 on a two-week extension to my current overdraft. At least I could pay to service Arthur's outboard, which I hadn't done yet, and fill my car so I could actually get to Land's End and the start line.

2
LAND'S END

'Hey mate, really sorry but I've missed my bus by two minutes.'

Jez hadn't got his bus from London to Penzance and therefore would not be here for the start of the swim, which was set for midday tomorrow.

'Shit. OK. When can you get here?' I asked, trying not to sound annoyed. He had quit his job for me after all. The reason I needed Jez there was because the only way to get to the tip of Land's End was to drive a mile up the coast to a place called Sennen Cove, which has a harbour and access to the sea. From there I was going to take the yacht to the tip of Land's End and jump in to start the swim.

'Tomorrow evening is when the next one comes in. Sorry,' he replied in an annoyingly calm voice. Why wasn't he stressed out? I would soon learn that Jez never gets stressed out about anything, which has its advantages.

'I guess there is nothing we can do. I'll try to find a fisherman or something.'

I put the phone down and put my head in my hands. Getting to the start line had been so difficult, but here we were. Everything was meant to be in place and I had hoped to have a relaxing evening, get some food and then an early night. I now needed to go and find a fisherman to help me, so I headed down to Sennen Cove for some advice. Em came along as I figured a girl might have more luck asking for things.

Em started working her magic straight away with a pretty convincing 'we're desperate' sob story. First stop was the café. They were incredibly friendly, and when Em told them what I was attempting they sent us to find a fisherman and also suggested that the RNLI might help.

So we asked the RNLI if they had a small dinghy that someone could take us in a mile up the coast and then drop me in the water.

'No, we can't do that!' the old lady replied as if it was absurd to ask. 'We take people out of dangerous situations and out of the water. We can't be seen to be putting people into the water and into dangerous situations!'

I was initially annoyed with their logic because I was going to swim no matter what and surely having them close to me was better than me going it alone but, after thinking about it, they did have a point. Imagine I did get into trouble and it was revealed that the RNLI had put me in that position. It would not look good for them. I guess I was just going to have to get used to the idea of this 'sorry we can't help in case you die' attitude for this swim.

The next stop was to ask a fisherman called Bob. Apparently he was still out fishing but was due back in about an hour, so Em and I sat on the beach and looked out to the sea. Although typically overcast, there weren't that many waves and conditions looked pretty good for swimming.

'I hope it's like this tomorrow,' Em said, looking a little worried. Em had actually never kayaked in the sea before; the only kayaking she had done was an hour on the Thames a few weeks before. (She had travelled down the Missouri by stand up paddle board as part of Dave Cornthwaite's crew.) It was a risky choice as we didn't know what the sea conditions would be like, but her swimming knowledge was well worth having and of all the people who had applied she was the most enthusiastic, and that counted for a lot.

'Me too. It's hard to imagine it all stormy and violent on days like today. Let's hope it stays like this,' I replied.

Off to our right was Sennen beach, which had a few kids building sandcastles and running around being mischievous. It was Saturday 29 June 2013, which meant the beach was probably at its busiest but, even so, it was still pretty quiet. Land's End is a very long way from anything really. So far away in fact that none of my friends had managed to visit. Just my mum and her friend Cathy had made it to see me off. I didn't really expect my mates to come all the way down, but it would have been nice.

My friends have become used to me doing big challenges after my round the world cycle, so they're not that surprised by anything I do now. It's fine because sometimes the planning of a big adventure like this can somehow turn into an all-encompassing monster that takes over your entire life. This can be a massive contradiction to the reasons you want to go off adventuring in the first place. You want to get away from the rat race, expand your mind, push yourself and not get caught up in the bullshit that modern living can throw at you. If you're not careful you can get just as caught up in the adventure bullshit, where your challenge starts to own you and all other parts of your life fall by the wayside. My friends keep me really grounded, and on occasions when I am telling someone at a party what I do, all my mates shamelessly just turn around and walk away yawning, as they've heard it a million times.

Mum, on the other hand, like all mums, loves everything I do and spent most of the preceding months telling everyone she met about the swim. Even people in the queue for an ATM, where engaging in conversation could be misinterpreted as an invasion of privacy, Mum doesn't care, she goes straight in with, 'My son is just about to swim the length of Britain.' No introduction or anything. Just bang, right for the jugular.

It was a shame Dad wasn't here but coming all the way from South Africa seemed a little over the top. He has always been bit more aware of the practicalities of what I do and worries a lot about my safety, especially after I got run over in America. It was a traumatic time for my family who could do nothing to help me from the other side of the world. But, although he was concerned, Dad was still supportive of the swim. I'd set him up with a Twitter account on his phone so he could keep up to date with my progress.

*

Bob eventually came ashore in his fishing boat. It was a lovely wooden open-top 15-foot boat, painted white with a blue rim. It was full of fishing boxes, various coloured nets and small plastic buoys. Bob was in his late fifties, wore typical fisherman dungarees and sported the most spectacular beard. I was envious.

'Hi Bob,' said Em, smiling from ear to ear.

'Hi there! You must be the swimmer. I've heard about you. Has anyone told you, you are mad?' He laughed.

'Mainly my mum!' I replied trying to keep the conversation light-hearted.

'Anyway, our skipper can't make the start for tomorrow,' continued Em, 'and we were wondering if there would be any chance we could hire your services for an hour to take us to the start? We need to leave at midday or thereabouts.'

'Midday? The tide would have just turned then. It won't be possible to swim.' He said with quite a worryingly stern look on his face, a stark contrast to his friendly smile earlier.

The way tides work in Britain is that for six hours you get the tide running north and then for another six hours the tide runs south. When it's running south, you can't swim northward as you'd just go backwards. This presented various logistical issues that we'd have to think about seriously because the tide affects where the boat can get to each night. Jez was in charge of all this but Jez wasn't here, so we were kind of in the dark.

The rest of the swim would be governed by tidal times that are related to High Water Dover. This is a sailing term which tells you when the tide is running in which direction, sort of like Greenwich Mean Time but for tides. High Water Dover is the benchmark for when the tide changes. The tide would turn at Land's End at High Water Dover +2. High water in Dover is at 10am. This means the tide at Land's End would turn at midday. My start time tomorrow, however, was determined by when the media could get here. I was set to start at midday and, although not ideal for the tides, I figured if I kept close enough to the shore I could avoid the big rush of tide that goes past Land's End. I had no research to back this idea up, more of a gut feeling really, as I was yet to do my first open-water sea swim. However, seeing as I was only going to swim one mile tomorrow and then carry on from Sennen on Monday, I wasn't too worried.

'I'm sorry. I wouldn't feel comfortable dropping you in the sea there. It's a nasty stretch of water and at full rush, not even my boat can cope against that tide,' said Bob while hauling large boxes of fish onto the sand.

Em tried everything and even explained it was all for charity, but nothing was going to make him budge. We asked if there was anyone else but he said we'd get the same answer from everyone.

Feeling a little terrified, we made our way back to the hotel at Land's End. Although I'd become quite used to people's default answer of 'no' or 'you can't do that' or 'it's not possible', I'd tended not to take them too seriously. This time was a bit different.

The sea can be a nasty place, and when it comes to nasty, Land's End is up there near the top of the list, apparently! Although I was hearing the local advice, I wasn't listening, or at least trying not to listen to it, and I was determined to display fake confidence, which was important for me and the crew. That this had never been attempted before meant there was always going to be a huge amount of guesswork involved, I just wished it wasn't on Day 1. A few days' easy swimming to get into the swing of things really would have been nice.

The hotel had kindly let us stay the night for free. If they hadn't I'd have probably had to spend the night in my car, as the last of £250 I had borrowed from the bank was gone. At least we had Stowaways to eat on the boat. All 500 meals were stuffed in the front of *Friday While*, or *Friday* as she was now known.

Once back at the hotel, Em, Owain and I tried a few more leads for getting a boat but no one was willing to help, so we sat down, ordered beers and decided what our options were. The first was to delay the start by a day, when Jez would be here. The problem was that we had arranged for the media to come on Sunday, and our friends and family who had come down for the weekend needed to get back to work on Monday. Too many people had made the effort – I couldn't let them down.

The second option, and the only really feasible one, was to swim from Sennen Cove to Land's End, turn around and then swim back. This meant that on one of the routes I'd be against the tide. We worked out that at midday I'd have tide heading away from Sennen Cove and then be fighting it on the way back. Any later than midday and the tide would be way too strong. In the grand scheme of things an extra mile didn't matter, but I liked the idea of waving at everyone on the cliffs from *Friday*, who was all kitted out in Swimming Britain stickers, having a big countdown and jumping in. Instead I was going to swim with Em in the kayak next to me. I then realised we didn't have the kayak. It was still on the yacht in Penzance, ten miles away. I'd have to go collect it in the morning.

I spotted *Friday* rafted four boats down in Penzance harbour. She seemed a lot smaller than I remembered. I hadn't seen her since I joined Jez and Lou taking her from Shoreham-by-Sea towards Land's End, but I was so seasick I had my eyes closed for half the time. She was now fully laden with everything we needed to survive for two months at sea.

Not really knowing what the etiquette was, I scrambled over other people's yachts and eventually stepped onto her. I was surprised at how much she heeled over to one side when I stood on her, but at 26 foot I guess that was to be expected. To put her size into perspective, most four-man Atlantic rowing boats, which are considered small and cramped, are just less than 30 foot. *Friday* really was tiny.

Her deck was made of wood and, although in fairly good condition, she had started to fade in patches where the sun had taken its toll over the last 52 years of her life. Her mast was made from one solid piece of wood and rose a good 30 foot or so into the sky. I looked up to the top of the mast and then felt a little seasick so looked back to the harbour wall to gather my balance. That didn't bode well considering the water was glass flat, as you'd expect in a marina.

At the stern was a wooden tiller arm for steering. This could be done while sitting on either side of the rear cockpit depending on which way she was listing. There was just enough room in the cockpit to sit four people but it would be a squeeze. Through the door and into the cabin was a really old paraffin stove on the port side and a chart table on the starboard side, each about half a square metre in size. Next along were two bunks just about long enough for Owain, who is 6 foot, 2 inches tall. It was so tight that the leg space went under the sink and the chart table on each side. Up against the wall was a fold-down table which we could use for meals and team bonding. The bunks were also the seats for the table.

The toilet (or 'heads') was on the starboard side and then a cupboard on the port side, which contained all my swimming kit, suncream, and carb/protein recovery nutrition powder.

Getting a yacht with a separate toilet was a bonus because most small yachts had the toilet under the V between the front two bunks. That would not have been ideal as there was no way I was going to let someone take a dump right where my head was going to be. I had also stuck a map of the UK on the toilet door and the plan was to mark off our progress each day. It looked dauntingly large so I opened the door to hide the map. I didn't need any more negative thoughts.

Moving to the front, there were two bunks angled together. Under the front part of the bunks were the

Stowaways meals and stuffed into the front (or 'forepeak' as Jez corrected me) were all our sails. Each of us had about one bin liner's worth of space under each of our bunks, and I did actually tell the crew to bring their kit in a bin liner as we didn't have enough space to store rucksacks and bags. So that was it, our little home for the next few months. 'Cosy' was a good way of putting it but 'claustrophobic' probably more apt. It would be a miracle if all four of us managed to survive on *Friday* without falling out at some point.

After some more faffing, I loaded the kayak onto the car and drove back to Land's End. It was 10am and I needed to get ready for a midday start.

Everything was laid out on the bed in the hotel room: wetsuit, goggles, thermal cap, outer cap, booties, fins, gloves and watch. This was the kit I was going to swim in. Next to that was some stuff I needed Em to take in the kayak. I had some bottles of water, some energy bars, some rope (you always need rope) and most importantly a SPOT tracker. The tracker would send a signal off every ten minutes showing my location on my website. This was primarily for my family to see where I was when I didn't have phone signal out at sea. There was also an SOS button that, if pressed, would alert the coastguard and send them our co-ordinates. Hopefully I'd never need to use it but it was good to know we had that as backup.

I hadn't had the time to feel nervous since arriving at Land's End due to all the admin I had to do, but walking out of the hotel in a wetsuit and onto the cliffs overlooking the Atlantic, knowing that I'd be out there for the next two months, suddenly made my stomach turn. Now it was real. I was also slightly embarrassed walking around in a wetsuit in front of so many onlookers. It was the first time I had tried on this wetsuit. Most people would have tested it out before but my local pool had a no-wetsuit policy, which meant I couldn't have done even if I wanted to.

It was pretty overcast again and the wind had picked up slightly. There were a few people around but generally Land's End was pretty empty. In fact, most of the people there were friends and family of Em and Owain, along with Ryan and Holly from Speedo, and the hotel staff who were keen to have a photo with me. There is a wall in the hotel with photos of various people who had made the length of Britain journey in interesting ways. Actually, there was already someone in a wetsuit but he was in a small pool on the back of a flatbed truck. I enquired as to what he did and was told he did laps of the pool as they drove from Land's End to John O'Groats. I liked that. Good old British sense of adventure and eccentricity. I also looked for a photo of my mate Dave, the one who swam the Missouri, from when he skateboarded the route but couldn't find it. I wondered if they would put a photo of me up there if I completed the swim.

There was a small queue for the official Land's End sign so I waited my turn. There were a few cyclists, some just starting and some finishing their adventures, both with equally big smiles on their faces. I cycled it in 2008 and know exactly how they were feeling. Back then it was by far the biggest thing I had ever done and I loved every moment of it.

Eventually it was my turn and I walked below the sign.

'What words would you like on the sign?' asked the lady in charge.

'I think let's go with SWIMMING BRITAIN and the date.'

'Are you swimming it?'

'That's the plan.'

She just smiled ever so slightly and kind of shook her head. I'm not sure what she meant by that but she didn't seem fazed at all and proceeded to get the relevant letters together in one hand. There was a slight buzz in the small crowd gathering as the letters went up. This was it. As soon as those letters spelt SWIMMING BRITAIN, it became official. There would be no turning back. The proof was there for everyone to see.

One man with his wife and kids shouted across to me.

'Mate, are you really swimming it? What? How? I don't understand?'

All of a sudden I noticed everyone looking at me and felt embarrassed.

'I'm getting in the water here and swimming up the west coast until I reach John O'Groats.'

'Shit! No way! Sorry, honey!' he apologised to his wife for swearing. 'That's amazing. How long will it take?'

'I hope two months but it all depends on the weather.'

'Fair play, mate. Good luck.'

'Cheers.'

At least he seemed impressed and didn't give me any 'you are going to die' vibes.

I stood under the sign for a while, having some photos taken by a press photographer. We had hoped the BBC or ITV might send a TV crew but in the end only one photographer turned up. Not even the local Cornish newspapers bothered. It wasn't that I wanted to be in the press for this, that's not the reason why I was doing the swim, but I had promised to raise £10,000 for War Child and getting publicity helps me spread the word. Maybe they thought it was a waste of their time as the risk of failure was quite high.

After the photographs, I went over to the edge of the cliff and looked out into the vast, empty Atlantic Ocean. It looked deceptively calm out there.

'Sean, come on, it's time to go,' said Em, taking control. That's exactly what I wanted from a crew captain. I wanted to be able to focus on the task at hand and let the crew make the decisions for me.

I walked away from the cliff and towards the car park, the sounds of the waves slowly disappearing into the distance. My stomach started turning on itself. I jumped in my car – which was a lot harder than expected wearing a wetsuit – and drove down to Sennen Cove.

I was a little behind schedule and it was 12.30pm by the time I got everything together and Em got in the kayak.

'You OK?' I asked, knowing this was Em's first time kayaking at sea.

'Yeah, totally fine.'

'Right, let's do this.'

I slowly walked into the water and was surprised at how cold it was. I turned around and waved at the few people who were there. I then sat in the water to put my fins on. Throughout the lead-up I had questioned whether I needed fins or not, and ideally would have liked to dispense with them as they put strain on your legs. However, after hearing that Martin Strel, the world's most accomplished open-water swimmer and the only person to have swum the Amazon River, used fins for his swims to fight currents, I figured I should at least try them out.

After faffing with the fins, I stood up again and looked out to sea. I was filled with apprehension and excitement at the same time. I turned back to the ten or so people on the shore. Everyone had huge smiles on their faces and a few were taking photos. In a weird way this made me feel quite pressured to succeed, as if those people were unconsciously saying, 'Sean I've come all this way to Land's End to see you off. You better bloody do it!' I knew that wasn't the case but I still didn't want to let them down.

I gave one last wave and dived in. Time stood still for those first few seconds as I was completely submerged before coming to the surface. This was it, I was now underway in the world's first ever length of Britain swim attempt. It was strange to think that for the next couple of months this would be my environment, my home, my life. Swim, eat, sleep, repeat. At two months long, it would be one of the longest swims in history, time-wise, and most certainly one of the longest sea-swims in history. I had no idea what lay ahead of me. What I did learn quickly, however, was that the sea was bloody cold. I hadn't thought to test the water temperature and although I knew it would probably be cold, I didn't think it would be that cold and immediately felt like an idiot.

Would there be animals? A few people online said I'd get eaten by killer whales. Turns out there are killer whales up in Scotland but luckily the figures were in my favour as no one has ever been killed by an orca in the wild. The few deaths that have occurred have been in captivity.

There was also the question of whirlpools, back-eddies, undercurrents and rip tides. These were some of the other reasons people told me this swim wasn't possible. I had convinced myself that they were incorrect and it couldn't be that bad, but the reality was I really had no idea.

Bursting through the surface to take my first breath of salty sea air, I felt a jet of cold water rush down the back of my wetsuit, which took my breath away. The water temperature was 13 degrees and it was a shock. The pool I trained in was around 20 degrees. I could feel the sting on my face and cheeks as I made my way out of the harbour, Em following close behind me.

I pushed on along the dramatic cliffs towering above me and headed towards the small island just off Land's End, which would be the official start point. I was about 100 metres offshore and seemed to be making good progress when I remembered I had the tide with me; I still had to turn around and fight it on the way back. On and on I swam, getting used to the new feeling of swimming in salt water and having to deal with, albeit small, waves for the first time. I reached the little island in about 40 minutes and was surprised how fast I zoomed past it. This tide was strong. I figured I'd swim another 50 metres past just to make sure I didn't miss anything. I'd hate to get back to Sennen and be told I wasn't quite at the End of Britain. I put my face down and suddenly something darted below me. My heart jumped. I looked up at Em and she had a look of fear on her face. Suddenly a fin popped out the water and went back again, and then another one. In a moment of panic I was certain they were sharks, but then realised they must be dolphins and I relaxed a bit. There were about ten of them that zoomed past me right as I was at the tip of Land's End. What an honour. It was as if they were coming to wish me luck. Then as fast as they appeared they disappeared again.

'How amazing was that?' I asked Em.

'Amazing!' replied Em, still looking concerned.

In the frenzy of dolphin activity, I had been swept quite far away from the island. It was definitely time to officially start my swim. I could see a crowd of people gathered at the top of the cliffs outside Land's End Hotel and waved at them. They all waved back. I turned around and started to swim back. I could feel the flood of water running over me. I felt like I was flying. It must have been the adrenalin from seeing the dolphins. I was still breathing to my left, which was away from the cliffs now. Stroke, stroke, breath. I did this for a good few minutes and then looked up expecting to be past the island again and heading back to Sennen. I was very surprised, then, and a little worried to see I was still 100 metres from the island.

'Em, can you come to my right?' I asked. 'Are we even moving?'

'Slowly, but we are moving.'

I carried on for another five minutes and didn't make much more than 20 metres progress. I looked up at Em again.

'Keep swimming. Every time you stop we drift back.'

I looked up at the cliff and could see some people coming down to the edge. It must look as if I was in trouble.

Again I pushed for another five minutes, but eventually Em shouted at me, 'Right, now we are not moving!'

She was also struggling to kayak against the tide.

My heart sank. This couldn't be happening. The tide was getting stronger and stronger, and the half hour delayed start might have meant I had missed my opportunity. What if I got swept way out to sea? There wasn't a beach for miles in the other direction to Sennen. I'd have to call a mayday, which involved pressing the SOS button on my tracker. This would alert the coastguard and probably the RNLI, and the old lady who laughed at us would get a message giving her our location. I could just imagine the look on her face. If there was ever a 'I told you so' moment, this was probably it.

I then remembered that I had planned to swim right along the edge of the cliffs. I was a good 100 metres offshore still, so decided to try swim towards the shore.

'Follow me Em. I'm going to swim to shore, maybe there is less tide there.'

'OK!' Em shouted back.

It took nearly ten minutes to swim the 100 metres to the shore but eventually, and utterly exhausted, I was just underneath the little island. The tide was kind of pushing past the island and flicking around, which meant I could rest in the water. There was no way of being able to fight the tide coming around the outside of the island. My only option was to try swim through the two-metre gap between the island and the mainland. It was hard to tell what it was like, how deep it was or whether I'd get smashed up against the rocks.

'Em, can you go have a look?'

'Are we going through there? It looks bad. Can't you go round?'

'Don't think so. It'll be fine! Please check it out.'

Em paddled off hesitantly towards the gap, which was being battered by a few waves. She went through and disappeared around the corner. I felt very exposed and alone. It felt like minutes but was most likely a few seconds before she came back through and waved to me to come. I put my head down and started towards the gap. The nearer I got the shallower it became. I was soon right between two rocks and the rise and fall of the water was about a metre. I looked down to see some very sharp rocks just below the surface. If I wasn't careful I could easily get washed onto one. I pushed hard with my head down and got another bucket load of freezing Atlantic water down the back of my wetsuit. My wetsuit was now full of water. Maybe I hadn't put it on properly?

Eventually, and completely out of breath, I pushed through the other side and into the open sea again. I was spent. It had been well over half an hour since I turned around to start the swim and I had done all of a few hundred metres.

'I need to rest, Em, and get the water out of my suit,' I called.

I went to a section of the cliff with a large flat rock and scrambled ashore, which wasn't easy wearing fins. It was a good thing I had fins though because there was no way anyone could swim against that tide without them. I stood there shivering, cold to the core, for a good ten minutes while Em circled around in the kayak. Em's boyfriend, Rob, who had been on the cliffs watching, appeared above us.

'You guys OK? That looked pretty sketchy.'

'Yeah, just a bit cold. I'll get back in in a bit. Tell everyone we're OK.'

I stood there for another five minutes and then decided to jump back in. It wasn't as cold this time and my theory of swimming along the shore worked. It took another hour to do that mile back to Sennen, and I arrived completely exhausted and collapsed on the beach.

'Well, that was a little harder than I thought,' I said to some onlookers, trying to keep it light-hearted, and so as to not stress out my mum who had an uncharacteristic look of worry on her face. Em got out the kayak and hugged Rob, who seemed relieved and also impressed that we survived and both made it back in one piece.

At least I had started and got all the chores out of the way. Tomorrow would be the real start to the adventure. We walked back up to the car and as I was getting in to head back to Penzance a chap came running up to me.

'Hi there. I'm Simon. I heard about your attempt. Amazing! I live in St Ives and do a lot of open-water swimming. Anyway, I see you're in a rush but here is my number. I'd love to come swim with you when you reach St Ives.'

'Sure thing. I hope to be there in a few days so keep a look out at my tracker online.'

'Will do.' With that he rushed off.

That afternoon Owain, Em and I said our goodbyes to friends and family, and headed to Penzance to sleep on the boat and wait for Jez. Although it was nice to have everyone around giving us support, it was hectic and I was looking forward to my first night on the boat.

Jez eventually arrived at 7pm and we had one beer each, which was all I could afford. The deal I made with the crew was that all expenses would be covered by me, and that would include a few beers and entertainment here and there. We all deserved a beer after today.

We retired to the boat for an early night. Jez and Owain took the two bunks in the main saloon, and Em and I had the shorter bunks up front. At least we'd have a calm sleep in the harbour. As I was getting into bed I noticed some pain on the inside of my left foot. I looked down to see a layer of skin, about one centimetre long, had rubbed off. I wasn't sure when it had happened but my feet had obviously been too cold to feel it. It wasn't bleeding or anything, so didn't think anything of it and fell fast asleep.

3

SEASICK AND SENNEN

It was good to have the whole team together finally and we were all keen to get going. We got up at 5am to make our way from Penzance to Sennen Cove. I had some porridge to fuel myself for the day, and then we left the harbour and started heading west with the RIB and the kayak dragging behind us on a long piece of rope.

'How long till we get there?' I asked Jez, as I started to get my wetsuit out of the cupboard.

'No rush, mate. Probably four or five hours,' replied Jez, while he loaded up the navigation app on his iPad.

'Really? How far away are we?'

'About 15 miles or so, but *Friday* can only go three or four knots, maybe five or six if we have a good wind, but we don't have a good wind.'

This was the first time I properly understood just how slow *Friday* was. The reviews I read weren't wrong.

It was great to be at sea finally and although overcast it was warm. It always takes a while to get a system together on expeditions. We were all still bumping into each other and falling over while we got used to the motion of the ocean, as they say, especially Owain, as he was the tallest by quite a bit. Within the first half hour he had hit his head on the roof in the main cabin about 20 times.

'Shit, bloody shit. Bloody roof! Argh!' he'd shout every time while rubbing his head, and we'd all burst out laughing. Our spirits were high and we were all thrilled to be underway.

'Right, first person to get seasick has to have two Jägerbombs,' I joked.

I was making light of it to the crew but the reality was that seasickness could in theory end my swim and I was quite nervous. I wasn't worried about Em and Owain as they both said they didn't get seasick on the questionnaire when applying to be part of the crew, and I knew Jez would be fine as he had already sailed *Friday* down to Penzance. But if I threw up too often I'd have no energy in my stomach to swim efficiently and keep warm, and therefore not be able to make the mileage I needed each day. Seasickness on a trip like this can completely ruin you. It is dehydrating, saps your energy and is one of the worst feelings in the world.

The next half an hour went by as we powered, slowly, through the averagely sized three-foot waves along the Cornish coast taking in the scenery. We were even joined by a pod of dolphins dancing in front of the boat like happy children. I wondered if they were the same ones from yesterday. I'd like to have thought they were coming back to make sure we were having a safe journey onwards. They gave me a strange sense of safety as they jumped in and out of the bow waves almost smiling at us. Then as soon as they came they were gone, back down into the depth of the sea, looking up at us. I liked the idea that the dolphins were making sure no other nasty animals were coming to bite me.

Another hour went by and I started to feel seasick, so went below and closed my eyes, which helped a bit.

'Please, don't get sick. Please don't get sick,' I kept saying to myself in a kind of anti-seasickness chant, hoping Neptune would hear me. Em too decided to have a nap, although she said it wasn't because of seasickness. I had my doubts though; yawning and sleepiness are often the first symptoms.

Seasickness is an imbalance of the inner ear that confuses your brain. I'm not sure why it makes you throw up or feel uncontrollably ill but that's just how our bodies cope with it. However, if you close your eyes you can't see that you are moving so your body doesn't get as confused.

I slept for another hour and rose again happy to be feeling a little better. Maybe I would be all right after all. I walked into the main cabin. Jez and Owain were in the rear cockpit and not talking much. Owain had his gaze fixed on the horizon.

'How you feeling, Owain?'

He just shook his head slightly.

'Seasick, mate?'

He nodded while keeping his eyes fixed on the horizon. Jez had given him the tiller arm to hold to give him something to do and take his mind off feeling nauseous. Then I saw Owain let the tiller go, do a kind of backward side bend over the edge and begin vomiting, while Jez tried to regain control of *Friday* as she veered off-course.

'We have a winner!' Jez shouted. 'Two Jägerbombs for Owain,' he laughed, now with *Friday* under control again.

Em came running through from her bunk.

'Owain, did you vom?' laughed Em. 'I feel a bit sick too,' she admitted.

'But you both said "no" to getting seasick on your questionnaire!' I exclaimed.

'Actually I said: Not that I know of!' she replied.

Owain still had his head overboard and clearly wasn't in the mood for any banter.

After a good five hours, we eventually reached Sennen Cove. Owain had retired to his bunk and Em was getting my swim kit ready. I had started to feel sick again and it was quiet on *Friday*. The waves were a lot bigger than they had been the day before and anchoring in the bay was pretty hairy. I went up on deck with Jez to help. *Friday* started to go side-on to the waves, throwing me left and right. I immediately felt really sick. I started to walk to the bow of the yacht and about halfway along, and without much warning, a torrent of the previous night's food mixed with this morning's oats came rushing up from the depths of my stomach. I leant over the side rails, while holding on to one of the shrouds to avoid ending up in the sea, as I turned the dark blue water into a murky white haze, vomit coming out of my nose. I hung over the edge for about a minute until there was nothing left in my stomach, my nose and throat burning. I was just dry heaving. I was frustrated because I hadn't lasted more than a few hours at sea and I had also just wasted some pretty important calories, which were now feeding the fish. I really didn't feel like eating so would have to have a liquid nutrition shake to fuel me instead. It wasn't ideal but I really needed to get calories in me.

Owain had thrown up once more too, and Em didn't look any better but was putting on a brave face. We just needed to get to land. We dropped anchor and Jez rowed the RIB to shore (I didn't have enough money to buy fuel for the engine yet) while Em kayaked alongside. I had all my swimming kit in a bag ready for the day's session but honestly didn't feel like swimming at all. Owain unfortunately had to stay on the yacht as it was too rough to leave it unattended at anchor. I knew the pain he was going through and I felt incredibly guilty. I knew if I were in his shoes, feeling like that, I'd have let the boat sink instead of stay on it. He looked helpless sitting in the back cockpit by himself as we rowed away from him, his head close to the edge of *Friday* in case he needed to throw up again. Eventually we got to shore and I collapsed on the sand, my world still swaying from side to side.

'You guys all right? Why did you row in?' asked a man standing halfway up the slipway.

'We haven't got any fuel for the RIB yet,' I replied.

'You're the swimmer, right? Hi. I'm Norman, nice to meet you. I'll tell you what, I'll go get you some if you want?' he said with a big smile on his face. He was from

Yorkshire. I didn't know what to say because I had no money to buy any fuel so just made an excuse.

'Thank you but I left my wallet on the boat. We'll get some in St Ives.'

'No, don't be silly. I'll donate it to you. Come, give me the tank. The wife and I will go now. It'll take us half an hour. Hope that's OK?'

'Wow, thank you so, so much. Very kind of you.' I said, as the sense of gratitude I felt unfortunately coincided with another sudden urge to vomit.

'Ah shit, Em, sorry! I forgot my energy shakes on the boat. Any chance you could kayak back and get them?'

In my haste to get off the boat I had left them in the cupboard. I really needed my shakes today as I was all out of nutrition in my stomach. As well as crew captain, Em's job was to get my nutrition and kit ready each day. She would basically be like my mum on the swim. I had some carb and protein powder, which Em would carry in the kayak.

Each shake was around 500kcal and that was a much-needed energy source between meals to keep me going. Em kayaked back to *Friday* and Jez faffed round with bits on the RIB, like attaching a small anchor to it and fixing a bigger rope used to drag it behind *Friday*. I slowly started to get dressed but started to feel sick again. I was still swaying from side to side. I hoped that getting back into the freezing water might snap me back to life.

Twenty minutes later Norman came back with our outboard tank filled. Jez could now motor back to *Friday* instead of having to row. I looked to see where Em was.

She wasn't on deck and the kayak was still rafted alongside *Friday*. Jez connected the fuel tank and decided to go and see what was happening. He zoomed out the harbour and into the now worryingly big waves. On one occasion he hit a wave so big I thought he might topple over backwards he went up so high.

When he arrived back on *Friday*, both Em and Owain weren't in a good state. Em was throwing up in a bucket and Owain was throwing up in the toilet. Em eventually managed to get up and back into the kayak, and paddled back to shore looking a little dishevelled.

'You all right?' I asked, not knowing what had happened.

'Yeah, fine, just been vomming, like, everywhere.'

'Really, can you kayak? Let me know if you can't.'

'No, I'm fine. Let's go Ginge,' joked Em, obviously trying to stay positive.

I was now in my wetsuit and ready to go. I jumped in and got the same shock from the cold water on my face as I had before.

This was it. This was my first proper day of swimming. I was a day behind because of Jez missing his bus and was hoping to get eight to ten miles up towards St Ives in the six-hour tide window before it swapped direction and I'd have to stop. The waves were coming at me from the left as I made my way towards *Friday*, bobbing from left to right in the bay. I tried bilateral breathing, where you breathe on every third stroke, which helps with your rhythm, but after drinking a few waves and nearly throwing up again whenever I breathed to the left, I settled with breathing only to my right on every stroke. This meant I was also looking at land, which gave me something to keep my mind busy.

I reached *Friday*, which was on my route north, and Jez was battling to get the anchor up with his hands because the waves kept knocking him off balance and he'd let it go. I later found out that he was even considering cutting the anchor because it was so hard to haul up.

The waves were starting to pick up as I carried on swimming towards the end of Sennen bay. Every now and then a jet of cold water rushed down inside my suit taking my breath away. I had tried to drink some of my energy shake but there wasn't nearly enough food in my stomach to help keep me warm. When your body is metabolising food and creating energy, it acts as a heater. When your heater runs out of fuel, you get cold very quickly. My heater had been out of fuel for hours. I was shivering with every stroke.

Em wasn't looking happy either, although managed to force a smile. I looked back to see Jez had finally hauled up the anchor and was coming towards us. Owain was nowhere to be seen and was apparently lying down with his eyes closed in his bunk. I waited for *Friday* to get alongside us.

'Mate, I'm freezing and everyone is feeling sick. Should we call it a day?' I asked Jez.

'Up to you, but it's another five hours to St Ives which is our only safe anchorage.'

I turned around and started to take a few more strokes. I really needed to get some miles in, and get away from bloody Sennen. It seemed cursed. I went another 50 metres and as I went to breathe, a wave engulfed my face and I swallowed what must have been a pint of seawater. I came up for air and nearly vomited again. I looked up at Jez running around the boat trying to sort out ropes, sails and steer all by himself because Owain was down below. Although *Friday* was a small boat that could be sailed single-handedly, if there was an emergency situation, having a second pair of hands was critical.

I had come up with a set of priorities for the swim and priority one was crew and boat safety. Nothing else mattered. If the crew or the boat was in danger everything stopped and we needed to make for cover. Second priority was for me to make progress. Me spending time in the water was more important than media, photos or exploring. Third priority was to document the adventure as much as possible, share the story and blog about it.

This was a time when there was a bit of a blurred line between priority one and two, but seeing as we were all feeling ill and probably not in any state to help Jez should we need to, I decided to abandon the day's session, get some proper food in me, take some seasick tablets and start again in the morning. I climbed back on the yacht feeling pretty disappointed with myself. I knew there would inevitably be problems to iron out in the beginning, but when the problem is not being able to do the main thing you're meant to be doing – i.e., swimming – then that makes it worse. I had wanted to start with a bang and get some good miles in. I knew if I swam like a fish on Red

Bull for the first few days everyone would start believing in me and the swim. I'd talked a big game in the lead-up, partly to try to convince people the 'impossible' is possible, and party because I listened to too many Muhammad Ali speeches on YouTube. I also put a lot of pressure on myself to do well at the start. Right now though I had swum two miles in two days and was very behind schedule. I could feel the naysayers' words in my ears. If I carried on like this it would take me just over two years to complete the swim.

I hoped tomorrow would be better. I had heard that you do eventually get your sea legs and prayed that we'd get them soon because there was no way we could carry on like this.

It was early evening by the time we reached St Ives and were all pretty desperate to get to land. We clambered into the RIB and motored to the harbour. Feeling our feet on solid soil was incredible. Even though we were still swaying from side to side after the long day at sea, especially Owain who had been in the yacht all day and still looked a little green. The one bit of good news was that my sponsorship money had cleared, which meant I could now get some proper food. First on the list was a nice big plate of lasagne from the closest restaurant to the harbour. It was the best lasagne I have ever eaten.

It was only halfway through the meal that I realised we had one big logistical problem to solve. How were we going to get the kayak to Sennen in the morning? Taking *Friday* all the way back wasn't an option and it was nearly a 20 mile drive. I then remembered Simon, who we'd met on the beach. He said he lived in St Ives and wanted to swim with me. I had his number so Owain decided to call him to ask if he could help us. It was a long shot but I wasn't sure we had any other options as hitch-hiking with a kayak would be near impossible.

'Morning. How you feeling? Owain tells me you were all seasick yesterday,' joked Simon, as he pulled up in his little silver Peugeot.

I'm glad he saw the funny side; although we tried to make light of it, it really hadn't been great for team morale. Simon and his wife Innes had really gone out of their way to help us. As they had lent out their van, which could have taken the kayak easily, to a friend, they had gone to the effort of finding some roof racks for their small car late last night. I was blown away by their kindness.

We spent half an hour trying to tie the kayak and paddle to the small roof rack before Em and I jumped into the back of the car and zoomed back to Sennen Cove. Simon and Innes chatted away, asking me questions and insisted we give him a call in the afternoon if we needed picking up from somewhere. It had started to rain slightly by the time we reached Sennen and unpacked our gear. We said our thank yous and decided to get a quick bacon and egg sandwich before my session. Just as I was finishing up and getting into my wetsuit, a large van with a satellite dish came into the car park. A lady jumped out holding a microphone.

'Are you Sean, the swimmer?' She asked with a big smile on her face.

'Yes, that's me.'

'Great. I'm from BBC Radio Cornwall and wanted to get a few quick words if that's OK.'

I told her all about what I was going to expect from the swim and also how we were all seasick, which is why I was a few days behind schedule already. She seemed to love that we were all seasick; I guess there was some sort of tragicomedy in the fact that everyone, on a sea-going adventure, couldn't actually handle the sea at all. I finished the interview and helped Em carry the kayak down to the beach. Sennen bloody Cove. We had been here for the best part of four days and I couldn't wait to get away from it. I knew that once we were round the corner from the bay I'd feel the journey was properly underway.

It was just Em and I today as Jez and Owain still had some boat admin to do in St Ives, and it would have taken too long to sail back to Sennen anyway. Both Em and I were really nervous as this part of the coast is lined with towering, jagged cliffs and the nearest beach is just over seven miles away, which meant there would be nowhere to get out if we got into trouble. If the tide changed before I reached the beach then I'd land up floating all the way back to Sennen again. So I had five hours (I was an hour behind schedule) to swim seven miles. To the average open-water swimmer that's a simple task, but I had no idea how I would cope and what my speed would be in the big Atlantic waves.

Em got in the kayak and I tried to push her into the sea but she just got caught in the mud. It took us three attempts before she was finally away. I had made it to the far side of Sennen beach the day before, so I ran around so that I didn't have to swim across the bay again. It also helped me warm up a little as the typical Cornish drizzle started to settle in.

Having a good night's sleep and a good meal certainly helped and I didn't feel nearly as cold as I had previously when I'd got in the water, and felt much better than yesterday. I swam through the breakers towards the end of the bay where I'd told Em to meet me, but when I got there I couldn't see her anywhere. The waves were just big enough that we both needed to be on the crest of a wave at exactly the same time to see each other. If either of us were in the trough we were hidden from each other's sight. After a good few minutes I eventually saw the end of a paddle above a wave. Em was kayaking away from me. I shouted and she turned around and we made our way towards each other.

'I thought you had started swimming without me,' she said.

'Yeah, can't believe how hard it was to see you in these waves. We need to come up with a system, like put your paddle straight up in the air if you can't see me,' I suggested.

Just then Em let out a huge gasp.

'What?' I asked nervously.

'I dunno, there is something big in the water over there and it wasn't a dolphin.' She looked worried.

My heart began to race. I looked all around and into the water below me.

'Look! There it is,' Em shouted.

I looked over to see a seal about 20 metres away, poking his head up and looking at us inquisitively.

'It's only a seal.' I said.

'Can they bite?' Asked Em nervously.

'I'm not sure. Come on. We need to go to make that beach.' I had never questioned if seals would bite someone but was almost certain they didn't. You never see pictures or graphics of angry seals, do you? They are always fluffy and cute. That was my logic anyway.

Within a few minutes I was finally around the corner from Sennen Cove and alone at sea. It was a strange feeling. There was no turning back now. I wasn't feeling confident at all in my ability to swim in big waves and knew these first few days would be a steep learning curve. I only wished that I was doing my first real session along a nice calm stretch of water with loads of beaches to get out and rest on should I need to. This was literally being thrown in at the deep end, the very deep and treacherous end at that.

That first mile seemed to take forever; I was trying to work out what to do with my arms as they kept getting pushed all over the place with every wave that came from my left. I hadn't quite achieved the muscle memory and had to concentrate really hard on every stroke in order to actually make progress. There were a few times when my hands and feet were doing the right things but I was in fact staying completely stationary.

On and on I swam, trying my best not to drink any salt water as I knew it would make me vomit. I stayed within

30 metres or so from the edge of the towering Cornish cliffs that rose from the crashing sea to a dramatically dark sky above. I didn't want to stop swimming as I knew my pace was slow, so just kept my head down. Stroke, stroke, breath. Stroke, stroke, breath.

It was coming up to the end of my five-hour tidal window and it had rained for most of the day. My body was starting to shut down. I could feel my pace dropping even further and I knew the tide was starting to turn against me. I still had no idea how far away the beach was. I knew it was just north of Pendeen Lighthouse but we hadn't seen a lighthouse all day. Would I make it? I was starting to get nervous that I wouldn't. I felt so very tired both physically and mentally, trying to remember what to do with each arm and then making that arm fight each battering wave.

'You all right Em?' I asked looking up at Em, who was soaked to the core. She looked freezing. I was at least keeping relatively warm due to being active.

'I'm OK, Ginge. Keep swimming.'

The waves were picking up and the tide was starting to push me backwards. I told Em to go ahead and it was then that I heard the foghorn, and thought it might be a rescue siren for me. I knew the bit at Land's End would be hard because I got my timing wrong but right here, right now, I should have been able to make some progress. I felt afraid for the first time, both for my safety and at the increasing reality that maybe I had bitten off more than I could chew.

'You go ahead Em. I'll stop here.'

'Are you sure?'

'Yeah, I'll be fine. I'll see you at the beach.'

Em paddled away from me and I eventually managed to clamber ashore and fell onto the grass, exhausted.

'You OK, mate?' a voice asked as I lay there with my eyes closed. A young guy had seen me struggling and came down the bank to see how I was. I barely heard him over the sound of the foghorn still blaring over the ocean.

'Yeah, just tired. Quite strong tides on that corner.'

We chatted for a bit and I got the impression he hadn't heard about my attempt so I decided to keep quiet. I wasn't in the mood for many questions. I just wanted to rest. After a bit more general chat about the weather and other irrelevant small talk I started to make my way round to the beach. I eventually reached it and found Em trying to empty the kayak, which was filled with a mixture of rainwater and seawater from waves that had crashed over her. She was wearing a spray deck – a waterproof covering for the kayak's cockpit that encircles you when you are sat in the kayak – but some water was still seeping in. Too much water and she'd eventually sink. It was unlikely, but she still really needed to tighten the straps on the spray deck.

'What a day, hey?' I said as I used up the last of my energy to help her empty the kayak.

'Well done. That bit on the rocks looked scary.'

I had made the seven miles stretch to the beach and that was enough for the day. There was no way I could attempt the next section now. I was just too tired.

Em and I needed to get back to St Ives, which was about 15 miles away on the roads but that would involve carrying the kayak about a mile up the steep cliff path. I had no energy left in my arms and it was far too heavy for Em to carry on her own.

'Should we call Simon? He said we should,' suggested Em.

'I feel bad. He's been so helpful already.'

'I know, but he did offer. I'll call him.'

There was no reception on the beach so Em headed back up the path to try and call Simon. I lay down on the beach and closed my eyes. I don't remember falling asleep but when I next opened my eyes, Em and a sweaty man carrying a huge tripod and broadcast camera were standing over me.

'Hi Sean, I'm Chris from BBC Points West. I followed the tracker and am here to do a piece on the swim. Hope that's OK?'

Chris was sweating profusely from having to carry all that kit about a mile from the car park. I felt sorry for him but he sure had dedication. I repeated most of the same things I had said in the morning's radio interview, including the bit about us all being seasick. This seemed to be the story everyone wanted to hear, and not the fact I was attempting the first ever length of Britain swim. I wasn't bothered though. The seasickness joke gave us all something to smile about and kept the mood light-hearted, instead of us getting overwhelmed and serious by the enormity of the swim and just how badly we were coping. I didn't want the swimming side of things to dominate. I wanted to have a coastal adventure that was using swimming as the means of transport. Much like you would on a cycle trip. The cycling gets you from A to B but the adventure is what you have in the middle.

I found it quite funny that no media bothered to come to Land's End to see me off but one mention that we were all seasick and they were all over us.

After the interview, Chris asked if I would just get back in the water and do a few lengths of the bay. It was the last thing I wanted to do as I had just started to dry out but I agreed nevertheless. I'm sure he got the shot in the first 30 seconds but I had to do about 300 metres up and down before he waved me in. Chris packed up and slowly walked back along the steep path carrying his heavy gear. His report would air on the news later that night.

'Simon is coming in an hour,' said Em, excited that we had a lift to St Ives.

'Awesome. Thanks for sorting that. I'm not carrying the kayak up there. I think we should leave it here. We can bury it by those rocks.' I pointed to a hidden part of the beach where no one would see it. It was unlikely that anyone would even come to this beach between now and tomorrow morning but it was Jez's pride and joy and I would feel happier if we hid it. So Em and I dragged the kayak up, hid it behind some rocks and then spent 20 minutes covering it in sand and seaweed.

We walked up to Pendeen Lighthouse and waited in the car park for Simon to arrive. He zoomed in, all smiles, in his little Peugeot.

'Good work, guys. I've been following your tracker all day. It's addictive seeing how far you go every ten minutes,' said Simon with great enthusiasm. 'I've spoken to Owain already, and Innes and I would like to have you round for dinner. She's making spag bol. Hope that's OK.'

Spaghetti bolognese is actually one of the best meals for recovery as it is high in fat, carbs and protein. I sure could do with a hearty meal.

Not only did we get an amazing meal and a few beers but we also had a shower. *Friday* had no running water, let alone hot water, so we knew having a shower would be a luxury to be taken at every opportunity possible. It was a nice ending to a pretty tough day and good to make new friends.

Unsurprisingly, I slept incredibly well. This was going to be the first day where I would swim on both north-going tides, one in the morning and one in the evening. The northerly tide would start running at High Water Dover +4. (The time of high water moves forward each day.) I needed to do ten miles to get to St Ives but had two tides to do it in. Jez had shown me one beach about halfway along that was inaccessible from land but we could get out of the water there and wait out the southerly tide. The only thing we didn't know for certain was if Google Earth had taken the photo at low or high water. If at low water then the beach might actually be covered at high water. The charts, however, showed some sort of sand, which gave us a little security. If that were to happen then we could always call Jez to come and collect us. High Water +4 meant I needed to start swimming at 7am.

Simon couldn't take us back to Pendeen because of work commitments, so the only way to get back to the beach was to take the 7.05am local bus from St Ives harbour, change somewhere along the route to another bus and then walk for 45 minutes. I'd then get in the water at around 8.30am, which was a little later than I wanted but at least meant I would have a faster tide to help me along. The middle three hours of every tide are the most important hours to be in the water as that's when I would make the biggest dent in my daily mileage goal.

So at 7.05am, already dressed in my wetsuit, Em, Owain and I caught the bus towards Pendeen. It was pretty surreal as the few people on the bus knew I was the swimmer and that we were all seasick. It seemed to be the running joke and certainly lifted our moods as we chugged along the Cornish country lanes laughing and joking with other passengers.

Just before getting in the water, I noticed the rubbing on my foot had turned to a small scab. I showed Em and asked her to look for something in the first aid kit. There was nothing but as it wasn't painful I put my booties on and jumped in. The sea was a lot calmer, which was a nice change. I also felt much warmer than I had the day before. I think it was a mixture of acclimatising and eating more food. The flatter water gave me the opportunity to work on my style somewhat. I tried various techniques to see what was best.

Eventually I settled on pretending to crawl along a ladder that was on the floor. Reach ahead, grab a rung, pull it towards me keeping my hand fairly close to my body and then push the rung below, then repeat that with the other hand. I wasn't sure if that was even correct, and was pretty certain my coach Mark would be pulling his hair out if he knew how bad it was, but it felt the best and with every stroke I was gaining confidence. It's amazing how a sunny day without waves can completely change your mental state. Yesterday, I had doubted whether the swim was possible, but today I felt good.

The only thing that was still a problem was the freezing cold jet of water that kept shooting into my wetsuit. That mixed with all my pee (you have no option but to urinate in your wetsuit when swimming for hours), which would gather around my torso area, meant that three hours of swimming made me not only look like the Michelin Man but also weigh me down a lot. I had been for a wetsuit fitting at Speedo and we had decided on a men's small wetsuit at the time because I was planning to put on some weight before the swim. Unfortunately I hadn't put on much weight at all and probably needed a men's extra small. This size was too big for me now and I was only going to get thinner. My starting weight was 67kg, which was far too light, but I've always battled to put on weight. This is normally a good thing but this time I could have done with a few extra pounds. My lack of body fat was definitely contributing to my inability to deal with cold conditions.

Settling into my ladder-crawl swimming technique for the day meant I could now begin to appreciate the incredible Cornish coastline. In the sunshine it wasn't nearly as dramatic as before, but the towering cliffs and jagged rocks were spectacular to swim along. I hadn't drunk nearly enough water the previous day so asked Em to make sure I had some every 20 minutes. Em too was getting more confident in the kayak and we managed to have some fun as we went along. The tide was due to turn around 1pm and we managed to get to our beach just in time. It wasn't the easiest of beach landings for Em due to the steepness of the rocks. It wasn't a beach at all really and had only become one due to what must have been a pretty big landslide once. I swam ashore and then Em did a run up to the rocks where I was ready to help pull her ashore. Even though the waves were no more than a foot high Em still managed to fall out the kayak.

'Noooo! I had just got dry.'

This tiny rocky beach would be our little home for the next five hours or so. The plan was to wait again for High Water +4 which was at around 6pm, but I figured I'd try swimming at relatively slack water, which would start at around 5pm. If the tide was too strong I'd just wait until I could make progress.

Both Em and I were pretty tired and it wasn't long before we had both found a little nook in the rocks and were fast asleep.

Crack!!! I heard some rocks smashing together a few feet from my head. I jumped up to see the remains of a cricket ball-sized rock split up into five or six different pieces and shoot off in all directions. I looked above me to see a few more pebbles rolling down the hill. A beach created by a landslide wasn't an ideal place to sleep but we had no option. I woke up Em and told her to find another large rock to hide behind in case more rocks came tumbling down. I found another spot behind another suitably large rock and soon passed out again. I was too tired to actually care. I just needed to sleep.

I got back in the water at 5pm and, although slightly against the end of the weakening southerly tide, I was still making progress so decided to get on with it. Having a nap certainly helped and along with hydrating every 20 minutes, I felt strong. It always takes a while to get into the flow of things and work out a system. It was incredibly reassuring to know that the struggles I had over the first few days were in fact teething problems and not challenge-ending problems. For the first time since I started I felt a smidgeon of hope that I could do this.

We reached St Ives at 8pm, and were too tired to do anything much other than eat a Stowaways dinner and go to sleep. The ten miles we'd managed was below the average I needed to do, but I knew this would be the case in the first week as I found my legs, and arms, so to speak.

4

CORNISH HOSPITALITY

Friday was rocking up and down more than usual when I went to bed but after finding a comfortable position I eventually fell asleep. I couldn't have been asleep more than an hour when all of a sudden the rocking changed from lengthways to sideways and I was flung right over and onto Em's bunk, pinning her against the side of the boat.

'So sorry! What happened there?' I apologised, while frantically trying to move back to my side of the bunk. I still didn't know Em well enough to know how she'd react to me invading her bunk.

'Don't worry, I can't sleep anyway,' she said.

I tried to get back into a comfortable position but the sideways rocking meant that with every wave I was still flung over towards Em's bunk. Unlike Jez and Owain's bunks, our front bunks didn't have sides preventing us from falling off in rough weather. Generally the wind and the waves come from the same direction, but sometimes in harbours the waves get flicked around the wall or headland and come in at a different angle to the wind. A yacht will always stay into the wind/tide so if the waves are coming from the side you will rock from side to side. It took a good few hours to work out the best position for my legs to create some sort of anchorage to avoid falling out of bed again. Eventually I fell asleep at around 3am.

Breakfast was dry oats and an energy shake which I was starting to dislike already. Normally I made the shakes with milk, but milk was at a premium on a boat with no fridge. So instead I had them with water which made them taste pretty disgusting. We all then went ashore to say goodbye to Simon who worked in the café along the edge of the bay. I decided to have a second breakfast from the café, which Simon said was on the house. What an amazing chap.

The section from here was a lot easier logistically. There was a town or beach every five miles, which meant I could get out and rest every few hours. Also, today I'd have *Friday* following me. The plan was to swim as far as I could and then anchor in St Agnes bay.

Em got ready in the kayak and instead of walking through the town, Jez decided to take me round in the RIB. We jumped in and fired her up. This was the first time I had been in the RIB properly and it was a good feeling bombing through the waves. We went round the corner of the bay heading west and then all of a sudden the engine died. Jez and I looked at each other as we came to an abrupt halt. Jez tried to start her again but she just spluttered. We were now drifting in the wrong direction and slightly out to sea. Jez tried a few more times and was getting tired so I decided to give it a go. Eventually after five attempts she fired up. Jez and I gave each other a ceremonial high five and carried on along the coast to yesterday's end point.

'Good luck, mate. We'll see you in a bit,' said Jez as I jumped in.

Jez followed me for the first few hundred metres until I was at the edge of the bay where Em was waiting in the kayak. He then waved us off and as he was zooming away I heard the engine die again. I looked up.

'Don't worry,' he shouted. 'I can row from here anyway. See you later.'

The tide was quite strong but I completed the four-mile crossing of St Ives Bay in just less than two hours. I looked back across the bay to see where Jez was but I could still see *Friday* anchored up near the harbour. Maybe they had gone for breakfast or Owain was arranging some media from shore. There was no real reason for them to be right by our sides all day, and as long as they met us at some point we'd be fine.

Our first beach was just east of St Ives Bay and as we came ashore the sun came out. The sand was white and the sea crystal clear. We could have been in the Caribbean if it wasn't for the freezing water. This was another beach that you could only access from the sea and at only 50 metres long we felt as if it was our own little paradise. I found a chair that had been washed up and sat down to rest and have an energy shake while the sun warmed up the rubber on my wetsuit. It suddenly dawned on me why wetsuits are black: to help absorb more heat, which certainly made a difference.

After about half an hour it was time to leave, so I got up and turned and got the fright of my life. There on the beach about 20 metres behind us was a guy in his late twenties sunbathing. He was completely naked with his blindingly white bum on full show. Em and I looked at each other. How did he get here and why was he naked?! There were 100 foot vertical cliffs all around the beach. He was just lying there reading a book and didn't even acknowledge us. It was all too strange so we just decided to get back in the water and keep going. We left the naked bum man and continued along the coast. The sun was out, the water was clear and there were no waves. The only thing still on our minds was that Jez hadn't passed us and we had no way of getting hold of him as we had no phone reception.

The next stop was Portreath, five miles away. I was making good progress and reached the beach by mid-afternoon. There were some slightly larger waves in the bay and Em took a pretty impressive tumble, which resulted in a Baywatch-style run in from a few of the ridiculously toned lifeguards on duty. I think Em capsized on purpose. They were exquisite examples of the human form as they ran in to help her drag her flooded kayak onto the shore. I too got dunked by a wave from behind as I walked into the beach but didn't even get a second glance.

At last, we had phone reception so Em called Jez. After a lot of chatting Em put the phone down with a concerned look on her face.

'He had engine failure.'

'On *Friday*?' I asked, worried.

'No, the RIB. He said he'd tell us later. They are about half an hour from us.'

Damn RIB engine. I had spent £220 getting it serviced and it still didn't work. That left us with the small problem of food. Em and I hadn't brought our wallets as we thought we'd have the boat with us, and I was all out of recovery shakes and really needed to eat something.

'I'll go beg for some food,' Em said confidently, as if that was a totally normal thing to do.

'Really, are you sure?' I've always hated asking people for things.

'Yeah, I'll find something.'

With that, Em wandered off and I lay down on the sand soaking up the warmth of the sun above and the hot sand below me. I could feel the tightness draining out of me.

Em came back about half an hour later with some soup, hot dogs and two flakes. Amazing! We gobbled it down with our hands while sitting on a pavement in a somewhat caveman style. We didn't care though, we were so hungry.

The next tide was only due to start running at around 7pm so we had a good few hours to kill before carrying on. I had done just over nine miles and wanted to at least get to Porthtowan by nightfall to bring my total up to 12 miles.

Half an hour later we saw *Friday* sail past, bobbing up and down in the waves. We called Jez again.

'Hey. How's it going?' I asked.

'Nightmare. Couldn't start the RIB and wind was stronger than I could row. I ended up drifting across St Ives Bay for two hours before embarrassingly giving up and calling the coastguard to drag me in. Damn Arthur's engine.'

'Shit. You all right?'

'Yeah, just very sore arms now,' joked Jez. It was good to see he still had a sense of humour.

'So where we anchoring tonight?' I asked.

'That's the other thing. Looking at the wind and the waves there might be nowhere to anchor except Newquay, which is six hours from here. We'll try in St Agnes but I think it will be too rough.'

If *Friday* went all the way to Newquay then I'd have no support boat for the next three days and Em and I would be stuck with the kayak each night, and have to hitch rides to and from Newquay, which would take forever. My heart sank. I hadn't thought these logistics through at all in preparation. There were just so many factors to take into consideration.

Jez continued, 'Owain and I need to go ahead to see if St Agnes is OK otherwise we'll have to push on to Newquay so we can't hang around. Sorry, but we gotta keep sailing.'

'OK, mate. Let us know.'

I now had a decision to make. Em and I had no clothes, no money and no food. If I did the next section to Porthtowan I'd get there at around 9pm. Jez would potentially be in St Agnes, which we could probably hitchhike to, but he could also very well be on his way to Newquay. We'd then be stranded at night at Porthtowan with nothing.

'What if we stop for the day? I'm sure we can find a place to crash here tonight. We still have time to do that,' Em suggested.

I hated the fact I was cutting another day short.

'I could then hitch to St Agnes, get our sleeping bags, clothes and wallets off Jez there before he needs to carry on, if he does.'

It did make sense. For the sake of losing three miles I guess it was the only option we had. I agreed and Em jumped into action. I called Jez to tell him to wait in St Agnes so we could get our stuff while Em went off to find somewhere to stay. About 10 minutes later Em came back.

'I found the most amazing lady. She is called Beth and she said we can stay in her house tonight. She's coming down for a surf in an hour so I said you'd be here. You'll like her.'

Em was buzzing with excitement. We now had a bed. All we needed was our spare clothes and money so Em decided to go and hitchhike to St Agnes.

With Em gone, I had some time alone to take things in. The last few weeks before the swim and these first few days in Cornwall had been so hectic that I hadn't had much time to absorb it all. The sun was still high in the sky, people were laughing and playing on the beach and I had swum here from Land's End. Although I had only swum 25 miles it still felt good to say that. My one concern was that I was still quite far behind schedule. I knew it would be slow to start but my competitive side was eating away at my fatigued mind because I wanted to do more miles. I was yet to hit double figures in one day and that annoyed me. In the lead-up I had planned to swim around 15 miles per day. That was worked out at a pace of 2–2.5mph for seven to eight hours a day in the water. Five hours in one tide and three hours in a second tide. My route was said to be 1,000 miles but I figured it might be a bit shorter if I cut across some of the big bays. A distance of 900 miles at 15 miles per day gives me 60 swimming days. I thought I'd have at least one rest day a week and a few bad weather days, bringing my expected swim time to be around two-and-a-half months, which meant finishing around the middle of September.

The waters stay warm until the end of September but the weather gets worse and worse the closer you get to October, so it's a case of make hay while the sun is shining. All these figures were good to write on paper but in reality it was complete guesswork. I really had no idea how the sea would treat us and how we'd cope mentally being cramped up in a small yacht for 75 days. Many expeditions in history have failed not because of the enormity of the task, but because of people's state of mind. With no one to ask for advice we knew there would be a lot of thumb sucking and supposition, especially in the first few weeks while we worked things out.

Jez had also said the first week would be hard from an anchoring point of view and that it would get easier. It was just difficult to think that way when there were so many things that weren't related to my swimming ability getting in my way. I lay down and closed my eyes for a while waiting for Beth.

'Sean? I'm Beth,' I heard a voice say and opened my eyes to see a lady standing over me. She had very short greying hair and was wearing a pretty well-used and characterful wetsuit. I felt very unadventurous in my shiny new suit that hadn't seen nearly as many stories as Beth's. I stood up immediately and then nearly fell over again because of a head rush. That was a sign I needed to eat and drink more.

'Listen, you're more than welcome to stay at mine but I'm just going for a surf for an hour if that's OK.'

'Of course. Thank you so much,' I said, still a bit dizzy as Beth went to get her board from the clubhouse and then disappeared into the waves. It had been a few hours since Em left and I had had a call from her to tell me she had got lost, been given a lift to someone's house, had a shower, some tea and cake, and was now on her way to meet Jez in St Agnes. She sounded like she had everything under control and gave me confidence in her ability to just get things done. Her bubbly personality mixed with her shameless ability to approach anyone and ask them for help was certainly going to be a good asset for the expedition.

Beth eventually came back from her surf and arranged with one of the lifeguards for me to leave the kayak in their clubhouse. She had cycled down to the beach from her cottage a mile up the road and instead of just giving me directions insisted on walking with me. I didn't have any shoes so was a bit slow over the pebbles but I was grateful to Beth for being so kind and patient.

I quickly noticed that Beth's bike had a Rohloff hub on it. Now, if you're into cycle-touring the Rohloff hub is the Rolls-Royce of gearing systems. You only buy one if you are going to be having some serious adventures. I have one on my touring bike and it's done over 16,000 miles and still hasn't missed a beat. It's amazing. Naturally I asked Beth what cycling she has done and she began listing off all the off-beat places she had cycled. Burma, Morocco, (back in the days when cycling in Morocco alone, as a woman, was pretty adventurous) and other far-flung places. Beth said she had been one of the first people to surf in Cornwall in the 1960s. When she started so few people surfed that she knew who owned every surfboard and who had owned them previously. This was before they even had built-in rip-cords and she told me how she experimented with doctor's tubes, the ones used on drips, which she would tie to her ankles. She had some wonderful stories. I was captivated by her adventurous life, which she seemed to still be living. Just then my phone rang. It was Em.

'Quickly, my phone is dying. Jez tried to anchor on St Agnes but too rough so has gone to Newquay. I'll hitch back. See you in a few hours. Gotta go. Bye!' With that she put the phone down.

I told Beth what had happened and she immediately said to tell Em we'd go and collect her. I was blown away. Cornish people are so very generous. I texted Em and she replied so I knew she had got the message.

Beth's house was at the end of a terrace, surrounded by all sorts of flowers and plants. I didn't want to get in Beth's car all smelly so quickly jumped in the shower. I had no clothes but borrowed a shirt and towel to go fetch Em. Yes, I was going commando. I'm not sure Beth was up to lending me her underwear just yet.

That evening we were treated to a delicious dinner, which included a salad made entirely with veg from Beth's garden. Em and I listened all night to her stories. She really was a remarkable woman. Considering we landed on Portreath beach with no food, clothing or money, we had done pretty well for ourselves. It was the best day of the swim so far.

The slight downer to the day was that we found a blog written by a guy at the café at Sennen Cove (not our friend Simon from St Ives café) who helped Em and I look for a skipper on Day 1 to get me to the tip of Land's End – completely mocking my swim attempt. What a back-stabbing idiot. Nice to my face but once back in the safety of his computer, he wrote:

> 'The poor boy is doomed. The tides around here may be bad but around Wales they are ten times worse and in some places downright dangerous. If he does complete his challenge he will certainly have every right to quote the cliché "they said it could not be done". From where I am standing just now they are saying it for a very good reason.'

The one other worry was the scab on my foot. It seemed to be getting bigger. I showed Em again.

'Ah, Stuart is back!' she said.

'Stuart?' I asked.

'Yeah, Stuart the Scab, that's his name now.' Em's light-hearted reaction made me feel a bit better.

'Damn Stuart. It seems to be getting worse, bigger and deeper.'

'We'll get some iodine or something at Newquay.'

I towel-dried Stuart, who was seeping a little, and fell asleep.

After we had big bowls of porridge for breakfast, Beth drove Em and me back to the beach for an early start. After missing three miles yesterday I was keen to get going. It was sunny again and fairly calm as I swam out of Portreath bay. A seal decided to come and say hi briefly, which was nice. I decided to try and push on to St Agnes for my first stop. It was seven miles away, which was the same distance that I had done on the first day out of Sennen that had nearly killed me. I felt a lot stronger and with a shorter day yesterday was confident I'd make it. We passed Porthtowan to our right and pushed on towards the far headland. That was my main marker for this session as I knew St Agnes was just round the corner.

My ladder-pulling technique seemed to be working and my pace was a steady 2mph. Em and I didn't talk much as I kept my head down, working on my style and breathing. My neck was starting to hurt and chafe on the right side from all the single-sided breathing. I figured I was turning my head too much so decided to try and roll my body more to breathe.

It took a while to master the technique but after a while I noticed I wasn't straining my neck as much and didn't chafe either. The only downside was that rolling my left shoulder in the water meant I kept swimming off to the left. I did that anyway because of an old injury I got while cheese-rolling in Gloucestershire a few years ago and this new technique was definitely making it worse.

My mother has lived about a mile from the bottom of Cooper's Hill, which is near the little village of Brockworth, for years. Every year on the late May bank holiday thousands of spectators gather to watch a few dozen people chase a large cheese down an incredibly steep hill. No one knows when exactly the tradition started or where it comes from, but in recent years it's become world famous. Probably because of the sheer eccentricity of this funny English event!

I'd kept promising to get involved, but when it came to it I would always wimp out (this hill is seriously high!). Then in 2009 I decided to tell my friends I was definitely doing it and that they should come and watch me. Then I'd be committed.

To get a place in one of the official races you have to get there early. The first race was at midday, but when I arrived at 9am it was already packed. I managed to make it into the second race and went to the top of the hill. My heart was thumping. I had just seen the first 15 people tumble down the hill and it looked way worse than the YouTube videos. According to the rules the cheese gets a one-second head start, and then the chasers are allowed to start running/falling down the hill. Being the honest guy I am, I followed the rules whereas most of the other guys went as soon as the cheese went!

I bolted down as fast as I could, lasting about three metres before everything became a blur: sky/grass/sky/grass ... I took a massive bump to the head when I collided with another tumbler. For a moment we were entangled together in one ball of craziness. Then I broke free and somehow landed up on my feet again, running, arms flailing in a double windmill fashion. I was heading down the steepest bit, which was just about to flatten out, and had managed to work my way into third place by now. However, as the flatter bottom of the hill neared, I realised I couldn't stop, and I was inevitably going to end up in a huge heap, face-planting the ground. Before I knew it I was face-first in the dirt, bounced twice and then skidded and rolled over the line where some hefty rugby players from the local team were waiting to stop us.

I had somehow managed to come a close second. I was a bit gutted as I would have won with a better start but at least I was uninjured... or so I thought. Once the adrenaline had worn off, I discovered I had actually dislocated my shoulder and torn muscles in my back.

It was one of the most exhilarating 23 seconds of my life, so I didn't mind the injuries too much. However, it did mean that my left shoulder was always a bit weaker than my right, so I had to pay attention to Em to make sure I didn't swim off in completely the wrong direction, which when tired, was happening in a worryingly short distance. If I didn't concentrate I was swimming at 90 degrees within 100 metres.

It took just under three hours to get to the far headland and I was ready for a break. On passing the headland we came across a huge patch of foam. It was about ten inches thick and covered an area the size of a football pitch. I didn't know what it was and whether I could swim through it. Em and I discussed it for a while but decided it was probably fine and going round it was going to take too long. The first few strokes were very strange because I couldn't breathe at my normal height otherwise I'd breathe in some foam. It also didn't smell too good. I therefore had to roll onto my back with each stroke just to breathe. Eventually I made it through and started to head inland for St Agnes. Going right into the bay was a good mile detour but there was no other choice. Just then I started to feel a rumble in my stomach. I hadn't been to the toilet in days, a number two that is. I think my body was still in shock from what I was putting it through. I looked up but couldn't see St Agnes at all. I was certain it was just around the headland. Em got out her phone and checked on Google Maps.

'It's a good mile and a half still.'

'Really? That's at least an hour, 50 minutes if I push it!'

'Why? What's the problem?'

'I might need the, er, actual toilet, if you know what I mean.' With that, I cramped up immediately, as if saying it out loud was my body finally giving up.

Em burst out laughing – she didn't seem to have an ounce of sympathy for my predicament.

'It's not funny, dude,' I said lightly, but was worried.

I pushed on for another 20 minutes as the pressure built up in my stomach. It was getting worse and worse, and still a mile from the beach I had to curl into a ball to try to stop a disaster. There was no way I was going to shit in my wetsuit. If it came to it I'd unzip it and then swim the last bit without a suit. It was just so cold though and I really didn't want to do that.

'Sean's going to shit himself. Sean's going to shit himself, la la la la laaaaa,' Em was singing away, happily.

'No! I won't. I can't!' I curled up in a ball, face-down in the water as if I had just done a splash bomb. If I wasn't careful I'd do a different kind of bomb pretty soon.

I carried on and eventually could see St Agnes bay. I scoured the beach for a place I could run and go to the loo but there were kids everywhere. I'd definitely get arrested for shitting on a beach near small children. There was no other option but to swim all the way into the beach and find a public toilet. Those last minutes were agonising as I swam through the breakers. Em's beach landings hadn't improved at all and she had another Baywatch lifeguard run in, but I didn't have time to help her and hobbled out the waves towards somewhere that might have a toilet, past a very smiley man with a dog who looked like he wanted to talk. Desperately, I rushed past him. There was a toilet in the car park, which I was directed to as I clinched my bum cheeks with so much force they started to hurt. Eventually I made it into the cubical and proceeded to make that cubical 'out of order' for the next, I'd say, year or so thereafter. I did, however, feel like a new man, when I came out.

I headed back to Em to find she was completely soaking wet from her little tumble. She really needed to work on her beach landings. She was chatting away to the friendly chap with the dog who I'd rudely ignored. I felt guilty and went over to say hi.

'You must be THE Sean?'

I laughed. I've never have anyone refer to me with an accentuated THE before my name.

'I'm Steve. I've been following you along the cliff top for the past hour. You've made good progress today. How's the seasickness?'

Steve knew everything about me, the crew and our journey so far, and informed me that his wife was a keen swimmer.

'Yeah, it's not bad. Good to make the beach though as I've needed the loo for the last hour.'

We all laughed. I was honoured to have someone actually go out their way to not only come and find me but also to follow me along the cliff tops. It was easy to forget that anyone was actually watching, let alone caring enough about my swim to come out and find me.

'So where are you staying tonight?' he asked.

'Our yacht is in Newquay, so probably swim to Perranporth and hitch a ride from there.'

'My wife and I would love to have you over for dinner, and if you wanted a shower and an actual bed, we've got the space.'

'Really? Thank you! We might take you up on that.'

We chatted for a bit longer before Steve left and Em and I went to find some lunch, and to wait out some of the southerly tide.

After a good break the plan was to swim round to Perranporth, have some more food as I needed to start eating more, and then try to do another three miles towards the north end of Perranporth beach. It was beautifully sunny and still fairly calm, but getting out of St Agnes bay seemed to take forever.

A few hours later we were starting our approach towards the beach at Perranporth when something felt wrong. We started to hear huge waves crashing. Em and I stopped. I climbed onto the back of the kayak to get a better view. Then we heard someone shout. There were a group of people on the cliffs above us shouting and signalling for us to get back and go further out to sea. Just then a huge roller came in from behind us. It wasn't breaking yet but it lifted us a good 10 feet in the air. From the top of the wave we could see why they had been shouting at us. Perranporth beach was experiencing some of the biggest swells it had seen all year. They were so big that not even the surfers were out.

'Shit, Em. I'm knackered. I'm not sure I can carry on.'

'Yeah, but they look huge. I can't do beach landings in one-foot waves. These would kill me.' Em said, looking scared.

I hadn't seen that look on her face before. I really needed some food and had run out of water too because

I'd drank it all thinking we'd stop. We looked back up at the cliffs where more people had gathered. They seemed to be pointing to the far end of Perranporth beach, which was a good three miles away.

'I might go in and just rest and get some food. Would you wait here?' I asked.

Em didn't reply but I knew she wasn't comfortable with that. Our only other option was to carry on swimming. The next beach, which was just round the corner from the far end of the long Perranporth beach, was four miles away. Doing this with no food and water would take me three hours. I just had no more energy and at times, even though I looked like I was swimming, I was just flapping around in the same spot.

I carried on swimming, getting lifted high into the air with every long roller that came through. I was questioning whether we could have made it to the beach and getting slightly annoyed with Em's inability to stay upright in waves, when I looked back to see the now even larger Atlantic waves crashing up against the cliffs. We had definitely made the right choice. Not even an experienced kayaker would have managed those waves. Knowing I had no other choice meant I just put my head down and forgot the 'but we might have made it if we tried' thoughts going through my mind. It was time to commit to the task at hand and get to the next beach.

By early evening I had made it round to Holywell Bay. I was exhausted. I couldn't move my arms any more and was starting to shiver. The problem was that we couldn't get into Holywell either because of the surf. No matter how I put it to Em she didn't want to do it. My heart sank. What were we going to do? Em looked terrified and I was so tired that treading water became so difficult that without the kayak to hold on too I feared I'd sink.

'We could call Jez,' Em suggested

Newquay was three miles away, which would take Jez at least an hour to get to us. Em and I would then have to just float at sea for an hour. The tide was turning, which meant even if my now-broken body wanted to I couldn't carry on swimming.

'Do we even have reception?' I asked.

Em took out my phone.

'One bar!'

We tried to call Jez but lost reception. It seemed to come and go but eventually Em got through. The conversation didn't last long before we were cut off again. I started to shiver uncontrollably as my core temperature dropped now that I wasn't swimming to keep me warm.

I tried to climb onto the back of the kayak and nearly tipped Em over as I fell off over the other side, like a lazy seal sliding into the water off an icy ledge.

On the fifth attempt, we managed to get through to Jez and tell him our situation. There was nothing we could do now except float aimlessly at sea until he arrived in *Friday*.

Eventually, after many tries, I found a way of getting onto the back of the kayak, and I lay there shivering and fatigued. I could feel my body burning away my muscle tissue in an effort to recover. This was the last thing I

◁
Riding a rhino for a conservation publicity shot as a kid. Growing up in a national park in Zimbabwe this was, believe it or not, fairly standard

My first ever open water swim aged 14 in the Midmar Mile. I obviously thought the water was 'cold'. Ha!
▽

◁
Clean shaven at the start with my mum

Standing under the iconic Land's End sign looking seriously nervous
▽

Friday in all her glory. Jez is sailing, while Em's in the kayak and I'm swimming ahead

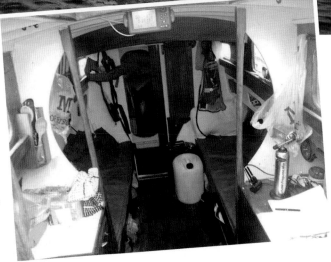

▷

Friday's rather cramped and somewhat leaky interior. Four of us lived in here for over four months. I don't know how we didn't kill each other!

△

Coming back in the RIB from a trip to shore to get supplies. Judging by the look on Em's face she's forgotten something she wanted!

◁

Jez (otherwise known as 'The Hoarder') was always finding interesting ways of using flotsam and jetsam

△
Waiting out the southerly tide
on a landslide in Cornwall. It
wasn't the safest place to have
a nap, admittedly…

Em, despite later admitting that
she was actually terrified of
water, was always smiling

Trying to prepare mentally for another difficult session

△

Swimming with seals

▷

My arch enemy: the lion's mane jellyfish. I grew my own lion's mane to try to stop them stinging me in the face

Enjoying a night ashore round the campfire cooking the fish Owain had caught that day. It was moments like this that really made the swim

▽

△
An ocean selfie
with *Friday* in the
background

◁
Trying to stay out of
the way of the huge
container ships
around the Bristol
Channel gave us
a few hair-raising
moments

needed. Less muscle means less power in the water. I was already below weight and couldn't afford to lose any more.

An hour later Jez arrived in *Friday*. To get out the water I had to wait for the RIB we were towing to come near me and grab one of the straps and haul myself into it. I then had to accomplish the even more acrobatic task of waiting for the back of *Friday*, which was moving up and down about a metre every second, to be at the right height before jumping on. This was hard normally, and after swimming for five hours, I wasn't sure how I was going to do it. Once on board I collapsed on my bunk and decided to nap on the way back to Newquay. I'd been asleep all of five minutes when I heard Jez shout.

'Sean! Can you help us?'

I got up slowly and walked into the cabin still half asleep.

'What's up?'

'The kayak has overturned, can you come help me?'

Friday was too small to bring the kayak on board so we were dragging it along with the RIB. A wave must have knocked it over and it was filling with water fast. Jez needed someone to help pull it onto the RIB and empty it.

Owain took the tiller arm and Jez did a very impressive Indiana Jones-style flying jump into the RIB, which was a good few metres behind *Friday*.

'Shit Jez, how'd you do that?' Em shouted.

There was no way I was going to manage that as I had started to stiffen up already from the swim.

It took Jez and me about ten minutes to try and bring the kayak onto the RIB, turn it upside down – which then just put the water in the RIB – before letting it go back into the sea.

Once back in Newquay we got our kit and prepared for a land evening. We had to row into the harbour again as Arthur's engine was still not working even though both Jez and Owain, who knew about outboards, had both had a look at it. It was a nice surprise to find out Owain knew a thing or two about mechanics. I hadn't actually asked this in the interview or the questionnaire, which I really should have, as I am sure I'd be needing his expertise at some point in the future.

We were lucky enough to stay with Steve and Kate that night. I spent the evening getting loads of advice from Kate, who was a seasoned open-water swimmer, while we all had a few beers, ate good food and had the hottest shower in the world. It was a great end to my longest day at sea. To top it off, when they found out we'd probably use Newquay as a base tomorrow they invited us back again for a barbecue. Cornwall seemed to be full of such kind, generous people. It was reassuring my faith in humanity.

I had finally done my first double-figure mileage day. Although completely shattered from doing the last few hours using muscle tissue as an energy source, I felt happy. Total distance swam: 12 miles.

I had the best night's sleep in a king-sized bed. It was nice not to have to try and hook my legs into anything, although a few times in the night I still felt I was rocking from side to side. Jez was the only one who didn't have a land-bed, as we now called them, because he said he didn't feel safe leaving *Friday* unattended on a mooring buoy outside Newquay harbour all night, so went back at around 11pm. His row back to *Friday* had all the ingredients for something bad to happen: dark, a few beers under the belt, a broken engine and some large Cornish waves, but thankfully he was safe.

I decided that I was only going to swim the four miles to Newquay the next day as I felt we could do with an afternoon off and a few beers to celebrate getting there; Newquay was the first major town on the map and something we had been looking at for days. Originally we were going to use *Friday* to get back to Holywell Bay where I ended my swim yesterday, but Steve and Kate insisted they take Em and me there with the kayak on their roof. After heading back to *Friday* to get my kit, Jez rowed me back to the harbour. Em kayaked and predictably fell out at the first sign of a wave, which was still hilarious. Her inability to kayak in any sort of wave was a skill in itself. Luckily she saw the funny side of it.

I absorbed as much open-water swimming advice as possible from Kate as we drove round to my swim start, especially on the diet side of things, which I had truly failed at. She said I should be eating every 45 minutes to avoid getting cold. Up till now, I was just drinking water every half an hour and eating every few hours. She also recommended I get a hooded thermal to fill out my chest space if my suit was too big. This seemed like a good idea and also helped with stopping cold water hitting my skin directly as it went down my neck. I figured if there was a place to get surf gear, Newquay would be it, and I'd sort it out in the afternoon.

It was a calm and sunny day, and knowing I only had four miles to swim meant there was time for some joking around on the beach before heading out. Em kayaked through the breakers, and didn't fall out, and I followed a few minutes later. I was just out of the other side of the breakers when I swam right into something hard, and sudden thoughts of swimming into a shark came rushing into my mind. I looked up and it was one of my water bottles that Em carried in the netting part of the kayak. I grabbed it and swam towards Em. She hadn't even noticed but had lost it in the breakers. We needed to come up with a better system for carrying water and food on the kayak. If I had been planning to swim further that day, not having water would have been disastrous.

I made it round to Newquay without much problem and then took the crew out for a few beers. It was nice to have the afternoon off and relax a bit.

Rest time not only allowed my muscles to recover but, essentially, allowed the crew to let their hair down. I knew all too well that following a swimmer doing 2mph was pretty boring and I wanted to show that I appreciated what they were doing for me. My way to do this was beer. It seemed to work. After a few hard days at sea, I could see the crew losing motivation. Three pints in the pub though and all of a sudden they were raring to go again. I have to admit the theory worked on me too. Added to that, beers are calories too. 200kcal a pint in fact.

We also stocked up on some supplies and fresh food, which included luxuries like toilet paper, red meat, pasta, potatoes, broccoli, cheese and milk. It was hard to keep food fresh and the only place we found that was remotely cool was under the floorboards in the bilge of the main cabin. The problem with this area was that it was always wet because poor little *Friday* leaked a lot, not to mention the fact there was excess diesel from many spillages over the years. I also managed to find a hooded thermal top without sleeves which would go under my suit. This would add more volume to my chest area thus avoiding the rush of water running down my back.

That evening Steve and Kate put on a barbecue the size of Russia for us, and we sat outside chatting and laughing. We were at the end of our first week and it was exactly what we needed. Just when we thought our friends couldn't get any more generous, on hearing about our problems with Arthur's engine, Steve offered to lend us his outboard, take ours to be fixed and then come find us in a few days to do the swap back. What a true gentleman.

I had another amazing night's sleep, which of course had nothing to do with the four beers I had the night before. Jez had again missed out on a land-bed and went back to *Friday* after even more beers than the previous night. He didn't answer his phone the first few times we tried to call him but happily it was because he was fast asleep and not washed up on a beach somewhere.

We said our goodbyes to Kate but knew we'd see Steve again in a few days with Arthur's engine. We did the swap over and motored back to the yacht. What a difference it made not having to row.

Today was going to be the first day where I'd be swimming with the yacht next to me. This meant I could eat a lot more, but more importantly it reduced the risk of me shitting myself as I could always get out if I needed to. It also meant that I could swim directly from headland to headland. Up till now I had been following the shoreline, even though there were so many cliffs I couldn't have gone ashore anyway. I still wasn't that comfortable at sea, and the idea of being a mile offshore with only Em was terrifying.

The going was steady and seeing *Friday* in action, zooming past as Jez sailed circles around me, was a joy to watch. She really was beautiful, despite her faults. Today's main challenge was to come up with a system of eating and drinking in the water. Kate's other recommendation was to drink warm liquids, which would keep my core temperature up. Owain was set the task of boiling the kettle and filling my flask with warm water, adding some juice and then working a way of getting the flask to me in the water and then me being able to get it back to him, bearing in mind once *Friday*'s sails were up it was hard to keep her in one place for long. He initially tried to throw the flask to me, which was attached to a piece of string, but inevitably Owain ran out of string as *Friday* slowly moved away from me in the wind, and he'd have to let his end go. There would then be 15 metres of cord in the water that we didn't want to get caught on *Friday*'s rudder or around the propeller, which still spins freely when the engine isn't running, so I'd have to frantically gather it in.

The next stage in the process was for me to try and launch the flask back at Owain. This felt like grenade-throwing practice as the only way I could throw it was with a straight arm and over my head, back at the boat. This obviously didn't work as I have never thrown a grenade before and I missed the boat by a mile.

Next, Em, who was trying to assist from the yacht today instead of the kayak, tried jumping into the RIB being dragged behind *Friday*. This made things a little easier but inevitably we had the same problems as from the yacht. After an hour, Em decided that it would actually be better if she kayaked next to me and did the food collecting. This was better not only for feeding but because my cheese-rolling shoulder meant I was swimming off to the left a lot more without her next to me. Every 100 metres I would hear everyone shouting, 'Swim straight!' and pointing to where I needed to go. It was almost impossible to get the direction right being so close to the surface of the water. Em said she was feeling seasick in *Friday* anyway, so all in all it made perfect sense.

It was great swimming with the whole team near me and it finally felt like the adventure I wanted it to be. Em was enjoying kayaking. Owain, being a keen photographer, was taking photos and videos, both of me swimming and some amazing landscapes for himself. Jez was happy sailing and playing with ropes, looking at charts and various other sailing-related things I didn't understand. Everyone was in high spirits.

We were in the switch-over tide period where all of the second tide was at night, so I had only had one session to swim in. By early evening I had swum a distance of 11 miles, all the way up to Polventon bay. This was just around from Booby's Bay, which, when reading the name on the map resulted in at least 15 minutes of predictable childishness between Owain and Em.

We managed to find a perfectly calm anchorage in a secluded bay near a lifeguard station and, while Em prepared our Stowaways dinner, Jez went for a swim and then a quick kayak to explore some of the coastline. It was a beautiful evening and we didn't want to waste it, so we went ashore and decided to make a beach fire and cook some marshmallows that Em's friend had given us. There wasn't much in the way of firewood so I went inland to see what I could find.

One hundred metres down the road I found a few chopped down trees that were lying in a pile of overgrown weeds and bramble. They were in a field but there was no gate so I went in. I untangled one branch, which was just big enough to have a fire to roast marshmallows and make a great end to our best day. Just then I heard a voice shout from one of houses on the other side of the road.

'Put it back!'

I turned around to see an old lady shouting from her fence, reading glasses on the end of her nose and kitchen towel over her shoulder. I dropped the branch and went over to her.

'Put it back. You didn't ask for permission.'

'I'm so sorry. Is this your field?'

'No, but you didn't ask.'

I was confused. It wasn't her field. Why did she care? Also it was a rotting tree in a pile of weeds, hardly a stack of prime wood.

'I'm so sorry. Who owns the field? I'll go and ask them.'

'No it's too late, you should have asked first.'

She then shrugged and turned away from me and gave one more flying comment, 'Now go away!' while flicking her hands at me. What a grumpy old lady. If I had scaled a fence to take an organised pile of wood then yes, but surely this was just foraging? I decided it wasn't worth the conflict and sulked all the way back to the beach empty-handed. Our marshmallows would have to wait for another night.

It was strange sleeping back on *Friday* and I struggled to get a good night's sleep. She was just rocking way too much. I had, however, managed to work out a way of locking my legs into the corners, which, although not comfortable, meant I wouldn't land up on Em's bunk in the night.

We had another day where I only had one tide to swim in, which meant a late start of 1pm. We could have got up at 5am for the end of the last northerly tide but figured for the sake of a few miles we'd get more sleep, which with hindsight didn't matter because I didn't sleep anyway. The crew did though and it was just as important for them to be rested.

We pushed on to Polzeath and then along to Port Isaac, and the going was similar to the day before. I was slowly finding my rhythm. Swim for 90 minutes and then rest for 20 while having a meal. I was tired but making good progress. My muscle memory was slowly starting to form and, now that I didn't have to think as much about what each arm was doing, I could start enjoying the journey.

This part of Cornwall is notoriously busy in the summer. Car parks are full, beaches are overcrowded and traffic is a nightmare. Being at sea meant we didn't see any of it. In fact, because I was only swimming past a few towns each day, most of the time we really did feel like we were completely alone. On my second feed break of the day, I lay on my back in the water balancing a bowl of Lancashire Hot Pot on my belly while trying to eat. I looked up towards the towering cliffs and couldn't help but think we were discovering a new and exotic land. It felt like Jurassic Park and I half expected a pterodactyl to swoop over the cliffs at any moment. Looking to my left and seeing *Friday*, a rickety old wooden yacht, added even more to the sense of early exploration. Somehow, we felt we were discovering things no one else had. Many of the beaches and coves were only accessible from the water and it was likely that some of them hadn't seen people for years. It's very rare to have good enough weather to get ashore even if you wanted to. I started to wonder how long it would take someone to find you if you decided to build a small shelter on one of these secluded beaches.

'Oi, keep swimming!' Jez shouted loudly, bringing me back to reality. He was right. I needed to make the most of each tide if I had any chance of reaching Scotland before the weather started to deteriorate at the end of the summer. Em took my empty bowl and I turned back onto my stomach. I took a few strokes and suddenly something soft and squidgy brushed past my face. I looked up to see a beautiful opaque purple jellyfish calmly floating a few inches below the surface of the water. It looked so graceful and peaceful but I knew what was to come. Pain! It had practically just molested my face. There was no way I had escaped being stung. I braced myself for the pain to start, but it didn't come. Turns out these purple ones don't sting at all, which was a huge relief, because about two metres further along was a bloom of about 100 of them covering an area the size of a small bedroom. If they had been stinging jellyfish, that would have been the end of me, I fear.

The most common stinging jellyfish in Britain is the lion's mane jellyfish. They can grow to the size of a football with tentacles that spread about three metres out in all directions. Luckily, these purples ones were harmless and after making a quick video of me swimming with them, I continued north.

Steve had called to say Arthur's engine was now fixed, at an extra cost of £160. On top of the £220 I had paid before, this was turning out to be an expensive option. Arthur had better be grateful when he gets his practically new engine back, I thought. Our next anchorage was going to be Port Isaac. It had a harbour so I told Steve to meet us there at around 8pm to do the swap. My progress was good and by the end of the tide I had managed to swim a few miles past Port Isaac. Swimming ahead of our anchorage was always good because it meant we could then use the southerly tide to get back. If we had to anchor north of my last swim spot then *Friday* was usually fighting the tide to get there. All these logistics took a lot of planning and decision making. Jez was doing a great job ensuring we made the most of the tides.

After my session we turned around and went to Port Isaac. On arriving we discovered that Port Isaac did indeed have a harbour but it was a drying one. Jez's app didn't show this so he opened the chart which confirmed it. This means that at low tide all the water drains out and boats are left on the mud. Unlike boats that are designed for harbours like this, *Friday* had one long fin keel which meant we couldn't ground her. We could anchor just outside the harbour but she wouldn't be sheltered from the waves. It was quite choppy, which would make it pretty uncomfortable on board, but we didn't have much other choice.

We anchored up and went ashore to meet Steve and get Arthur's engine. We offered him a meal and a pint but he said he needed to get back to Newquay. I was still blown away by Steve and Kate's kindness.

We fitted Arthur's engine and looked back to *Friday* to see her mast sticking up behind the harbour wall. The top of it was moving a good three or four metres from side to side. I knew it was going to be another rough night's sleep. We started to get back into the RIB when Owain's phone rang.

'Really? Thank you so, so much. That's very kind of you. We'll be up shortly.' And he put his phone down with a huge smile on his face.

He said, 'While you were swimming, I tried to get us a B&B and one of them said yes, so we all have a land-bed tonight.'

'No way! That's awesome!' shouted Em. She too was having trouble sleeping in the front bunks with no sides.

'Thanks Owain but I'm going to stay on the yacht again,' Jez said.

'Really?' I asked.

'Yeah, I wouldn't sleep well anyway being away from her. I don't think we can leave *Friday* unattended all night in these conditions. The anchor could drag or even worse the chain could break. It can happen. Also, I'm starting to kinda like *Friday.*'

Jez liked his own space and enjoyed tinkering with things by himself. Owain, on the other hand, was fairly social and always keen to help out. They were very different individuals but it was too early to tell whether they were getting along on the boat while Em and I were out swimming. All seemed good so far.

I also felt slightly bad that I wasn't really getting to know Owain. He was the person I was spending the least amount of time with and also the crew member who was the best at going off on his own and sourcing media and logistical things, not to mention free land-beds.

'Are you sure, mate?' I asked feeling really guilty that Jez was still yet to have a land-bed.

'Yeah. Don't worry, but if you feel that guilty give me a tenner for an ale before bed. That'll help me sleep!' Jez laughed.

It was the least I could do. I had budgeted for beer and pub food for the crew and Jez certainly deserved a few beers tonight.

5

HIGH PRESSURE HEAVEN

The alarm went at 3.45am as I wanted to catch the last few hours of the morning tide. Unfortunately I hadn't slept well at all because the room didn't have much ventilation and was extremely hot. Still bleary eyed, we stumbled in the dark down to the harbour. Jez was there waiting for us in the RIB looking quite tired too.

'Sleep well?' I asked.

'Not bad, not bad,' is all he said. Which probably meant it wasn't that good but Jez wasn't one for complaining.

We motored back to *Friday* and then did the half-hour journey to my last swim point marked on Jez's navigation app on his iPad. At the end of each session he'd drop a pin and write down the co-ordinates as a backup. These co-ordinates could be logged into *Friday*'s GPS, which would tell us where to go. Our third backup was actual charts just in case all else failed. We had two batteries on *Friday*, one for charging phones, laptops and VHF radios, and the other used solely for starting the engine. You never knew when these might fail so having paper backups was really important.

This was the first time I was getting in the water before the sun had risen. Although the water was a constant 14 degrees it somehow felt a lot colder. It's strange how your mind can play such a big role in how you feel.

There is even a general open-water swimming rule that is 'never mention the C word'. That C word is cold. If you don't mention it, it won't affect you, so the thinking goes. I'm not sure I believed it because I was still really chilly. That first minute in the water was always the worst as my outer layer of skin would acclimatise to the sudden change in temperature. Ideally, you'd try do some running and jumping to get warmed up before you got in the water, but *Friday* was way too small for that. The best I could do were some fast squats on deck while holding on to the mast to stop me falling overboard. Once in the water I'd swim as fast as I could to get my heart rate up. I'd also often turn upside down and do some dolphin style kicks underwater for as far as I could go before coming to the surface.

I only had two hours of tide and hoped to get to the next possible safe anchorage four miles away. I put my head down and switched off my brain and churned out the miles. People often ask me what I think about, but the truth is I try and think about nothing. I learned to do this on the round the world cycle when I had to push 16 hours a day on the bike. If your brain is not telling you how tired, cold and fatigued you are then you tend to keep going.

Anything to minimise negative thoughts is always a good thing. Doing this while cycling was, however, a lot easier as I had things to look at to keep me busy. With swimming all you see is sky, water, sky, water, for hours on end so it's a lot harder to switch off.

Left arm, right arm, breathe in, breathe out, repeat. While I was swimming, Em was taking in the sun, Jez was practising his tacking and Owain was doing a spot of fishing for lunch.

I just managed the four miles before the tide started to change direction. I had made it to Tintagel bay, which was by far the best anchorage we had been in. The bay was sunk into the Cornish cliffs and flanked by ancient ruins: crumbling stone walls and right at the very top a breathtakingly old castle overlooking the ocean. This wasn't just any old castle, it was in fact the castle where King Arthur was said to have been born. As picnic spots go, this was certainly one of the best. Just when I thought it couldn't be a better place for lunch Owain showed me a bucket containing four large mackerel he had caught. We had six hours in this anchorage before the next tide so there was no rush to do anything except relax, eat and potentially go ashore for some exploring. I gutted the mackerel, as Owain wasn't too keen, and we fried them as a starter. They were one of the most delicious fish I had ever eaten. There is something special about eating fresh fish you have just caught.

Jez and Em decided to have naps while Owain put on his wetsuit and went for a quick swim.

'Is it cold?' I shouted, as soon as he'd jumped in, knowing full well it was freezing.

'Not … too … bad!' he replied, trying to catch his breath.

'Whatever mate, admit it, it's cold!'

'Yeah OK, bloody freezing!'

A small part of me was glad he was freezing. He now knew what I had to deal with all day, every day. Owain lasted 15 minutes before throwing in the towel and coming back on board.

It was a busy day on the coast with loads of tourists walking along the cliffs, a few of them shouting and waving at us. *Friday* had a huge banner and stickers on her side which said 'Swimming Britain'. I wondered if they were waving at us because they'd heard about us, or just because *Friday* must have looked pretty special anchored up in this idyllic bay on such a sunny day.

After lunch we did some *Friday* DIY. Up till now we had 120 litres of water in a bladder under the floorboards, but had no way of getting it because the foot pump had broken off the floor. We'd been using a spare 20-litre jerrycan but that was running out quickly. Eventually we managed to screw the foot pump back onto the floor again but it was a pretty slapdash effort.

We spent the last hour of downtide exploring the shore and getting some land time to keep us sane. Four of us living in such close proximity, where even standing up straight was nearly impossible, certainly pushed us to our limits. Maximising land time was important to fend off the ever-encroaching cabin fever; an illness that I'm sure can make you clinically insane. It's actually well known that your decision-making ability is vastly reduced when you are confined to small spaces.

Within 15 minutes of getting back into the water the waves started to pick up again. The wind had changed direction and was now coming from the north. This meant the wind and the tide were running against each other. When this happens the sea becomes extremely choppy. The waves were only about one and a half metres in height but were very close together and steep. They were coming at me with such speed that I'd swim up one side of the wave and almost get thrust off the top and right into the front of the next wave. I'd then spend a few strokes almost completely submerged before coming to the surface close to the top of the wave and becoming almost airborne again into the next wave. It was relentless, wave after wave hitting me in the face, sending me underwater. All attempts to have any sort of style were hopeless and it became a fight to just keep afloat. It was hard to believe I was making any sort of progress but Jez assured me it was worth continuing.

We had made the decision that if my pace ever dropped below one mile per hour then it would be more beneficial to stop swimming and rest than to try and fight bad conditions while becoming more fatigued. On endurance events that last more than three weeks it's important to manage your energy efficiently as you can easily fall into deep fatigue, which takes weeks to recover from. With shorter races of less than three weeks you can almost operate on adrenalin and body reserves, and you don't need to worry about long-term fatigue. As I was expecting this swim to take between eight and ten weeks, I always needed to factor in proper recovery time and make the most of the good conditions. It was pointless spending two hours trying to swim two miles in bad weather when I could do that in 45 minutes the next day when things looked better. This was all good in theory but if we were hit with a week of bad weather then I may not have much option but to sluggishly move forward. However, for now, the weather was good and, although it was hard fighting the headwind and waves, I was still making progress, so pushed on.

It was 9pm and just getting dark by the time the tide turned. I was surprised to find I had swum over seven miles, which was a lot more than I had expected considering the waves were probably the hardest to swim in so far. My confidence was slowly growing as I was getting stronger. The first week had been a fast learning experience but I was gradually getting into the swing of things, as were the crew.

We had reached Crackington Haven and decided because I had an early start again to get the morning tide, we would skip a shore visit and just go to bed. For dinner, we had sausage casserole and I opened a bottle of wine for the crew.

After a good feed we all went to bed. It was fairly calm, which meant we should have a good night's sleep. As I was drifting off I felt my stomach rumbling again. I knew what was about to come and immediately felt embarrassed as I was only a few feet away from Em. Most athletes will know what I'm talking about when I say 'protein farts'.

I needed to eat probably twice as much protein as I normally would and I got most of this extra protein in the form of powder which I would have after every session. This noticeably helped me recover for the next day. The downside is that your body then produces farts that can end marriages. They really are bad. I had been supplementing my protein for a week now and it was only a matter of time before they'd arrive. I lay there and sneakily looked over to Em. She was facing the other direction. I got my sleeping bag and tightened the neck hole. I then let out a silent one. Within seconds I could smell it. I turned to see if Em had noticed and in doing so loosened the hole a little and a rush of fumes came up my neck. I started to cough. Em turned around.

'Are you … ahhhhhhhhh dude! What the hell?' she barely had time to finish her sentence and was gagging while covering her nose.

'I know right. Damn protein farts,' I was quick to try shift the blame.

'Ahhhhh! Come on!'

With all the commotion, Owain who hadn't gone to bed yet, opened our door and nearly fell over.

'Jeez, dude! What did you eat?' he said with horror, and quickly closed the door again. I could hear him chuckling on the other side.

'Owain! Open the door, you're hot-boxing me in. I think I might die,' Em shouted.

'No way are we letting that into our room!' he called back.

'Well it was nice knowing you all. Tell my parents I love them.'

I was lost for words. It seemed to linger for about ten minutes and just when it seemed safe to breathe normally, I let out another ripper. It's safe to say Em was not impressed but what was I to do. Better out than in right?

Another 5am start and we were greeted with by far the best sea state I think I've ever seen in my life. It was glass smooth; even flatter than the pool I trained in. I could finally start working on my style again. There was no wind for Jez to sail, so they just floated a few hundred metres away. If only the entire swim would stay like this, I kept thinking to myself. It made life so much easier.

Em and I carried on while I basked in the glory of not drinking any sea water, not having to roll my head so high to breathe and not being dunked by huge waves. I was just falling into a trance when I heard the distinctive sound of a full throttle outboard engine. I looked up expecting to see a fishing boat but instead saw Jez bombing along at around 20mph in the RIB, Arthur's engine finally working to its full potential. Jez was sitting near the front of the RIB to get the nose down onto the plane. With his hair blowing in the wind and his neck stretched out, he looked like an excited spaniel with his head out of a car window. I've never seen Jez so happy.

'Mate, you got to give this a go,' he said as he rushed up next to me. It did look fun. I'd probably never get conditions like this again but didn't want to waste swimming time.

'OK. Tell Owain to get some food ready and I'll have a go in 20 minutes and eat at the same time.'

'Cool,' replied Jez, as he opened full throttle and bombed away again.

I was really excited to have a go in our improved RIB and for the next 20 minutes I had an extra spring in my stroke. Jez then came round with *Friday*, and Em and I jumped in the RIB and proceeded to act like rebellious teenagers, doing circles and bombing up and down the coast as fast as possible. I'm not a speed freak by any means, I drive a 20-year-old Land Rover called Mana that only does 60mph, but I have to admit I enjoyed ripping it up, as they say, in the RIB that morning.

Getting into the water seemed a lot easier this time. It's amazing how much your mind plays a role in how you feel in the water. Normally those first few minutes were freezing cold, but the combination of high spirits, some adrenalin and glass-smooth water meant I was actually, for the first time, looking forward to getting swimming again.

I carried on swimming along across the bay towards Bude, and by the end of the tide had done six miles. I got out and we headed for Bude. It was 10am and we had a good six hours of downtide again to do some exploring and get some food. Also, going to land meant we could have a bit of our own space to avoid the ever-threatening case of cabin fever in *Friday*'s confined spaces.

Bude was bustling with people as we ribbed into shore. We found a spot to leave the RIB and went into town for my third breakfast, and then, for a spot of team morale, we decided to start a series of games. First on the list was crazy golf, for no other reason than we saw a course right next to breakfast and decided to add it to the list. We played one round and it's safe to say Tiger Woods has nothing to worry about just yet. I was so bad I gave up counting. Owain took a close win over Jez by two shots.

We then did some errands, a food shop and got the obligatory 99 ice cream, then settled into a pub to write the blog and do a quick radio interview with BBC Gloucestershire, before heading back to *Friday*. We got back to the RIB to discover that it was now low water and the RIB was a good 200 metres up on the sand. Jez managed to find a RIB trailer to borrow, which made getting back to the sea a lot easier. The RIB, with engine and other crap now collected in it, weighed well over 150kg. All four of us could just about push it along the sand for 20 metres before needing to rest.

Just like yesterday, the afternoon headwind picked up and the glassy flat sea had turned into huge waves intent on smashing me in the face. One wave slapped the side of my head so hard that my ears started to ring, slightly disorienting me and sending me swimming off to the left. Em too was taking loads of water into the kayak because she had got rid of the spray deck so that she could keep my water bottles by her feet as the netting wasn't holding them. We'd cut a water bottle in half that she used as a scoop to get the water out when it got too full. She seemed to be scooping more than paddling at the moment.

For the entire afternoon, wave after wave battered my head and shoulders. I swam till early evening before I started to get cold and tired so gave up for the day. I could have gone on for another half hour but my progress was slowing as the tide started to turn. I clambered on board and Jez and Owain had huge smiles on their faces. Something was up?

'Mate! You did your biggest day – 14 miles in total. Well done,' said Jez, patting me on the back. I was knackered but felt good for it.

Owain shouted 'dinner!', while holding a huge pollock right in front of my face, and then spent a few seconds pretending the fish was a puppet while saying, 'Eat me, eat me.' I couldn't help but laugh. I was glad they were having a good time on the boat, because following a swimmer with his face in the water for six or more hours a day can be very boring.

From *Friday*'s deck we could see an amazing beach with a waterfall running down the cliffs, falling onto a flock of seagulls all taking their evening shower. It was idyllic and deserved some exploration. We got some Stowaways and everything needed to make a fire and cook the pollock, and ribbed ashore. Within seconds of getting to the beach Jez had wandered off. Em and Owain collected driftwood for the fire while I gutted the fish. Twenty minutes later the fire was ablaze and Jez came back carrying, and wearing, an array of things he had found on the beach. He wore one odd boot, one small flipper and a diving mask with one screen missing. He was also carrying two different wellies and some rope. This was nothing compared to what he was dragging behind him. He had found a huge fender used to stop ships hitting the side of the harbour wall. It was teardrop shaped and about a metre tall.

'You look ridiculous Jez,' laughed Em.

'I know, I know,' he admitted. 'Most of it is rubbish but we're keeping the buoy, the rope and the wellies.'

Jez had mentioned his hoarding tendencies but this was the first time we saw him in action.

We sat around the fire, cooking the pollock and boiling up a pot of chicken and bacon pasta, our favourite of the Stowaway meals. Dessert was some more marshmallows and some leftover wine from the night before. As I sat there staring onto the dancing flames of the fire, I couldn't help but feel incredibly happy. I had really hoped that this swim would not only be a huge physical challenge, but also a chance to explore places we would never have otherwise seen. The last few days had proved to be exactly that. I was managing to swim hard when the conditions and tides were right, and then spend the rest of the time seeing the Great British coastline. After a tough first week at sea, I finally felt that everything was coming together, and that we were now having what would surely be the adventure of a lifetime.

Clank! Clank! Clank! The jib – the front sail – on the deck flapped around just inches from my and Em's heads all night as the wind rattled. I got up three times to try to secure it but there was also a scraping metal sound which I couldn't identify. The next morning Jez told us it was the anchor dragging along the seabed as the wind and tide pushed us. Jez said he had been keeping an eye on things to make sure we weren't pushed too far off our position and onto rocks. We definitely needed to make a plan with the jib though as neither Em nor I could handle too many more nights like that.

I got up slowly and felt the worst I had all swim. I had been swimming for ten days now and the last two afternoons of fighting head-waves, and a few nights of not much sleep, was starting to take its toll on my now fairly thin body. I started the swim at a reasonable 67kg and in ten days I had dropped down to 63kg. Considering I didn't have much fat to lose I was starting to eat into my muscle reserves. Once that starts happening you risk falling into long-term fatigue, which I really needed to avoid.

Today was the last day along the Cornish coast before cutting north, across the Bristol Channel, and towards Wales. It was going to be a big crossing so I had originally planned to take a day or two off before it to recover. I wanted to be fit as possible. However, while the weather was good I was thinking that maybe I should just go for it. I was also now a few days behind schedule, which added extra pressure. Luckily I hadn't yet told the crew I was hoping to be able to push on as I didn't want to promise anything. I would see how I felt at the end of today's session.

My last GPS point was two miles further south from our overnight anchorage so Jez said he would RIB us there. He also admitted it was because he saw some stuff on the beach he wanted to forage. Brilliant, more crap for *Friday*! We motored back to the start while dragging the kayak and I was in the water by 8am. Jez then went to shore and I carried on swimming back north towards *Friday*. I was feeling very tired and there also seemed to be a weird tide as we approached Hartland Quay. The going was so slow that I was making the least progress all swim: it took me well over two hours to do the two miles to *Friday*.

Eventually, by the end of the tide, I had only done three miles. I felt quite depressed and sat in silence drinking my shake. Em could sense my distress and was trying to comfort me.

'You've been swimming for nearly two weeks solid, Ginge. Of course you are tired.'

'I think I might take the weekend off.' That was in two days' time.

'This weekend, mate?' Jez butted in.

'Yeah, I think I need to rest before the crossing.'

'Well if you do, and tell me if you're not happy with it, but my local pub have a cart entered into the Red Bull soap box derby in London and I'd love to be there.'

I remembered Jez talking about this. They built a cart out of a coffin and called themselves the Coffin Dodgers. It was genius. It certainly added pressure to my decision.

Em then added, 'Also, if you do decide to take the weekend off, my boyfriend and all my friends have booked a cottage in Devon for the weekend.' That was just the excuse I was looking for. If I was going to have a weekend off and not feel guilty then this was probably going to be the best one.

'Awesome, I'll get the wife down too,' said Owain.

'Great! Well then, let's try and push as far as we can for the next two days and take the weekend off.'

'Perfect. There is an amazing village called Clovelly just along a bit. It has a harbour and a good place to leave the boat for the weekend.' Jez said, while looking on Google Maps for safe anchorages. Although tired I was ready to jump back in the water and make the most of the next few days.

'Come on. Let's do this.' I shouted enthusiastically, stood up, hit my head on the roof, sat back down again, and then realised I couldn't swim for the next six hours because we were against tide.

The sun was out and we were once again anchored up right next to an incredible beach. Jez managed to find a shipwreck that was so old you could barely make it out from the rocks except for some quite obvious water or fuel tanks and one huge propeller protruding from the sand. We really did feel like we were following in the footsteps of ancient explorers led by a crazy hoarding skipper. All Jez needed was a silly parrot to complete the look. Even his clothes were starting to tatter.

The afternoon session was a lot more productive than the morning one. I did five miles in the first three hours with a break and still had 90 minutes of tide left, which was very much needed to make up for the disastrous morning session. We could finally see Lundy Island through the low-lying haze across the ocean. Lundy is ten miles offshore or a third of the way into the Bristol Channel towards Wales. It's a small island, about three or four miles in length, and was once occupied by pirates who would commandeer all the cargo ships heading into Bristol. It now has 23 inhabitants who look after the farmlands, small cottages you can rent and the amazing sea life, including seals and puffins. I was really looking forward to exploring it.

Our plan was to use Lundy as an anchorage base for a few days as I crossed the daunting Bristol Channel to Pembrokeshire. We were now at Hartland Quay, which was two miles south of Hartland Point, where I'd start swimming towards Lundy. I was quite nervous about this next section because the Bristol Channel is not only notoriously rough but is also one of the busiest shipping channels in the UK. The plan was to get to Hartland Point tonight and then try and get as far across to Lundy in tomorrow's morning session before the weekend off. I stopped for my last feed before pushing on for the final hour to Hartland Point when two kayakers came up to us.

'Are you the swimmer?' one of them asked.

'Yes, that's me.'

'Ah brill. Where you heading from here?'

'We're heading to Hartland Point and then start the crossing to Wales via Lundy.'

'Lundy? You should have been starting your crossing much further south. The tide is really strong. Even if you start here you will probably miss Lundy.'

We knew the tide was going to be strong but not that strong. In order to hit Lundy the kayakers were saying that I'd have had to start making my way out to sea ten miles back. Ideally by Hartland Quay, where I was now, I should have already been five miles offshore getting pushed towards Lundy. At this rate it was likely I'd pass a few miles south of Lundy with the strong tide.

'So what are the options?' I asked nervously.

'Well, I'd start from here at the end of the southerly tide and head out to sea. You'll get pushed a little further south but will make progress out from the coast. Then when the tide turns north you will hopefully get swept closer towards Lundy. If you go now you'll still get swept under it I reckon. That's just my opinion. I've kayaked these waters loads and that's the strategy I'd take if I was kayaking there.'

That was the last thing I wanted to hear. I had only done eight miles or thereabout so far today. By the sounds of things the next possible time for me to start the crossing would be at 6am tomorrow morning.

'So you wouldn't go now?' I asked, to confirm I understood.

'No, pal. Tomorrow at the end of southerly tide would be my choice.'

Cycling around the world had taught me who to take advice from. The overweight drunk guy in the pub telling you that you can't cycle up that hill was probably talking nonsense. A fit looking kayaker who was actually kayaking where I wanted to swim probably did know what he was talking about. So after more debate about logistics I eventually decided to trust the kayaker and go tomorrow morning.

I said thank you, got out the water and slowly unzipped my wetsuit feeling a little deflated about my short day.

'Well there's only one thing to do then,' joked Owain while pointing towards a pub on the cliffs. It did look bloody inviting, I admitted.

'We'll have a quick one then let's cook dinner on the beach before an early night for the morning.'

Owain had caught another pollock and a few mackerel, which I was keen to fry up again. My body was craving oils and protein.

We went to shore but I just wanted some time alone so sat outside for a while. I was still annoyed that I had done a sub-ten mile day. Up till now I was enjoying the forced exploration time due to downtides but this time it angered me. There were just so many things to consider outside swimming. I guess this is why most big swims in history have been river swims where you don't have to worry about tides.

We had a pint and looked at ye olde maps of all the shipwrecks along the north Cornish coast that were hung around the pub's walls. There were hundreds dating back a century and more. Looking at these maps was a good reminder of how treacherous these waters can be. I'd been extremely lucky so far with the weather. But I was worried that my luck was going to run out sometime. I hope it's not halfway across the Bristol Channel, I thought.

After the pub we went back to *Friday* to collect everything for a beach fire dinner, and jumped back in the

RIB and started the 200 metre trip to shore. I looked up into the cloudless sky, millions of stars winking at me in a gentle and motivating way as if to say, 'You're going to do this.' I wanted to be able to look at them all night.

'Guys, should we sleep on the beach?' I asked.

'We need to get our sleeping bags then,' said Jez, immediately turning the boat around and heading back to *Friday*.

Just then I changed my mind as it would add another half an hour of work getting back to the boat in the morning and the rocks were so uncomfortable I'd never get a good sleep.

'No, actually, let's sleep in the boat,' I said.

'Are you sure mate? Make up your mind now!' Jez said, as we were almost back at *Friday*.

'Nah, let's just get to the beach and make a fire,' I said, although I was disappointed in my choice. Normally I'd have jumped at the idea to sleep on the beach but I really needed a good night's sleep before crossing to Lundy.

Jez turned around again and we headed for land.

We all fell into the same routine. I gutted the fish. Owain and Em sourced wood and built a fire, and we lost Jez to all the flotsam and jetsam scattered along the beach. Within half an hour we were all huddled around the fire eating fish for starters served on flat rocks, Stowaways for mains and a cheeky Rattler cider for dessert. Most people think alcohol is bad for you when doing endurance events but actually, as long as you stay hydrated and don't get absolutely bladdered, it can be a good source of calories. A couple each night were the same calories as a meal and also helped keep the team morale up. However, the Rattlers were pretty strong and I gave the last bit of mine to the Hoarder, as we now called him.

We all sat in silence, now comfortable enough with each other not to feel the need to make small talk, and instead just soak up the environment and fall into a trance watching the flames.

Jez then calmly said, with a slight ironic laugh, 'Guys, um, we have a problem. Look at the tide.'

We all looked out to sea trying to adjust our eyes to the darkness. Then, slowly but surely, we all started to see what the problem was.

'Shit! How did that happen?' gasped Em.

We had come to shore at high water and since then the tide had gone out revealing 100 metres of huge jagged rocks protruding from the ocean floor creating what was almost certainly an impassable barrier between us and *Friday*. We took our torches to see if we could find a way out. Between us and *Friday* – whose anchor light was just barely visible in the distance – was a mini Mordor for us to cross. We looked for a way of getting the RIB over the rocks but not only would we probably damage the RIB, if there was a time when one of us would get injured then this was it.

'Well, what now then?' I asked Jez, finally giving in that we couldn't all get back to the boat.

'I guess we'll have to sleep here till the tide comes in.'

'When will that be?'

'At around 6am,' Jez laughed.

'6am. So basically we have to sleep here.'

'Yup!' said Jez in an annoyingly matter-of-fact way.

It was obvious that the tide would go out but we figured we'd just have to drag the RIB over the sand. Admittedly we had been slightly caught up in the moment, hypnotised by the dancing camp fire, and slightly mellow from a few too many ciders, and hadn't quite kept an eye on things.

After walking slowly back to the fire, we sat down in silence and tried to come to terms with the fact that we were actually going to have to sleep on the cold stones with no sleeping bags or camping mats.

'And we so nearly got our sleeping bags,' said Em.

I felt extremely guilty that I had made the call not to get them.

'Well I guess we need more wood and anything to try and sleep on,' said Owain, being the most proactive of us all. We spent the next half an hour collecting every bit of wood we could find and each found a spot next to the fire. There was a bit of a wind so the only place to get warmth was downwind, but every time the wind picked up the flames and sparks would get worryingly close.

We also scoured the beach for any form of mattress – seaweed, plastic bags, anything to stop the cold – but the only thing we could find was a two square metre pile of tangled up old rope covered in tar in places. We brought it near the fire but figured tar and flames would not be a good combination. Instead we used it as a windbreak to shelter from the now fairly cold wind coming in off the sea.

It was near impossible to find a comfortable position amongst the tennis ball-sized rocks, but after a lot of shuffling I managed to find a gap for my hips which only hurt a little and was bearable. I found two larger rocks and balanced them on top of each other for a pillow and tried to fall asleep.

'Good night chaps, and good luck,' I joked but no one responded. The reality was that it was going to be long cold night for us all.

The only person to fall asleep instantly was obviously Jez and he was happily snoring away, which was as irritating as you can imagine. Owain, Em and I kept moving places, shuffling on the rocks and restocking the fire to keep warm. Although summer, I guess it was still around 14 degrees at night, with the cold stones and wind chill making it feel a lot colder. Eventually, after half an hour, I decided to change location and try the pile of netting as a mattress. It kind of worked and Em decided to try it too. I soon found a fairly comfortable position in the net and even managed to use a section as a duvet. It was more psychological because the holes in the net were the size of grapefruit. I did, however, manage to sleep before I was awoken by a jumping ember from the fire burning my leg. The fire was dying out so I got up to stoke it. I looked over to Owain, who I could tell was awake. I then noticed the bottom of his shoes, which were too close to the fire, had started to melt.

'Owain,' I whispered, 'your shoes, mate.' He sat up looked at his shoes and kind of shrugged and rolled over. He was too tired to care. So was I.

I had managed to find a comfortable place to sleep but was now being kept awake by the cold wind blowing through camp. I decided I needed to make a shelter and the only thing I could find was a small wooden pallet we were going to use as firewood. I took the pallet and a stick and created a shelter from the wind. It wasn't ideal as pallets have huge gaps between each strut but it did help bounce some of the heat back onto me. I curled up again and managed some broken sleep here and there, in-between stoking the fire and checking to see if Mordor had been covered up again, getting progressively more annoyed each time with the minefield of razor sharp rocks preventing me from a good night's sleep.

It was light by 4.30am and with not much more than an hour's sleep I got up to see if we could get back to *Friday*. I was shattered and my heart rate was very high, quite a common side effect from sleep deprivation. Most of Mordor was now covered up but we still needed to wait a good hour or so before the sharp rocks were sufficiently below the water level for us to get back safely. We didn't want to break Arthur's engine or, worse, tear the side walls of the RIB. I looked over to Em who was curled up in the pile of fishing net shivering so I added more wood to the fire.

By 5.30am we all got up and just sat in a daze staring blankly into a pile a smouldering logs that had kept us from freezing to death in the night. We had battle wounds to show for it too. Owain's melted shoes, small burn marks on my legs and all of us with various holes in our jumpers from sparks. No one had slept much and we all felt like death. I also had a slightly tight chest from being cold all night. Looking at the state of us all I knew that doing a session this morning was not going to happen, besides I had also now missed the tide I needed to get to Lundy. It was so frustrating because what was meant to be two days of big miles turned into just one half day. I was hoping to have made it at least to Lundy by now but instead was still on mainland and now had three days of no swimming.

I had swam just shy of 90 miles in 12 days which was about 10% of my total distance but it had taken me twice as long as I had expected with my daily average being a miserable seven and a half miles per day. I really needed to step up my game. Chasing the miles so early on was playing on my mind as the knock-on effect could be catastrophic if I got to Scotland too late in the season. I had a window of about three and a half months and was already nearly a week behind, even before my weekend off.

I had a pretty productive weekend in Clovelly, a village on the north coast of Devon tucked into the forested cliffs. There are no cars and the only way to get into the village is down a pretty steep cobbled path. The entire village is privately owned and has been that way for 800 years with only three families ever owning it. The current family have owned it for nearly 300 years. This means that all 80 properties, every hotel, restaurant and pub are all owned by the one family and you have to lease or rent from them. Not everyone can just rent though. You have to be interviewed to see if you will fit into the village. It was an interesting social dynamic but it seemed to work.

It was strange being there alone without the crew but I made the most of it by meeting the locals, eating as much as my shrivelled stomach could handle, getting a much needed shoulder massage from Emma, the village masseuse who also moonlights as the hotel receptionist, and updating my blog. Stuart the Scab had been getting increasingly big and deep. He went about three millimetres into my foot and I could now see flesh. Being in the water each day meant he wasn't having much time to heal. Spending the weekend out of the water at least meant he had the chance to dry out a bit.

The only thing that was slightly annoying was that I seemed to have pulled my shoulder muscle while trying to start Arthur's RIB engine, which was playing up again. It was however a much-needed weekend's rest.

The crew returned on Sunday looking as fresh as ever too. Jez's Coffin Dodgers had come a close second in the race, Em had seen her mates and Owain had entertained his family in Devon for the weekend. We were all as ready as ever for the next leg – the Bristol Channel. We'd head off in the morning to start the next session.

6

THE BRISTOL CHANNEL

Da! Da! Da! Da! Da! The vibrations from *Friday*'s single cylinder engine were sending shock waves through my skull and down my spine. It was 2.30am and I hadn't slept much because, if I'm honest, I was bricking it for my next section, finally crossing the Bristol Channel. Jez and Owain got up and started the long journey from Clovelly, back to Hartland Quay. It was going to take us at least four or five hours and I was hoping to be in the water by 8am to make the most of the tides. This was by far the longest commute so far and lying in the front bunk for four hours not being able to sleep was increasingly frustrating. Although tired and nursing the niggle in my right shoulder, I was feeling a lot stronger and was glad I had taken the weekend off.

I was nervous getting in the water again but was surprised that I didn't feel nearly as cold as I had done before the weekend. It's amazing how just a little bit of extra body fat can make all the difference. I had purposefully made an effort to eat plenty of carbs and fat over the weekend. A high mixture of both is the best way to gain weight.

To try to play the tides correctly, I swam directly away from Hartland Quay heading in a westerly direction. When the tide turned I'd eventually get swept north-east towards Lundy. The chap in the kayak wasn't lying about the strength of the tide as I was pushed sideways at nearly 4mph. For every 100 metres I swam west, I'd get pushed 400 metres north-east. No matter how fast I swam it soon became clear that I'd get swept quite far south of Lundy and therefore have to swim the slightly further route along the east side of the island instead of the west side as originally planned. At least the weather was good. I'd have been pretty annoyed if I was faced with huge waves after a weekend of glass smooth water sitting in Clovelly, not swimming.

It was a lot harder to work out where I was going because I no longer had land to look at. Instead I had to rely on Em next to me who, at times, looked like she might actually be asleep in the kayak. My right shoulder was still a little fragile but the cold water helped numb the niggle as I pushed on, resting for a few minutes every hour and a half and having a Stowaways meal with nearly half a tub of butter to add more calories and fat. It had to be butter from grass-fed cows (as opposed to grain-fed) because Steve, my nutritionist, told me that was best. Trying to find grass-fed butter is a lot harder than you think. It's not often on the packaging. In fact, the only butter I'd been told for certain was grass-fed was Kerrygold so we had stocked up on ten blocks of it that was now in the wet bilge-fridge. I really needed to get some more weight back on. I carried on right through to the next southerly tide, hoping it would sweep me west and on to Lundy but it started pushing me back towards Cornwall, so I called it a day. I had made it about two miles south-east of Lundy, which wasn't as bad as feared. With a little tidal planning I should make it past the north end of the island by the end of the next tide.

We now had our six hour break so we decided to go on to Lundy to do some exploring. We anchored in the main bay and ribbed ashore and started the long walk up to the top of the island to pay the £5 anchoring fee. We also needed some diesel for *Friday* so took the jerrycan to see if we could buy some.

Lundy was beautiful. It was three miles long and comprised of mostly grassland, one church and a lighthouse. Jez walked up the hill with a strange sense of built-in navigation, straight for the pub, naturally.

In the pub, Jez managed to ask about diesel. Five minutes later the warden of the island, a chap called Derek, came over and chatted to us for a while, telling us all about Lundy. On hearing about my swim he then gave us a free round at the bar and said he'd happily donate us a jerrycan of diesel for *Friday*. What an amazing guy.

Butterflies started dancing in my stomach as we headed back down the hill. The tide times, which move forward each day, were now going well into the evening. Tonight would be my first session where I might have to swim in the dark. I had just about managed to not think about all the scary monsters lurking in the depths below me while it was light, but night-time swimming was going to be a real test for me.

We arrived back at the RIB to find it was full of water and the two oars were washed up the beach 100 metres away. From where we tied it up, we thought it would have just risen with the tide slowly and landed up a bit higher on the beach. It was a wonder that the oars were still around. The RIB was too heavy to lift so we all spent ten minutes bailing enough water out with bits of driftwood and the oars before it was light enough to lift and empty out. At least it got a thorough cleaning.

It was a good hour to get back to my last swim point and I took the time to have a meal and prepare for my first night session. Jez would give the ten minute countdown and then five minutes before we reached our spot, Em and I would clamber over the back of *Friday* and into the RIB where I'd put on my goggles and cap. Em would do the acrobatic task of getting from the RIB into the kayak. She was surprisingly good at this, which was baffling to me. She was still unable to paddle ashore in one-foot waves, but balancing between RIB and kayak in five-foot waves didn't seem to be a problem. Jez would then circle around the GPS pinpoint and when he was eventually on top of the exact spot he'd shout, 'Go!', and I'd fall backward into the freezing water. Once or twice, I took too long and we'd drift past the pinpoint by 10 or 20 metres. If that was further back from where I finished that was fine, but if we had drifted ahead Jez would then shout 'hold on', shake his head and have to turn around and go back again. I have to admit I secretly missed a few on purpose just to get another minute of warmth. Those first few minutes in the water weren't getting easier.

Today was the same as any other day, but as the sun started to set over the horizon so began the noticeable increase in heartbeats. I'm not normally a nervous person but today felt like the time I had to do a duet with my little sister at primary school in front of everyone. I tried not to think about it and decided to keep my eyes closed while face-down and only briefly open them when I breathed to see I was still swimming in the right direction. This seemed to work – out of sight, out of mind.

At least it was dead calm, which made things a lot less trouble. I pushed on, trying my very best to not think about a huge whale coming up from the depths and swallowing me whole. I don't know why I was constantly thinking about the extremely unlikely event of deep-sea creatures lurking in the darkness below when in fact there were far more real and present risks for swimming at night like tides, waves, getting run over by a ship, drifting away from the boat or even getting run over by *Friday* if I swam off to the left too sharply. I think I was subconsciously stressing over the *unlikely*, which somehow seemed to make the *very likely* less daunting. If I actually thought about it properly I may very well have chickened out. Swimming across the Bristol Channel at night was certainly the most brave/stupid thing I'd ever done in my entire life.

Just then, as I took a stroke with my left arm, my hand went straight into something. In a moment of panic I pictured a shark biting off my hand and with lightning reflexes I pulled my arm away and felt a sharp pain in my left tricep. I came up for a breath and looked ahead. Thankfully it was only one of the purple jellyfish but because my nerves were on edge, the knee-jerk reaction had caused me to pull the muscle in my left arm. I rubbed it for a minute or two trying to get blood flow, hoping it wasn't a pulled muscle and just a bit of cramp but it was no use. I had suffered my first swimming injury and all because of a stupid little harmless jellyfish.

I tried to carry on swimming but had no power in my left arm at all. This was adding extra strain to my right shoulder, which was still a bit sore from Arthur's engine. I didn't know what to do. I needed to push on but didn't want to worsen the injury. I hadn't done much more than a mile but after a lot of failed attempts to try and swim I decided to call it quits for the day. The one positive was I didn't have to do a night session. If I'm really honest with myself I think I was probably using the injury as a bit of an excuse to delay the inevitable. Had it been a warm sunny day I may very well have continued, slowly. But for now I wasn't feeling very confident and could put it out of mind as that would be tomorrow's task, which was now even more daunting with an injury. As soon as I was out the water I felt extremely guilty for not carrying on considering I should have been fighting to make the most of every tide. Luckily for my psyche, my arm got progressively worse in the night as the adrenalin wore off, which somewhat helped me cope with the decision to end the session early.

The fact that the second northerly tide was in the evening meant the morning tide wasn't at stupid o'clock and we could all have a relative lie in till 7am. I had a surprisingly good sleep, considering my sore shoulder and arm. I tentatively flexed the sore muscles. My left tricep was still quite painful but nothing a bit of cold water and painkillers couldn't numb.

We were still south-east of Lundy and the plan was to hopefully do about eight miles in the tide and get a good chunk north by the end of the session. I worked out that if I changed my style slightly I didn't have to use my tricep as much, and, although not nearly as efficient, I was still able to make relatively pain-free progress north. We had another calm and sunny day at sea and I managed the eight miles I'd planned.

After my session, we went back and anchored in a bay right in the north of Lundy. Owain then ribbed to the southerly bay to collect the diesel that Derek said he'd leave for us while Em, Jez and I clambered ashore and walked the full length of the island and back to the tavern in the glorious early afternoon sun. From the cliffs we could see hundreds of puffins and even spotted a few seals swimming in the clear blue sea below. From up here the ocean looked so incredibly tropical and inviting, a stark contrast from its finger-and-toe-numbing reality. The water in the UK reaches its warmest temperatures in August/September, which was at least something I was looking forward to. I'd definitely be done by the end of September at the latest just when it would start getting cold again.

We spent the afternoon in the tavern chatting to people and telling them all about the adventure so far. There were four types of reactions from the public. First there was the 'dumbfounded'. This is when people just looked at you blankly, with their mouths slightly open and would often just say one phrase like, 'You're mad,' or, 'Did your parents drop you as a kid?' and then walk off shaking their heads. The second type were the 'questioners'. They would bombard me and the crew with a million questions like, 'How many miles each day?' or, 'How many calories do you eat?' or, 'Do you pee in your wetsuit?' They were really friendly and were most likely to donate a bit to charity. Third were the 'critics'. They were generally people who thought they had some sea experience because they'd gone on a fishing holiday once or took a ferry during a storm. They would concentrate on all the issues that lay ahead of me like, 'The Bristol Channel has the strongest tide in the UK and is a big shipping lane,' or they 'spotted killer whales in Scotland last week you know'. To start with I'd try and defend my decision but eventually gave up and came up with a few stock answers like, 'I'll cross that bridge when it comes', or, 'Jez has that covered.' Fourth were the people who were generally not interested at all but in a typically British way wanted to be polite so would just say 'fair play' give a half-hearted nod and walk off. Luckily we sat next to a family who were 'questioners' and they gave us £40 for War Child, which was incredibly kind – £10 of which came from the young daughters who donated some of their pocket money. Moments like that certainly gave me a boost to get up and go.

At 7.00pm it was time to get back in the water. It was a lovely evening with the setting sun bouncing a rainbow of colour over the smooth water. The colour slowly turned from rich yellows and oranges to deep purples and blues as soon as the sun slowly set. Being midsummer meant it would only get completely dark at around 10pm. This hopefully gave me time to slowly build up the courage for night-time swimming. I'm not sure I'd have been able to start my session in complete darkness. As the session continued my left tricep was becoming more and more painful with each stroke. I think my eight miles morning session had taken its toll. It was so frustrating because this evening had perfect conditions and not making the most of them could have a huge knock-on effect towards the end of the swim when the weather would get worse. If I dropped two miles a day it would add nearly ten days to the swim. That could mean bad weather in Scotland.

At 9.30pm, and just before it was completely dark, I decided to call it a day and rest my arm, which was still painful enough to hinder performance. Not only had it been a short session, which again made me feel pretty depressed, but I was still putting off my first proper night session. No matter what happened, I'd definitely have to do a night session tomorrow. There was no way of getting around it. I needed to make up some miles. It was now 18

July and I had been swimming for nearly three weeks and had only covered 110 miles.

It was so calm in the night you could forget you were even on a boat at all. The windless night, however, meant it was boiling hot. I had borrowed my friend's minus-15 degree sleeping bag too, which didn't help, and I landed up in a pool of my own sweat on the slippery faux leather bunk mattresses.

Three things were certain for today's session, which were making me incredibly nervous. One, I was most definitely going to swim at night. Two, we had no idea where we were going to anchor at all. I'd most likely swim to the exact halfway point between Lundy and Wales, which would be way too far for us to get back to land, so either I'd need to cut my day short so we could get back to Lundy or swim harder to try get closer to Wales. Three, we had to cross a pretty busy shipping lane.

'Am I allowed to just swim across the Bristol Channel. Who owns it?' I asked Jez.

It sounded ridiculous but surely there are rules for this? Who does own the Bristol Channel? The Queen, I guess.

'The sea is free, mate,' Jez replied with a rebellious grin on his face. Turns out, no one, not even the coastguard can stop you. We did however make sure we radioed in our intention so that all tankers knew what they were looking at when they saw a tiny yacht trailed by a red kayak and a swimmer who looked like he was drowning due to the new style he'd adopted to avoid injury.

I started my morning session at around 9am and put in a steady pace. Within a few hours we lost Lundy to the haze behind us and couldn't see Wales ahead of us either. This was the first time that I couldn't see land at all and I started to feel quite alone. With no fixed marker on the shore it was also now near-impossible to swim in the right direction and at times Em and I veered off at nearly 90 degrees until Jez and Owain would shout from *Friday* and point us back on track. It was so disorienting. Eventually, after the fifth time, Jez found a compass and gave it to Em and told her which direction to aim for. There was a bit of science in this because I was now getting pushed sideways so needed to aim slightly off our true direction in order to avoid landing up too far east. This should have worked but only caused more confusion as it was a pretty cheap compass. The combination of me swimming like a drowning sloth and Em trying to use a compass as if firing a gun would certainly have been fit for any Laurel and Hardy sketch. That thought did cause me to chuckle involuntarily a few times, which, when face-down in the water, was the closest I'd come to actually drowning all swim. The irony.

There was a huge shipping lane ahead of us too and for most of the morning we could see enormous tankers bombing up and down. Luckily none of them were ever close enough to be an actual threat, but nevertheless I felt incredibly insignificant and unimportant in comparison.

I did my eight miles in the morning session as per usual. This seemed to be my optimal pace for conserving energy and not burning out. Ideally, I was hoping it would have been closer to ten miles but considering I was fighting a strong side current I was fairly happy with the progress. We had nowhere to anchor for lunch so just turned the engine off and let the tide take us where it wanted to. Jez would monitor things and start to head back to the GPS pinpoint depending on how far we drifted. We all kept to ourselves that afternoon. I lay on deck listening to music and trying to warm up like a seal on a rock. Owain did some fishing. Jez did sailing stuff and tinkered with *Friday* and Em went for a nap.

By 8.30pm it was time to get back in the water. Unless I did in fact get swallowed by a whale before sunset, I would be swimming right through till midnight. The reality of this suddenly brought on the question of whether or not this was actually a safe thing to do and also whether the crew were actually happy with it considering the swim priorities. We hadn't really talked about it. I had just kind of figured we needed to do this. I called a crew meeting.

'Guys. We haven't really talked about this but I wanted to ask whether you are happy to do this night session? Jez, what's the real risk here?' I asked.

'As long as Em has a head torch, you wear your wrist reflector and Owain stays on deck to keep a look-out, we should be fine.'

'What about ships?' asked Owain, being the most sensible of us all.

'We'll see them from miles off. It's a pretty clear night.'

'Em. You happy to kayak at night?' I asked.

'Yes, Ginge. As long as you bloody swim straight,' she joked. It was hard to tell her real feelings as she was always extremely upbeat but I detected a hint of worry.

'Sure, Em?'

'Yes, we have to. We can't fall any further behind.'

'Come on, mate. Get your kit on. We got some mileage to make up,' said Jez.

In a weird way hearing the crew say they were happy to take this risk really helped me. We were after all, all in the same boat. Every pun intended.

'One stroke at a time. One stroke at a time.' I kept repeating to myself. At least it was flat again.

Stroke, stroke, breath. Stroke, stroke, breath. Each hundred metres gained was further into the heart of the busy shipping lanes of the Bristol Channel, and getting darker and darker at the same time. It wasn't long before the orange and reds turned to blues and purples, and then I heard Em shout.

'I need a torch and can you bring his reflectors?'

This was it. There was no getting out of it. I had bought some reflective armbands so that the crew could see me in the water. Em had a head torch on, both so that she could see me and also for me to be able to see her next to me so that I carried on swimming in the right direction. *Friday* was also just on the other side of Em so that she knew where to go.

'I am bricking it,' I confided in Em, as she brought me my reflectors.

'Me too, but you'll get eaten first so I'm OK,' Em said.

'Ah thanks.'

By 10pm, it was completely dark. Suddenly the rest of my senses became far more alert. I could hear Em's paddles going into the water next to me, and *Friday*'s single cylinder engine tutting away off to my right sending small vibrations through the water. Are sharks scared of these vibrations or, like dolphins, attracted to them? I decided it was best not to think about it. Along with extra audio sensitivity I was feeling everything in the water. I could feel the water rushing over my cheeks and across my lips. I could feel all the bubbles from my breath running over my wetsuit. It was a whole new experience and took some time to get used to.

Time seemed to stand still and what felt like an hour in the water would turn out to be 15 minutes. I knew I had to push it to at least try and get nearer to Wales, so I decided to skip a proper meal and just have a recovery shake in the water with extra carb powder. By 11pm I was still not even halfway and knew I had to dig deep and try get within 10–12 miles of Wales. Any further and we'd be stuck in the middle of the channel all night and unable to get to shore and back again in time for the next tide.

I put my face back down and started to pick up my pace. I couldn't have gone further than 10 metres when all of a sudden I felt an electrifying shock across my nose and cheeks, followed by a rush of warmth and then a burning sensation as if I'd fallen flat on a bed of red-hot coals. I let out a yell and turned onto my back. My scream nearly toppled Em over. I knew immediately what had happened. I had been warned about lion's mane jellyfish but was hoping I'd meet them a lot further north, and not on my first night swim, in the middle of busy shipping lane.

'Ginge! Don't move. There are tentacles all over your face.' Em said as she shone her head torch on me. I could see them stretching from my cap and down my cheeks, glistening in the light. Em came over and with her gloves on tried to take the tentacles off me but in doing so let more of the burning toxins onto other parts of my cheeks. I felt like I was on fire.

'Where is it?' I frantically asked in case it was right near me.

'Don't worry it's over there.' Em shone her torch about a metre away from me. There it was, a jellyfish about the size of a football with tentacles reaching well over a metre in all directions. It was just floating there as if nothing had happened, the bastard!

'Can I pee on you?' shouted Owain from *Friday*. I didn't know if he was serious or just trying to lighten the mood, but either way that definitely wasn't going to happen. If anything I'd try and pee on myself, a sentence I never thought I'd say. I'm not entirely certain how you'd even do that. I'd pee in a bottle, I guess, and then pour it all over my face. The thought of that nearly made me vomit. I was ready to try anything though.

'Sorry to put a damper on things mate, but we've only got 45 more minutes of tide and we need to push on,' suggested Jez. He was right. If anything the stinging face was now the most painful thing in my body making my shoulder and tricep secondary concerns. I nervously turned around and put my face back in the water to find the cold surprisingly soothing. This was the one and only time I was grateful for cold water. I carried on until midnight with my face burning with every breath as my face came out of the soothing cold water.

Em was now on jellyfish watch. Whenever she saw one she had to stop me swimming and try and move them out the way with her paddle. There seemed to be hundreds of them and they were all on the surface of the water which was typical for jellyfish when the water was calm. When the waves pick up they tend to go a few metres down. At this moment I'd take bad waves any day over captain fire-face. I had to change my style to look slightly ahead for jellyfish that Em might not see a foot below the surface. This was adding extra strain to my neck but it was worth not getting stung again.

By midnight I had made it to the exact place we didn't want to be – slap bang in the middle of the Bristol Channel. We were pretty much equidistant from both Lundy and Wales. It would be a five-hour sail just to get to a safe anchorage. We had no option but to just stay in the channel all night, much like we did during the lunch break, and drift with the tide.

'Right guys, we need to do shifts to look out for ships, etc.,' explained Jez. I'm not sure what 'etc.' was but was too scared to ask.

'Em, you do now till 2am – a two-hour shift as you need some rest. Owain, you do 2am to 6am and then I'll do the rest until we get back in the water at around 10am.'

Jez then went on to explain what navigation lights to look out for. Red light means you are looking at the port side of the boat. Green means it's the starboard side. Either of those meant the ship was probably passing parallel to us. If however they saw red and green side by side, that meant the ship would be coming straight for us. If that happened they'd need to wake Jez up and we'd move out the way or radio it in. Ships can travel at up to 20 knots, which meant we'd have about ten minutes to move out the way if one was coming directly for us. We knew where we were on the chart and knew where the ships were likely to pass but, even so, going to bed was quite worrying. To make things worse, my face carried on pulsating for a few hours. That, mixed with Stuart the Scab, who was still getting progressively deeper and not healing at all, throbbing away, made sleeping near impossible. I was resigned to the fact I'd have a gaping hole in my foot for the entire swim, all because of a small scratch on the first day. At least the cold water made my foot numb so that I didn't feel the pain while swimming.

After some broken sleep, I saw the sun rise over the glistening ocean at 5am. I knew we didn't risk getting run over in the light, as much anyway, although we were still a tiny speck in the sea from the point of view of these huge container ships. I nevertheless managed a few more hours' sleep till 8.30am. Being in the middle of the Bristol Channel meant that the tide was coming directly from each side. From my left all morning until high water and then from my right all the way back down to low water. The downside was I had no tide to help me along, but the plus side was that I could now swim on both tides. I'd land up swimming a big 'S' shape as the tide pushed me towards Bristol until around 2pm and then back out towards, well, America till around 8pm. This meant that today I had to change my strategy. I needed to slow my pace so that I could swim for longer. I'd also need to eat a lot more as I'd most likely be in the water most of the day burning around 800kcal per hour.

I started my session at 10am and asked Em to make sure I drank every 20 minutes. I'd then stop every 90 minutes for some food and rest up. There wasn't as much of a rush to get going each time I had a break as I had all day to swim but, nevertheless, I really wanted to get across to Wales by the end of the day.

At 3pm *Friday* came alongside me, which was unusual. Jez usually stayed a few hundred metres away. I stopped swimming.

'Sean, look up!' Owain excitedly shouted and pointed ahead while standing on the front of *Friday*. From down here he looked like Leonardo DiCaprio in *Titanic*, only a lot scruffier. I looked ahead of me and in the distance, if I squinted my eyes, through all the haze I could just make out some land. It was Wales. I could see my destination.

'Woohoo!' I let out a worryingly girly scream and everyone cheered. Seeing land gave me a new boost of energy. I now had something to aim towards. It was still ten miles away but I almost felt like I could touch it.

For the next few hours Wales didn't get any closer and my pace started to get slower and slower. I was convinced I was swimming in one spot and the crew were playing a cruel game on me. By 6pm I decided I had had enough. We were about five miles offshore and close enough to get to land and find a pub. Crossing the Bristol Channel was as good as in the bag and we needed to celebrate.

We found a safe anchorage in a calm bay and ribbed ashore. The nearest pub we could find was a good hour's walk but we were willing to do it. We also urgently needed to fill up *Friday*'s water bladder so we all took it in turns carrying the 20-litre empty jerrycan up the green lanes to a small town called Stackpole where we found the inn. It was a quaint pub and I had a dark ale as I felt it was better for me than a lager. We then all sat down in the beer garden with a sense of achievement. It had been a tough few days with torn muscles, not much sleep and jellyfish stings, and it was good to be on dry land again. Although pretty excited to have made the crossing I think we were all too exhausted to really show it. For me it felt like when you're at university, have a few too many pints and then decide to do something stupid like climb up a high tree or try and tightrope walk a sharp metal fence. You wake up in the morning, with the world's worst hangover, and although you haven't impaled yourself you shiver at the thought of what could have happened. I felt like I was in a post-Bristol Channel hangover.

On our second round, Jez got out his iPad to look at the week ahead. Being so far behind schedule meant

I now had no idea when I'd likely hit Scotland. From my last point I'd start swimming slightly west towards St David's Head and then north along the Welsh Coast towards Anglesey. The next big crossing would be in a few weeks' time from north Wales to the Isle of Man and then again a few days later to Scotland. They would be much tougher crossings but hopefully I'd be stronger then. Jez was then scrolling across when I caught some land in the top left corner of his screen, just off to the north-west of St David's Head.

'What's that? Is there an island out in the Irish Sea like Lundy?'

'I dunno,' Jez admitted and started to zoom out slowly. It was an island – Ireland! It looked a lot closer than I remembered when planning my route.

'I had no idea it was that close. How far is it?' I asked.

Jez did his calculations.

'41 nautical miles.'

'How far is it from Wales to Isle of Man?'

'40 nautical miles, only 1 mile shorter.'

My brain immediately jumped to one amazing, scary, adventurous idea.

'How cool would it be if I swam to Ireland?' I said, with a sudden surge of excitement again.

'Yes Ginge. I have never been to Ireland!' said Em, with a huge smile on her face. How had a 28-year-old never been to Ireland?

'I can't see why not,' said Jez in his usual matter-of-fact way. 'It's definitely doable.'

'Right. Let's get another round and think about it.' I got up and went to the bar feeling the most excited I had been since thinking of the idea to swim the length of Britain, before all the detractors started to ruin my excitement. I came back with a tray of beer expecting to celebrate but the mood was very different on my return.

'What's up?' I asked. Jez and Em looked sheepishly at Owain.

'You all right, Owain?'

'I've planned loads of media and stuff in Wales and changing it now means I've wasted my time. I have no contacts in Ireland and if we go there then I think I might go home instead. You'll have no use for me.'

I was shocked. Jez and Em just looked down at the table trying to stay out of it. I thought the crew would jump at the idea to do something adventurous at the spur of the moment.

I thought for a moment.

'I'll tell you what. We still need to get to St David's before we decide so let's think about the pros and cons for the next few days. Right now let's enjoy Wales while we are here.'

I then swiftly tried to change the subject. The mood was very sombre for the rest of the evening and at around 9pm we all took it in turns to carry the now full, and very heavy, water can back down the hill.

I hadn't slept well at all. Em and I stayed up late weighing up the case for swimming to Ireland. The pros were: we'd get the big crossing out of the way early while the weather was good. It also meant we didn't have to do three very big crossings later, instead just one short crossing back to Scotland from Northern Ireland. It was slightly shorter and would save me about 50 miles in total. There were more anchorages in Ireland and, most of all, I just really wanted to go. It excited me.

My family, on my dad's side, left Ireland to move to 'the colonies' 100 years ago and swimming there would be none other than just very cool. That was all. It was the kind of bonkers idea that makes me excited and I hated that Owain's ultimatum was affecting my decisions. We only found one downside to going to Ireland, other than losing Owain who was a great crew member, and that was the issue that my adventure, the website and the huge stickers on the boat all said 'Swimming Britain'. Ireland was not Britain. I didn't know how this would go down. At the end of the day I was still swimming the length of Britain but going via Ireland. At least all the stickers were on the right side of *Friday* for going up the west coast of the UK. They would be facing out to sea if we went up the inside of Ireland so hopefully no one would get offended.

By morning, I had made up my mind. I was going to swim to Ireland. It made the most sense almost to the point that not swimming to Ireland would jeopardise the swim because we'd need to do three big crossings later on when the weather might not be as good. I got out of bed ready to tell Owain my decision. I was really nervous. I didn't want to lose him. He had done so much work getting media connections, taken loads of photos and really knew what the trip was all about, but I knew what I had to do. I walked through to the main saloon, my heart racing. But even before I could open my mouth, Owain started talking.

'Sean. Sorry for last night. I was just dead keen on Wales and was looking forward to it. I've been thinking about it and, you know what, I've never been to Ireland either and arriving by yacht would be kinda cool. I'm in.'

What a huge relief. That was the best news I could have hoped for as trying to find another crew member would have been quite stressful. Plus Owain was awesome at fishing.

We all cheered. Ireland, here we come.

Because I had a potentially four or five-day crossing ahead of me, and now knowing just how difficult they were, I figured we needed to stock up on some supplies and potentially take a day off so that I was in peak shape. The weather was looking good for the next week or so, which was a relief. Besides those few choppy headwind days, we'd had amazing weather since Newquay. My luck was going to run out sooner or later but as long as I wasn't stuck in the middle of the Irish Sea when those big Atlantic rollers came in, I was happy.

I was quite tired from pushing it all day yesterday, as were the crew, so we skipped the morning session to do expedition work. We all went ashore. Jez went to find diesel. Owain went to call various media and sponsors to tell them of our change of plan, and Em and I walked up the green lane and hitched a ride from a lovely old lady called Pam to Pembroke to stock up on various supplies, including another thermal layer as I was still getting cold in the water.

The afternoon swim session went by really quickly. I was now back with some pretty strong tides and swam right up till it was almost dark. Having a new and exciting goal made me completely forget about my sore arm, shoulder, jellyfish and anything else that was playing on my mind before.

My session ended just outside Milford Haven and we anchored up in a quiet bay. Even though I had only done the evening session I had somehow managed to swim 12 miles. The tide certainly helped but also it's amazing what a new sense of excitement can do to your body. I was flying through the water and ready for the next big crossing.

Jez and Owain got up at 4am to get me back to my start point. The engine starting always woke me up but I waited in the front bunk trying to rest until I heard the 45-minute warning. I could tell it was quite wavy out as I rocked up and down listening to the bow crashing through the waves just centimetres from my head. About half an hour later I was amazed that it had calmed right down but then I heard the engine turn off. The door opened and Owain came through.

'We can't make any progress to the last GPS point. Headwinds are too strong. We're going to try a bit later again.'

This was the problem with such a small yacht. It was just way too slow. If there was a headwind, any sort of waves or we were against tide, we were going nowhere. It was so frustrating but there was nothing we could do.

A few hours later Jez tried again and luckily the wind had died down and we were able to get me to my start point.

The most noticeable thing about the day's swim was the sudden increase in wildlife. A lone dolphin came and swam with me again. It didn't get too close and I missed seeing it most of the time but Em saw it frolicking just behind us. There were also hundreds of little black birds bombing past only a few feet from my head. It looked exactly like they were initiating an air strike. They'd start a good 10 foot in the air, about 50 metres away, and then fly directly down towards me and pass a foot over my head before zooming up and circling round again. There was no squawking or any sounds coming from them so I knew they weren't actually feeling threatened by me. I think they generally search for scraps of food from animals like seals in the water. I looked like a seal, I guess. That thought sent sudden shivers down my spine because sharks eat seals. I really needed to stop this 'getting bitten by a shark' fantasy as there has never been a reported fatal shark attack in the UK.

It was coming towards the end of my session when I had the final mini crossing to do – the Milford Haven Waterway. It was by far the busiest port I had crossed all swim, and in the past hour we had seen about five very fast ferries and ships going in and out of it. Unlike the Bristol Channel where the shipping lanes were ten miles wide, here they were condensed down to around one mile. I was quite tired and knew that would take me around 40 minutes but once in the shipping lane we couldn't stop, we just had to keep going. Hanging around the busy shipping lane can result in an angry call from the coastguard who we could see on the top of the cliffs.

I had one last bit of Stowaways food with extra butter and then put my head down. My pace was slow and my arms were sore but I just had to get across to the other side. Jez went ahead as he too couldn't be seen to be hanging around. Eventually I popped out the other side of the shipping lane, exhausted and completely out of energy. Em waved her paddle in the air, the sign that we needed help and *Friday* came back and I called it a day. It had been two good days and although absolutely knackered, I felt good.

We found a typically picturesque Welsh cove to anchor in and all fell asleep pretty early.

The next morning I awoke to Owain chattering loudly. He then came into the front cabin and shoved his phone in my face.

'Hey! Check what they found off Milford Haven yesterday!'

I read the article on the BBC News website. The headline read, 'The fastest shark in the ocean – and a cousin of the Great White – has been caught by a crew fishing off the Pembrokeshire coast.'

'You cannot be serious!' I looked up at Owain. He looked worried. The article went on to say it was a mako shark, aggressive and fast, and has been known to jump into boats. They have attacked over 40 people since the

1980s, killing three of them, and have attacked 20 boats. This was the first time a mako shark had been caught in British waters for 42 years. The worst part is they then released it! To be fair they are pretty endangered but still, I now had a deadly, and probably rather angry, shark in the water somewhere just offshore from where we were.

You couldn't make this up. The first time a shark had been caught, not only happened to be a killer shark, and a cousin to the great white, but it was also caught right where I happened to be swimming on the very same day. My heart began to race. And it was just yesterday that I was thinking about looking like a seal. I couldn't believe it! I gave Owain his phone back.

'Well, now what?'

'Well the figures are still in your favour, no one has been attacked by a shark in the UK,' said Owain

'Yeah, but no one has swum the length of it either.'

Part of me wished he hadn't told me, but just then my phone beeped and it was a few Tweets from people sending me the article, so I would have found out anyway.

I slowly got ready trying not to think about sharks, because I knew it was ridiculous. There was nothing I could do anyway. If it was my time, it was my time. It was out of my control.

Our anchorage was only a few miles from my swim start so Jez ribbed me there for a change. It was a very calm and misty morning as I followed Jez up to coast towards Jack Sound, a notoriously dangerous narrow that is only passable at slack water and the place where I'd start heading towards Ireland.

Unfortunately I didn't swim fast enough and we missed the optimal time to get through the sound by about 20 minutes. We could see the rush of water flowing through at a worryingly fast rate. It looked like a river in full flood. The next time to swim through it would be in six hours' time and considering we were at the point where we would start heading to Ireland I decided now would be the time to take a few days off, rest my tired muscles, restock the boat properly, and most of all let the crew relax a bit.

Jack Sound was even too strong for *Friday* to go through so we went all the way around it, and made our way across towards St David's and anchored up in the bay.

We spent the next few days doing multiple trips from *Friday* to St David's, which involved a 30-minute walk. We couldn't carry everything we needed in one go so all had various tasks. Jez got the raw end of the deal and had to do three trips to get two tanks of diesel and some water, but he said he was happy to do so and became a master at balancing the heavy jerrycans on his shoulders with his head bent forward. I had also arranged for some supplies to be sent to a local tour operator who were happy to accept the delivery. It included a few more goggles from Speedo, more recovery powder and some much-needed suncream for me and the crew. My hands and right cheek were getting really burned. The only suncream that seemed to work was P20 and we were going through it fast.

It was also a time to update the blog and we even had the guys from Simply Swim, one of my kit sponsors, come out to Wales to film an interview.

It was a good and well-earned break for all of us.

7

SWIMMING TO IRELAND

Recovered and rested, we left the comfort of the bay near St David's and went back towards Jack Sound to start what would surely be the hardest section of my swim. Our successful Bristol Channel crossing certainly gave us all a lot more confidence but we had no idea what the tides would be like, how busy the traffic would be, or how big and strong the waves and the currents would be. They were all things we were just going to have to work out as we went along. Out there we'd have no shelter from the elements. If a storm came out of nowhere we'd almost certainly need to call a mayday. *Friday*'s maximum speed when conditions were good was 6mph, but she generally chugged along at around 3mph. If we got into trouble in the middle of the Irish Sea and needed to get to land it would take well over ten hours to get to shore. A very daunting reality but with the weather as good as it had been, it would take something seriously out of the ordinary to happen for us to call for backup.

We arrived at Jack Sound at slack water and I jumped in to swim through it. Because there was no tide it was just like any other swim. I popped out the other side and just before heading off towards Ireland Jez suggested I swim to land so that I can at least say I officially swam across the Bristol Channel. I wasn't that bothered about the 'official' but Jez convinced me to do it and I am glad he did because I think I would have regretted not doing it. I clambered onto the rocks, did a little dance, had my photo taken and then jumped back in the water and started heading north-west into nothingness.

I was feeling strong and together with the tide I managed to swim 18 miles. The waves were quite big too but I was powering through them gaining confidence with every stroke as Wales disappeared behind me. Em and Owain, however, were starting to get seasick again. I seemed to have got my sea legs from being in the water but after a week of flat conditions and a few days on land the others were suffering once again.

That night Em, Jez and Owain took it in turns to watch ship as I tried to get some sleep.

The Irish Sea was a lot rougher than the Bristol Channel. Long high rollers started to run through us lifting me ten foot in the air. By midday on the second day of our crossing I had done a further five miles into the Irish sea and was almost halfway. It was difficult for us to work out a strategy for swimming. Technically the tide, which runs diagonally from south-west to north-east and then in reverse, wasn't ideal. The northerly tide would take me nearer John O'Groats but further from Ireland. The southerly tide would take me further from John O'Groats but closer to Ireland. This meant I was swimming in big 'S' shapes which would add at least 10–20 miles to the crossing, which was already 41 miles long as the crow flies. Even with the extra distance it still seemed to be the correct decision.

By early afternoon the wind and rain started to pick up again. The dark clouds created a dramatic backdrop to an increasingly difficult sea to swim in. Waves were sometimes so big that they would roll me over sideways. Em too was struggling to keep with me, the side-winds often pushing her a hundred metres away from me. I pushed on for hours and hours, stopping every now and then to look up into the heavens as buckets of rain poured down. By 6pm I had had enough and decided to have rest as the southerly tide was pushing me too far in the wrong direction. I really needed to get more mileage west and the best time to do that would be at slack water at around 11pm. I decided to do a two-hour session in the dark to gain some much-needed ground closer to Ireland.

As we approached the mark that night I was even more terrified about swimming in the dark than I had been before. I wasn't sure why but I guess the last few night sessions I started when it was light and it gradually got darker. I couldn't shake the weird dread in my subconscious that as soon as I jumped in I'd go right into the mouth of a shark, even though I knew it was a stupid thought to have. Shivers went down my spine.

'Three ... Two ... One ... Go!' Jez shouted as we drifted over my swim start GPS point.

I jumped in and the first thing I noticed as how the lights from *Friday* were reflecting off the bubbles I created from jumping in. It looked magical. I started swimming and the bubbles kept glistening. I then looked up to ask Jez if we were going in the right direction only to discover he wasn't near me. What was lighting up the bubbles then? Em's head torch wasn't bright enough. I put my face back in the water and kicked my legs about. An explosion of light erupted from my legs. I then put my hands in the water and waved them around. A similar explosion of glistening lights engulfed my hands. It couldn't be? Were these phosphorescence?

'Em, look at this.'

Em came close and shone her head torch into the water but couldn't see anything.

'Turn off your torch.'

'Really? Why?' she asked nervously.

'Trust me.'

She did and I thrashed around in the water creating a cloud of light around me.

'No way. That's amazing!' Em shouted and proceeded to move her paddle around the water, creating even more lights. It was incredible and looked exactly like when Pi Patel was lost at sea in *Life of Pi* and the whale jumped out the water creating an underwater fireworks display.

For the next two hours I swam in a magical world of fantasy as trails of fairy lights followed my fingertips with every stroke. The light in the water created optical illusions and at times I didn't know which was real, as clumps of phosphorescence crowded so close together they created the illusion of larger sea creatures.

I could have swum all night but at 1am it was time to end my session. I got out of the water completely buzzing from the excitement of the night's session. I tried to describe it to Owain and Jez but it was near impossible to explain the experience. You really had to have been there. Those two hours were some of the best of my life and I'll take that experience to the grave.

The next morning we were getting pushed quite far north with the northerly tide and it looked like I'd hit Ireland halfway up towards Dublin at this rate. That would add an extra day at sea but once ten miles offshore we could logistically go to land each night. Today's big problem again was a 20-mile wide shipping lane we had to cross. The waves were picking up, which made swimming increasingly difficult. By early afternoon Jez came near us and shouted.

'Sean, we need to stop now and make for Rosslare. There's a tornado warning.'

'Funny, mate. Nice joke.' Surely there was no way there was a tornado coming. I'd never heard of an actual tornado ever touching down in the UK.

'I'm serious. Get out now. We are seven hours from shore and need to make a run for it. We can't stay at sea tonight.'

Jez had an uncharacteristically stern look on his face. Now I knew he was serious. I got out the water and we listened to the shipping forecast, and true to his word they mentioned a gale force eight or nine with tornado warning for southern Ireland.

The first shark in 40 years just where I was swimming and now surely the first tornado in Ireland for years just where I was swimming.

We chugged along towards Ireland, the waves getting bigger and bigger as we got closer. We had the sail out at full reach and were making good progress. Luckily we were heeled over towards the side of the boat my bunk was on so I could sleep lying almost on the side of the hull. It was surprisingly comfortable with *Friday*'s ribs digging into my back giving me some sort of massage. I was just dosing off when I heard Jez call from the cabin.

'Sean, I need your help.' He sounded quite calm so I got up slowly and went through to the main cabin. Still bleary eyed, I felt my foot go into some water. I looked down to see the floor completely underwater.

Shit! We were sinking! How was this possible? We hadn't hit a rock or anything. My mind suddenly went to thoughts of us all having to abandon *Friday* and get in the RIB, which certainly didn't have enough fuel to get to shore. Tornado versus RIB was a fight I didn't want to have. Everything went into slow motion. Jez was saying something but I didn't hear it. Eventually I snapped out of it.

'Sorry. What was that?' I asked Jez, preparing for the worst.

'We've got a leak.'

'No shit, mate. I can see we have a leak. How bad is it?'

Jez pointed to the side of the hull just above his bunk where water was pouring in. Just then we hit a huge wave and the foldaway table unhooked and came crashing down, completely shattering off its hinges.

'Help me get the floorboards up to see we don't have a more serious hole. Em, can you do the manual bilge pump outside. Owain, can you steer?' Jez jumped into full action mode.

Frantically we lifted the floorboards and felt through the very murky water along the hull to see if there was a bigger issue. There didn't seem to be one and after some frantic pumping from Em on the manual bilge we noticed with huge relief that the water wasn't getting any deeper. It looked like the issue was in fact with the automatic bilge pump, which had short-circuited while we were heeled over. We were at least three hours from Ireland and would have to take it in turns pumping out the water with the hand pump. As if my arms weren't tired enough.

It was 9.30pm when we finally reached Rosslare Harbour. All the fishing boats were rafted up together preparing for a stormy night. I was still sceptical about this tornado malarkey and none of us had any internet so we decided to find a pub with Wi-Fi to see if we would be able to swim tomorrow or not, and hope that the weather was good enough so we could fix the small hole and the bilge pump in time. It was 10.50pm but we might just make it up the hill before the pub closed. We wandered through the deserted harbour port looking for a way out. Owain then mentioned something none of us had even thought of.

'Aren't we in a new country? Shouldn't we have showed someone a passport or something? We could have sailed here from Somalia.'

He had a point. None of us had our passports on us and no one would know where we were from. In fact I had no ID on me whatsoever. From the point of view of anyone who met us wandering the harbour we had just sailed in and looking like a bunch of dirty refugees.

'We'll be fine,' said Jez and just grinned. I wasn't so confident. How did we overlook this?

Just then we saw a security guard waving at us. My heart sank. This was it. I was going to have to swim back to Wales or land up in jail for illegally entering a country. We walked over slowly trying to look as unthreatening as possible by putting Em at the front – although her hair now resembled a rat's nest and did us no favours in the refugee department.

'You must be looking for the pub,' said the security guard before we could even state our case. He had a pretty heavy Irish accent that was quite hard to understand. He continued.

'You better run like feck if you want to get last orders. Through that gate,' he pointed off to the left.

Brilliant. Possibly the worst security guard in the world. See four dirty people wandering around a port at 11pm and instead of ask what they are doing, send them to the pub. Welcome to Ireland. We didn't waste any time in case he started asking questions and immediately started running, shouting our thank yous as we disappeared into the darkness and up the hill towards the town above.

We found the pub just in time. It had Wi-Fi and true to the forecast we saw on an Irish news website that a tornado was due to hit Ireland in the night or early tomorrow. This would be an enforced bad weather rest day, which was slightly annoying because we had a few good weather rest days in Wales preparing for the crossing.

With all the drama of sinking boats and tornados we had neglected to get excited about finally reaching Ireland. We couldn't really celebrate because we technically hadn't made it across the Irish Sea yet as we were still a good 15 miles offshore. Also, Rosslare isn't exactly the most inspiring of places to land either, so all in all it felt a little underwhelming as we sat in the pub drinking Guinness in a corner. A far cry from the huge party I thought we'd have after completing the world's first ever Wales to Ireland swim.

We used the bad weather days to fix *Friday* and restock on supplies. Luckily *Friday*'s hole was above the waterline and only really affected us when we heeled over to the port side. We managed to plug it with a bit of wood and then rewired the automatic bilge pump. *Friday* was growing in character by the day with war wounds to show for her experiences.

Eventually, after three days in Rosslare without ever being asked for passports or any sort of ID whatsoever, we managed to get back to my swim point and I carried on heading north. I was close enough to Ireland now to only swim in the northerly tide and what a tide it was. Even in some pretty big rollers I managed to swim 18 miles in six hours heading towards Arklow, the point at which it was likely Swimming Britain would officially reach land in Ireland.

I was about to get ready to get into the water for the last session of the Irish Sea crossing when I heard a huge shout from Jez in the cockpit. He had a somewhat frantic tone to his voice. I'd never heard him sound distressed like this before, not even when *Friday* was sinking. I jumped out my bunk in a panic and burst into the cabin. I saw Jez bent over doing something on the floor of the cockpit, right above the engine, the stairs shielding what he was doing. It looked serious.

'What's up, mate? Everything all right?' I asked nervously.

'No, it's not all right. I spilt my coffee and I've waited ages for it to get to the right temperature,' he said, genuinely angry.

Making coffee isn't as easy as it sounds on a 50-year-old paraffin stove that takes a good 20 minutes to boil a kettle. I couldn't help but laugh though. The one thing that Jez can't do without is his coffee. *Friday* sinking was fixable. Not having coffee, a disaster.

Not having any land markers to swim towards was starting to be a real drain on morale as it often felt like I was swimming in the same spot. The waves too were pretty choppy, not big, just choppy because of the slight headwind making them shorten and bounce around. Also, because I had become so used to breathing to my right, in order to look at land in Cornwall, that changing to breathe on my left felt really weird. I was also swimming off to my left a lot more than usual. I could compensate for my wonkiness caused by the cheese rolling injury when I had something on shore to aim for, but without any markers within 100 metres I was swimming at 90 degrees to where I should have been going. It was pretty frustrating for the crew who would, every now and then, throw a fish at me to get my attention to swim in a straight line. With my earplugs in I could barely hear anything except my own breathing. This was happening a lot today but at least we were making good progress north.

I was also starting to feel incredibly cold in the water. I thought I was on top of my eating but obviously not. The cold was cutting me deep and I had lost most of my body fat. I decided to email Speedo and ask them for a smaller wetsuit.

Speedo later replied. They would post me two more adult extra small and one child extra large. I would not be impressed if I fit into a child's wetsuit, but anything to stop the cold water pouring down my back.

We got up early to head back to the swim spot. About 20 minutes into the commute we came to a sudden halt as if in a head-on collision. For a moment I thought we had hit a rock. The yacht then suddenly heeled over to the port side at quite a worrying angle. We went outside to have a look. Right off the side of *Friday* was a long rope going down into the depths. We followed it to the hull where we saw a black buoy tangled around the rudder. We had been caught on a lobster pot. This was far from ideal and was taking up precious swimming time.

Jez tried everything to try manoeuvre off the pot but nothing was working. This involved going full throttle back and forth, which inevitably involved us coming to a dead stop, sending most of *Friday*'s contents all over place.

'Someone's going to have to go in?' said Jez looking straight at me. That someone was obviously going to be me as I was already in my wetsuit.

'We need to cut the line unfortunately.'

I put the rest of my kit on and jumped overboard and went under *Friday*. The rope had been caught between the larger rudder and the hull. The only place I could cut the rope safely was about two metres down. I took a deep breath and feeling a little like James Bond swam with the knife in my teeth so that I had my hands free. The rope was at such tension that within a few cuts it snapped free, the recoil of the rope missing my face by a few inches. By the time I got up to the surface again *Friday* was a good 20 metres away, that's how strong the tide was. Jez then circled around and came back and picked me up. We carried on back to my swim point and I continued heading north.

The water was much calmer than it had been since we started the crossing to Ireland. We realised now that we were so close to land we were sheltered from the westerly wind. We hadn't planned this at all but we started to wonder and hope if we might have pretty calm waters all the way up the inside of Ireland. If the wind stayed from the west then surely we would? Of all the reasons to come to Ireland this was probably the best one, even though it hadn't been considered in our decision-making process.

The calm water stayed with us all morning and at around midday a thick blanket of low-lying mist mysteriously engulfed us. It became eerily quiet as I swam into nothingness, not being able to see much further than about 50 metres ahead. *Friday* would sail past and disappear into the mist like a stealthy pirate looking for treasure under the cover of fog. Moments later she'd reappeared and sail back past creating a small ripple, which was the only way we could tell the difference between water and sky. It was very eerie and certainly gave me fuel for my wild imagination, which helped me take my mind off the cold water.

We sat out the southerly tide and went again well into the night on the northerly tide. Again the phosphorescence were breathtaking and I kept asking Em to turn off her head torch so I could see them better. Jez didn't like this as he had no way of seeing where we were in the water. In hindsight this was very irresponsible but it was so calm and I figured they'd never be further than shouting distance from us. Although the sea was calm, the rain started to bucket down again. It didn't bother me but it was seriously miserable for Em and Jez who were out in the cold.

By 11pm we had made it to Arklow and technically finished the Irish crossing. We opened a bottle of champagne and had some cake to celebrate. It was good to be near land again. After one glass (or mug as we didn't have glasses) of champagne, I retired to my bunk as the next northerly tide was in five hours and I had to get up an hour before at 4am.

The wind picked up soon after getting into bed and both Em and I spent all night trying desperately to hold on to our bunks. There was also a very annoying BANG! whenever the front of *Friday* rose and dropped suddenly, making the anchor chain tighten suddenly. It was barely noticeable on deck but when our faces were 10 centimetres from where the anchor chain was, it would make the sound a million times worse. Slight vibration, BANG! Slight vibration, BANG! Every five seconds or so. It was torture.

When the alarm went at 3.45am, Em and I just laughed, in that overtired, 'I've given up' type of way. To make things worse, a headwind had picked up and the water seemed to be a lot colder but that was possibly because I had had no sleep and felt low. I swam past Arklow and did a good ten miles before nearly falling asleep in the water so called it a day and headed back to Arklow to stay in the marina and stock up on food.

I also had one of my best friends from South Africa coming to swim with me for a few days. It had all been a bit last-minute but he was waiting in Arklow to meet us. Although I knew it was going to be nice having a familiar face join the swim I was worried that we'd all get on each other's nerves on *Friday*, where things were already pretty cramped.

*

'Seano! My man. Bloody long time, bro,' said Kenton, as he swaggered through the pub to meet us.

Kenton is a 6 foot, 3 inch swimming machine. He has represented South Africa and even as a kid I remember him getting up at stupid o'clock to go training. When he heard I was doing this swim he decided he wanted to come all the way from South Africa to swim with me for a few days. Although I liked the idea I was concerned about how we'd all fit on *Friday*. Kent would have to sleep on the cold wet floor in between the two bunks in the main cabin, with his head slightly in the toilet because he is too tall. He's a proper bushman though so luckily that didn't bother him.

It was amazing having an outsider come and join us. Kent was so excited to be there it lifted all our spirits. He told us just how many people were following the swim in South Africa. My school was having weekly updates in assembly. It was nice to know that people were getting something from the swim. It definitely made me want to push harder.

That evening we had burgers on the boat and I got a visit from another close family friend who moved from Zimbabwe to Ireland. I felt like I was back home for a moment and the crew mocked me for slipping into a South African accent.

We woke up to perfectly calm and flat water. I was slightly annoyed as I wanted Kent to experience what we had experienced for the last week but welcomed the easy session. Having Kent there certainly made me step up my game. He was fresh-armed and a fast swimmer and at times I couldn't keep up with him. The one thing I had on him was he was not used to the cold, being African and all. He was constantly shivering, which made me laugh because the water was 16 degrees, the warmest it had been all swim. The tide was good and apart from a few jellyfish stings on our hands gained mostly from brushing them out the way, we swam a whopping 22 miles, my biggest day yet. We made it halfway across Dublin Bay. Kenton was like an excitable child and Em was enjoying the challenge of looking after two children at sea.

'Come now boys, swim together. Kenton! Stop swimming off like that. You're going to get lost,' she called to us. The mood of the crew was the highest it had been all swim and even though Kenton had to sleep on the manky floor he remained keen the entire time.

That evening we had yet another calm anchorage in Dublin Port. Kenton then took us out for dinner and a few pints before retiring for the night.

The next day, the wind finally picked up and Kenton got to experience what it was like to do some big wave swimming, as we headed across the rest of Dublin Bay and around the dramatic cliff-lined peninsula towards Howth. Kent loved it, and so did I for that matter, as we surfed down each wave below a lighthouse on the cliffs with a dark and stormy sky above. This was open-water swimming at its most extreme and what better way to share it than with a good mate.

We reached Howth in the early evening, still buzzing, and I was surprised to see Duane, Kenton's brother there.

He had flown over from London to visit us for the night. What a reunion, and a great end to a fantastic swim, the best so far. As we cracked into the beers we realised we had an email from the BBC to say that they were sending a cameraman down to film us for *The One Show* tomorrow. This would be great for the expedition and for War Child. It did however mean we weren't going to swim tomorrow, and I was disappointed for Kenton as I knew how keen he was to swim and he had to fly back to London tomorrow evening. Nevertheless, the few days he was with us were some of the best days of the swim so far.

Predictably, a few beers with Kenton and Duane turned out to be a few too many and I woke up with a pretty heavy head. *The One Show* presenter and crew had already arrived by the time we all frailly arose from the depths of *Friday*. The morning was spent filming on the boat, introducing everyone, including *Friday* and Stuart the Scab (who was now officially part of the crew) to the seven million-odd viewers who would watch it the following day. Everyone was enjoying getting creative with camera angles and telling their side of the story, except Jez, who has some sort of phobia of being photographed and spent most of the morning hiding behind one or all of us.

That afternoon we said our goodbyes to *The One Show* and sadly said goodbye to Kenton. Having him along for a few days was a much-needed boost to team morale and it was sad to see him walk down the pontoon with his bag over his shoulder like a sailor heading home.

That evening we headed off from Howth to make the most of the evening tide. As we left the harbour, Jez asked if I wanted to swim across the next bay or follow the coast, which was an extra 12 miles. The bay was 25 miles wide and I had been doing around 18 miles per day so decided we should cut across. I really needed to make up some mileage. Today was Day 41, which was a little over halfway in time but I had only covered just over a third of the distance.

8

SLACK BAY

We weren't quite at the start of the bay just yet, so the plan was to get as close as possible to it so that I could do most of the crossing the following day. Northern Ireland was on the other side of the bay and a definite psychological milestone to look forward to.

Another incredible evening of swimming with phosphorescence was slightly dampened by the sudden increase in jellyfish stings to the face. Normally, whenever I got stung I'd roll over onto my back and try to rub some of the stings off. This time I didn't bother and just pushed through. When you get stung once all over your face you stop caring about the next sting. The one thing I did notice was that where my beard was coming through I wasn't getting stung as badly. This must have been due to the fact my facial hair was stopping the tentacles from actually hitting my face. I had a hard decision to make. I could either shave and be more streamlined but get stung in the face, which would slow me down, or start growing a beard to protect me and hopefully not get stung so much. I'd see how the next week panned out before deciding.

I got stung so many times during the rest of the evening session that by the end I had already made up my mind. I'd happily sacrifice being streamlined for a facial-hair-jellyfish-protection-shield. They really were that bad. The beard not only needed to stay, it needed to get bigger.

Off in the distance I could see the other side of the bay. It looked a lot closer than 25 miles away. We needed to make this shortcut. We were a few weeks behind schedule now and I had to make it up some time somehow. And yet by the end of the day I had only covered ten miles in two sessions in the water. It dawned on me that the further and further I got into the bay the slower I was swimming. I was now only just over a third of the way across the bay, which also meant we were now too far into the heart of the bay to turn back for an anchorage, so we'd most likely need to spend the night at sea.

I looked at the tidal charts to see what we were dealing with. There in big letters it read 'slack' for most of the day. I asked Jez what this was all about.

'Basically, as the Atlantic fills up, the water rushes around the top and the bottom of Ireland and meets in the middle here. This means there is no tide. Instead, the water just rises up and down in one spot, and more often than not just swirls around in all directions.'

'Really? So basically I have no tide to help me get across the bay.'

'Probably not,' said Jez in his nonchalant way.

'Shit, man. I wish I had known this,' I said, bothered that it looked like we had inadvertently taken on another surprise crossing thrown at us without notice. At this rate it would take three days to cross 'Slack Bay'. That was as much time as it took us to cross from Wales to Ireland.

'We'll be fine, it's much quicker than going along the edge and you said you needed to make up some mileage,' replied Jez still looking at the charts. He had a point. Even if I had known I probably would have stubbornly said, 'Yes, let's do it.' I had become so used to doing proper mileage in the last week I couldn't have predicted just how hard and slow Slack Bay would be.

Annoyed, I retired to my bunk and tried to get into a positive mental attitude to smash out the miles tomorrow and get across the bay. There was no point in dwelling on it. We were too far into the bay to change anything. We just had to get on with it. The only thing slightly different to a normal crossing was that we could drop anchor, which meant the crew didn't need to do night shifts as we floated aimlessly. Incredibly, *Friday* had a 60-metre chain and we were in 33 metres of water, which meant, although not recommended, we could drop anchor. The general rule is you need three times as much anchor chain to allow the anchor to go out at an angle and take grip. An anchor going straight down from a boat is not effective. Technically, *Friday* could only anchor safely in 20 metres of water so 33m was a bit risky and we were likely to drift. Jez said he'd keep an eye on the GPS. In any case you could hear the anchor dragging along the bottom, which usually woke you up anyway.

As much as I tried to sleep, I just couldn't. This was the second night in a row that the rocking and the vibration BANG! of the anchor chain tightening prevented us from sleeping, pushing Em and I to the verge of sure madness. Four times in the night I went out the front hatch on deck and tried to put something under the chain to stop the banging. Nothing worked. Eventually the sun came up and it was time to get in the water again. My chest was tight and I was shivering even before I got in. This was the weakest I had felt all swim, which wasn't surprising considering I'd only had two to three hours' sleep in the past 48 hours.

We all got up slowly preparing for the next session. The mood on the boat was not good, a stark contrast to where we were only a few days earlier. I'd tried hard to get in a positive mindset, but no matter how good an attitude you have, sleep deprivation takes everything out of you. There wasn't much talking as we all did our various chores for the morning session.

The day was long and slow, my immune system was low and the cold was cutting right to my core. I vomited a few times too, which I hadn't done in a while, the slightest taste of salt water making me heave and retch. It was so demoralising swimming in water that didn't really know what it was doing. It was swirling all over the place, and in some patches I'd be against tide and other the tide would push me sideways. Progress was still slow and every time

I asked for a progress report it was usually around 1mph. As the hours went by, the colder I got, and I started to feel the swim slipping away from me. It seemed that every few days we'd somehow drop a day and fall further behind schedule, which was putting me under a lot of pressure. I was constantly thinking about the bad weather closing in or the crew deciding they had had enough. I really needed to be doing 15-20 miles a day to get to Scotland in time. I was very behind schedule already and if I carried on at this rate the swim would take another three months, taking us well into winter. Trying to swim in winter in Scotland would surely be impossible.

I began to sob quietly in the water while still swimming, my tears filling up the inside of my goggles. I didn't want the crew to know I was crying so started to breathe on the other side, away from Em. I knew the sleep deprivation was causing most of my negativity but that didn't help. For the next hour I increased the salt content in the Irish Sea as I let out tears from my goggles while pretending to cough and stretch my shoulder. By the end of the session we were still a good ten miles from the end of the bay and would again have to drop anchor in the middle of the bay, this time at a depth of 44 metres.

Just as we were going to bed Owain got another email from *The One Show* saying they wanted to do a live feed with us from Newcastle in Northern Island tomorrow evening as they had David Walliams, who has swum the English Channel as well as the length of the River Thames, on the show. That was about 15 miles ahead of where we were. There was no way I'd be able to swim there so we'd have to start making progress at around 10am in order to get there in time. This meant I could just about get four hours during the morning's session.

Again, I only managed about an hour's sleep. This surprise crossing was turning out to be the worst decision I had made all swim. I had now only had around three to four hours' sleep in the last 72 hours. That's four hours' sleep away from clinical insanity. Jez had let out all 60 metres of chain for our 44 metres' anchorage and it took him and Owain over an hour to ratchet the chain up using the mast winch, swapping from the left winch to the right winch as they pulled up 50 centimetres at a time. The chain weighed well over 100kg and was impossible to pull up by hand.

We had anchored on my swim point so Em and I left Jez and Owain hauling the anchor and began my session. Within seconds of being in the water I could feel my body seizing up. I had no energy and was shivering so profusely I could barely move my arms. I checked the water temp on my watch and it showed 12 degrees, four degrees colder than it had been. Although it didn't sound like much it really was making a difference. I could barely swim 1mph. My body was just too tired and cold.

Em sensed something wasn't right.

'Ginge, I think you need to stop, this is ridiculous.'

'I know, but I can't, we need to …' I stopped mid-sentence. I felt like crying as the fear of this swim not being possible crept into my thoughts again.

'Come on, Ginge, let's go to Newcastle and have a few days' rest and carry on faster. There is no point in doing 1mph.'

By now Jez and Owain had pulled up the anchor and were heading over to us.

'We're done,' Em shouted to them.

'OK, fair enough,' said Jez as he looped round bringing the RIB near me so I could get out the water. I felt like a failure. I only managed one mile and barely so. If I had known I was only going to swim one mile I would have asked Jez to take us to Newcastle last night and avoid a pretty horrendous anchorage. We were all feeling like shit and it was all my fault because I had said we should swim across the bay. Everything was on me now and the one thing I was meant to be doing, swimming, wasn't even happening. I lay down on my bunk and began to cry again and fell asleep for the first time in days as Jez did the six-hour journey to Newcastle fuelled by lots and lots of coffee.

We reached Newcastle by early evening and went straight to the hotel where they were going to film me. I was really nervous about being on the show again, so soon after the first time, when things really weren't going to plan and the likelihood of me actually completing this swim was growing ever more distant. I tried not to think about it and needed to stay positive, both for my own mindset and so as not to dissuade people from donating money to War Child. If it seemed that I might not make it then people surely wouldn't donate. I needed to be upbeat about the situation, even though I didn't feel remotely confident.

The hotel had kindly given us a free room and then on top of that the producer for *The One Show* had paid out of his own pocket to upgrade us to the suites. An actual bed for each of us. The last proper bed any of us had slept in was that weekend in Clovelly, which was nearly a month ago. At least something was looking up.

We did the live feed to *The One Show* where presenters Matt Baker and Alex Jones seemed genuinely interested in the swim. I had met Matt before when he did his rickshaw ride to London, but I was sure there was no way he would remember so kept quiet! They showed the footage of us that they filmed in Howth, which really did look incredible. They even somehow made me seem quite cool! David Walliams was on the show and he called me annoying for doing a harder swim than his, which I quite enjoyed. It was obviously tongue in cheek, but it cheered us up to be able to talk positively about the swim, and know people were interested. It took our minds off the fact that we still hadn't crossed Slack Bay, and we all ignored the fact that we needed to go back out there sooner or later.

After all the excitement of the TV activities, we went for an amazing Indian dinner, a few pints, the world's longest bath (the first proper bath for me) and then passed out. Beds, and dry ones at that, are seriously underrated and I vowed never to take my bed for granted ever again. Even Jez opted for a land-bed instead of going back to *Friday*.

I slept for 12 hours straight, but still had a tight chest so bought some chest medicine. We spent the day stocking up the boat and I tried to eat as much fatty foods as possible to put some weight on. I needed to do something about my increasing weight loss. The block of butter every couple of days wasn't working. I also bought some more iodine for Stuart the Scab. He hadn't grown over the last week or so and seemed to be settling down, but he was still revealing the red flesh inside my foot.

Arthur's RIB engine was playing up again. It took ages to start and would cut out sometimes. I hated RIB engines, especially this one, as I had spent nearly as much as buying one in getting it fixed and it still wasn't working well.

Technically I had had two full days of not swimming but I didn't feel rested at all. We were 15 miles from my swim point so we got up early to head back. I'd hopefully be able to do a night session.

In the end, it took us over two days to get back to my swim point. As soon as we left the comfort of Newcastle bay we were faced with strong headwinds and waves. *Friday*'s pace dropped down to 1mph as we nearly came to a standstill every time we hit an oncoming wave. Jez was doing all he could but by early afternoon, after being battered for 8 hours, we had only done just over eight miles. It was pointless trying to fight the waves so we headed to the nearest shore and anchored up for the night.

The following day was exactly the same as we were thrown around *Friday* all day as Jez heroically manned the fort for hour upon hour to get us back to my swim point. By the end of the day we were still two miles from the point. Instead of doing a 44 metre anchor in the middle of the bay like before, Jez decided to head another two hours towards the coast for a better anchorage, which was a much better plan. It was a lot calmer nearer the shore, which was incredibly annoying as if I had decided to follow the shore we'd have had good anchorages, calm water and better sleep. We were obviously falling further and further behind schedule, but after four full rest days I felt a whole lot better for it.

The weather took a turn for the better too and I had an easy morning session of flat water as I made my way towards Kilkeel. We had decided to start heading slightly in towards land so that we'd be closer to shore for calm anchoring. Even if it added another 20 miles we weren't going to drop anchor in 40 metres of water ever again. By the end of the session just as I was feeling good again, Jez announced that there was a gale warning and we needed to head to Kilkeel harbour for shelter. This was incredibly frustrating as I really did not need any more non-swimming days.

Kilkeel was a huge fishing port and *Friday* looked ever so dwarfed next to the huge trawlers all rafted up waiting out the imminent storm. Although old and rickety she really had done us well so far. What she lacked in amenities she made up for in pure guts and determination. Jez definitely had a soft spot for her. We all did. She was the fifth crew member and probably the most important.

We rafted alongside two trawlers that weren't going out due to engine problems and settled in for the night. It was likely that we would have to stay in the harbour for a few days due to bad weather.

'Ginge, I'm so sorry!' Em came into the front cabin. I was still half asleep.

'I've dropped your wallet and it's fallen in the water between the wall and a ship. It fell out my pocket when I was climbing up the ladder.'

Em, being crew captain, had been in charge of food shopping and general logistics and had my wallet to go and buy some supplies.

She looked so upset that I tried to make light of the situation. 'Don't worry, dude. It only had a hundred pounds in it. You'll just have to forfeit a few beers over the next few weeks.'

There wasn't anything in the wallet that I really needed and could easily get a new card sent out in a day or two. It wasn't worth stressing over. I had other issues to deal with, mainly in my mind and the number of non-swimming days I had had in the last week. Em, however, felt really guilty and left the cabin sheepishly apologising.

I got dressed and went out on deck to find a group of people gathering round the ladder trying to look down the one-foot wide gap between one of the fishing boats and the harbour wall. The next thing I saw was a guy called Steve dressing in full drysuit diving gear on the boat.

'What's going on?' I asked.

'This is Steve, he's going to dive for the wallet,' replied Em.

How on earth had this all happened so quickly? I was asleep ten minutes ago! Turns out the fisherman who we were rafted to, Joe, knew Steve and called him to come and help us. He didn't even question it and was there in a jiffy. How kind. Moments later, before I even had time to give my thanks, he was overboard and disappeared between the wall and the boat with a torch. We all waited anxiously, mostly for Steve's safety, as getting pinned between a 30-ton boat and a harbour wall would be fatal.

Steve tried for a good half an hour before giving up. The wallet probably floated away at an angle and with a slight tide could be 50 metres away in any direction. Steve was incredibly apologetic for not being able to find it, which made Em feel even more guilty. I too felt bad that he had gone out of his way to help some random strangers he hadn't even met before. What a true gentleman.

For some reason, Joe the fisherman also felt guilty and somehow managed to find us two huge fish and some seaweed-grown potatoes for dinner. I didn't know what fish they were but frying them in butter and lemon juice moments after gutting them made them taste heavenly.

That night I went to bed feeling a lot better for experiencing some real kindness from Joe and Steve. When people helped me, I felt I should repay their kindness by swimming harder and faster and completing the swim. That inspired me to stop messing around and feeling sorry for myself and just keep going.

The weather improved and we headed back out into the bay to hopefully do the last session before leaving the curse of Slack Bay behind us for good. Although feeling more positive there was nothing I could do to improve my pace, which was just over 1mph. I had been swimming now for 50 days and I guess my body had reached a state of fatigue that would take weeks to recover from. I didn't have weeks and just had to carry on as best I could. I only managed five and a half miles in the session and we headed to shore to sit out the tide. Just as we anchored up, a ray of sunshine broke below the dark and stormy sky creating the most glorious and wonderful full double rainbow any of us had ever seen. We all just stood there staring at the vivid colours contrasting against the dark grey clouds. Then, as quickly as it appeared, it disappeared again returning the momentarily magical oil painting back to a dull and murky seascape. We had four hours at this anchorage so Jez and Em decided to go ashore and do some exploring. I needed to get some sleep and fatten up. Owain, inspired by last night's fish, decided to catch some mackerel for dinner.

Owain caught five fish that we fried for dinner just before my night session, which started at 11pm. Fish have essential fats which are good for recovery and I really needed to make an effort to eat more. Luckily Owain loved fishing otherwise the only other option was to tie a line around my waist and try to catch some while I swam. I was actually intrigued to try this but didn't want to mess up my new extra small wetsuit that Speedo had sent me. (Happily I had retained my manliness: the child's wetsuit didn't fit me.)

Pace dropped even further and further as I pulled my way through millions of phosphorescence well into the night. I got out of the water at 2.45am, just five miles from the end of Slack Bay. Even if I did doggy paddle, I was determined to get out of this hellhole tomorrow and back into some tidal water again.

We were at the time of the month when most of the second tide was from midnight till 6am, so I decided to just make the most of the one daytime tide in the next few days. Although swimming at night was doable, it was putting a noticeable strain on the crew and at this point in time I was concerned that they'd stop enjoying the expedition and leave. I really didn't know how we would cope in that situation. None of them had hinted they weren't enjoying it but I didn't want to risk forcing the issue. They were, after all, volunteering their time. I needed to make sure it wasn't becoming a chore for them. Having a crew was very different from when I cycled around the world. Then I was on my own and didn't have anyone to look after me, or for me to think about. I really needed to keep the crew's experience in mind as I wanted them to have an adventure too.

9

THE DEPARTURE OF JEZ

'Sean, I've got some bad news,' said Jez sheepishly.

Still half asleep, I sat up and bumped my head on the ceiling above me. It hurt like hell.

'Really?' I asked nervously, rubbing my head. He looked more worried than the time he spilt his coffee.

'I've just been offered a job back in London and I think I'm going to take it …'

Jez carried on talking but I didn't hear any of it. My first thought was that I bloody jinxed it last night by thinking about the crew leaving. Without a skipper I couldn't carry on the swim. My heart sank. I had no luck whatsoever trying to find a skipper at the beginning. How was I going to find another one now? I then immediately started to think about all the times I didn't swim fast enough, for taking those four days off in Clovelly and another four days in Newcastle. A hundred 'if onlys' that could have put me closer to the end by now.

'When do you need to leave?' I eventually managed to open my mouth and speak coherently.

'I need to leave for London a week tomorrow.'

So I had a week to find a skipper. Not only did I need someone who could sail a yacht, I needed someone young and enthusiastic enough to deal with the pretty cramped and now very damp conditions on *Friday*.

'OK. You gotta do what you gotta do. Can you try and see if you can find someone though from your boat connections?'

'Yes, mate. I'll ask for sure. If we push it I can get you across to Scotland again and you and Em might be able to continue with land support in the worst case scenario,' Jez suggested.

It wasn't ideal, those first few days in Cornwall when it was just Em and me were a real struggle, but he did have a point. I could always ask my mum to drive my car up and get Owain to drive it along the coast. This was providing we got across to Scotland before Jez had to leave.

I got in the water feeling pretty helpless. There were just so many hurdles in this challenge that had nothing to do with my swimming ability that were hindering its success. Not having a skipper was potentially a deal-breaker, right up there with *Friday* sinking. Just when I thought things would get better once we left Slack Bay.

For the next two days my mind was consumed with ways to try and find a new skipper. I was swimming as much as possible trying to make as much progress as I could to get across to Scotland while using every break to

Tweet, Facebook, put posts on yachting forums and blog to find someone who might be interested.

At the end of the second day, we were hit with another blow. We anchored up to sit out the southerly tide and when we went to start the engine nothing worked. Click! Click! Click! There was a strong sulphur smell coming from the starter battery.

'Smells like battery problems,' said Owain straight away. I knew his engine knowledge would come in useful.

'I think we've fried them,' added Jez who also knew exactly what had happened.

Friday had two batteries, a starter one to get the engine going and a leisure one for charging things on the boat. For some reason the starter battery was fried and the leisure battery didn't have enough volts to start the engine. We sat for ages trying to decide what to do. It was 5pm and the nearest town was ten miles away. It was too late to get there tonight, and by the time we got there and back in the morning I'd have missed the tide, putting me yet another day behind schedule, a day I didn't have as it was tight whether I'd get to Scotland before Jez left already. I didn't need any more delays.

Just when we had resigned to the fact we were going to miss a session, a chap on a stand up paddle board and another guy on a blow-up kayak suddenly appeared out of nowhere. We had been so focused on the battery we hadn't seen them sneak up on us.

'How yous doin'?' said the guy on the SUP in a friendly Northern Irish accent.

'Not bad, just got a dead battery,' replied Owain.

'Really, what's wrong with it?'

'We fried it, I think.'

'Really? Well you're in luck today because I happen to have a spare battery in my van.'

'Seriously?' we all asked in unison.

'Any chance we could buy it off you?' Owain asked immediately.

'Well, let's see if it works first. Come on. It's just over there. We're Simon by the way. Both of us are Simon.'

Simon and Simon paddled towards the shore and we followed in the RIB, which had now finally given up all life, yet another thing adding to the list of things going wrong. Luckily Jez was good at rowing.

There were a few houses on the cliff tops but no sign of life whatsoever. Simon's black camper van was the only car in the car park. There was also a huge 'E' statue right next to the small harbour. Apparently we were at the most easterly part of Ireland. Em clambered on the statue for a few photos. The mood of the crew always lifted when we had company, mostly because none of us really wanted to admit just how hard things were, as this might open up the inevitable 'you didn't think this through' or 'we told you so' conversation. Instead it was easier to pretend all was well.

We chatted with the Simons for about an hour while charging up the spare battery. Simon not only had a spare battery, but also had jump leads and a voltmeter so we could see how charged it was. It was absolutely incredible.

The first time we see someone at sea since the kayaker at Hartland Point is when we have battery problems and he happens to have the solution for us.

Once the battery was charged Jez rowed it back to *Friday* and gave us the thumbs up to say all was well. Simon insisted we have the battery as he wasn't using it. Just when we thought we'd experienced all the kindness we could with Joe and Scuba Steve in Kilkeel, someone else comes to our rescue. We offered to buy Simon a pint but he said he had to get home so we said our goodbyes.

I managed to get almost to the Belfast crossing by the end of my first session. Things were looking up, the tide was strong again and I managed eight miles in four hours, double what I had been swimming in Slack Bay. We rested out the southerly tide and I managed to get some sleep as we prepared to cross the 10-mile Belfast Channel in one go. This would be by far the busiest shipping lane I would have to cross and conditions needed to be perfect. Unfortunately, when it was time to get back in the water a thick layer of fog engulfed most of the eastern coastline reducing visibility to less than 100 metres. There was no way we could cross a busy shipping lane in such dense fog. We'd most certainly get run over. To make things worse the weather forecast suggested tomorrow would be even worse. I seemed to be not swimming more than swimming at the moment. Besides those few glory days with Kenton, this Ireland leg was proving to be a lot harder than any of us had imagined: tornadoes, Slack Bay, broken engines and soon, I'd be skipperless. The mood on the boat was at an all-time low and there was only one way to fix that, I thought.

'Pub. Open bar on me, guys,' I suggested knowing we wouldn't be swimming tomorrow. Nothing a few beers couldn't fix. That was my way of showing my appreciation to the crew. And that was pretty much the last thing I remembered from that night.

'Mate, the forecast was wrong. We gotta go now,' said Jez, looking about as bad as I felt, peeping his head into the front cabin.

For a moment I had completely forgotten where I was and what I was doing as my head felt like it was about to explode.

'Hah?' I asked not sure if I had heard correctly.

'We need to go, the mist has cleared and it's glass,' Jez shouted.

'Shit? Really. OK, I'm up.'

I closed my eyes again. I had the enthusiasm of a sloth and sounded like Johnny Cash. Glimpses of last night started coming back, including Em trying to row us from the pub back to *Friday*, going in circles many, many times, crashing into three other boats and the harbour wall eventually giving up to Jez. I remember laughing so much I nearly fell into the water but recalled that at the time I wouldn't have minded a cold dip. It would have been a different scenario if I had in fact fallen in, although it might have sobered me up. All in all it had been a fun night and

I think was exactly what we all needed. I now, however, needed to pretend to know how to swim, and not any old swim either, swim across the dauntingly terrifying Belfast Channel. 'Right. It's very important you do as I say. If I say swim you swim hard. When I say stop, you stop. OK?' Jez told Em as I jumped in the freezing water, making my head pound even harder, which completely undermined the 'it'll sober you up notion'. It most certainly didn't.

I swam for about an hour before Jez gave the first order to stop. We stopped and let a terrifyingly fast ferry whizz past us creating a washing machine of water turbulence behind it. I then swam hard for 20 minutes to get ahead of the next ferry which went close behind us. We weren't using the sails but had them up anyway just so we'd become more visible to the oncoming ships. It took three hours to cross the Belfast Channel as we played chicken with various ferries and tankers and eventually were in the now even faster moving tide of the north-east coast.

All I remember for the rest of the session was throwing up a few times and getting one seriously bad jellyfish sting to the face, which on top of a pretty bad hangover, was possibly my least favourite life experience to date.

I somehow swam 18 miles that session, and only Hercules knows how, as I was feeling pretty horrendous. I had at least made up some mileage that I had lost and it looked like I would just get over to Scotland in time. The first smidgeon of positivity in a while was very welcome.

Later that evening, anchored up in one of the calmest bays yet, we met up again with Simon (who helped us with the battery). He had offered to collect a parcel of new thermals that I had had sent to Larne a few days earlier. Not only did he collect them but he then took us into Belfast to do some shopping as we were pretty low on food on the boat. He wanted nothing in return either and just really wanted to help us on our way. It was people like Simon who made me want to complete the swim more than ever and I went to bed that night with a new determination to find another skipper.

I was 13 miles away from the North Channel crossing and 24 or so miles away from reaching the Mull of Kintyre in Scotland, at which point I could potentially carry on with land support. I still hadn't had one reply from anyone even interested in being a skipper. I had two days to do this before Jez had to leave. A fairly tall order but after my 18-mile day yesterday, I was feeling confident.

The afternoon tide only started at 2pm and we were ready and in place, a few hundred metres offshore, a few hours before I needed to get in. *Friday* was pointing north facing the oncoming tide while anchored. As soon as her bow swung round to the south it meant the tide had changed and it was time to get in. The conditions started out calm but, typically, as I jumped in, the wind changed to headwind and the sea became very bouncy. Jez decided it would be best to start the crossing early on so that by the time we got to the narrow, and possibly dangerous, North Channel crossing, I'd be most of the way across already. I pushed hard all session but only managed eight miles as we started to make our way towards the Mull (of Kintyre) which was directly north of us, a disappointing distance, as this now meant I had to swim 16 miles tomorrow.

Here it was. My final day with Jez as my skipper. I was obviously gutted because I needed a skipper to continue but having someone leave the expedition halfway through was really sad. We had become a family and it was awful to see him go and not experience sailing through Scotland, which could arguably be the best section of all. Jez had put in some seriously long hours in the cold and rain getting me to and from each swim point and never once complained. So long as his coffee thermos was full, he was happy. It definitely wouldn't be the same without him.

I needed to give it everything in today's session. If I didn't make Scotland I'd be stuck in Northern Ireland and therefore need a skipper to get me over to the Mull. This is one of the most treacherous stretches of water in the UK, and only one person in history has ever swam it. Wayne Soutter swam it but started in Scotland and swam to Northern Ireland. He said he chose that direction because the tide was so strong he feared he'd miss Scotland if he started in NI. No one has ever swum it from Northern Ireland. I was finding it impossible to get a skipper for normal sailing so finding one that was happy to take the responsibility for me in that stretch of water would, dare I say it, be impossible. I had no option but to get to Scotland today. I jumped in with a new burst of energy.

Scotland would be mine by the end of the day.

10

SHATTERED DREAMS

I lay face-down on my bunk and, for the second time, began to weep uncontrollably. We'd been forced to abandon the crossing at the end of the last tide just four miles short from Scottish soil. We had no choice but to find the best anchorage to leave *Friday* and go ashore. This was a small harbour in Northern Ireland called Glenarm. That was two days ago and the sight of Jez walking down the pontoon and away from the expedition was haunting me. For the past two nights I'd dreamt that he got to the end of the pontoon and then turned around and said, 'Actually. I'm staying now.' I'd wake up and go through to his bunk to see an empty space and realise it was just a dream.

I sent the crew home to see their families and was now all alone in Northern Ireland in a last bid to see if I could find a new skipper, but I knew that the odds were against me.

Friday was an eerily weird place to be all alone. Some important things, like Owain's laptop, Jez's sleeping bag and Em's rucksack, all things that symbolised the adventure was still happening, were gone, and without them there was an overwhelming sense that this adventure was over. *Friday* felt old and dishevelled and her flaws that were once a sign of character and perseverance, now seemed unfixable faults resulting in her being unable to continue.

She was finally broken.

I was finally broken, physically and mentally.

Together we lay there engulfed by the reality that neither of us might ever go back out to sea again.

In all my searching, both before the swim and in the past week, I hadn't even got an, 'I'm interested, tell me more,' email or Tweet. Nothing! Deep down I knew that this was the end of the swim. I didn't get out of bed for two days except to go to the toilet. Nothing mattered any more. All I could think about was packing up everything on *Friday*, who I'd have to sell here in Northern Ireland, and heading home, no doubt to a bombardment of 'I told you so' emails from all the negative voices. Every time I thought of that an overwhelming sense of panic engulfed me. I closed my eyes again and fell asleep.

After three days, I decided to actually do something about it instead of sitting and crying and staring blankly at the last marked day on the toilet door map – Scotland still blank, daunting and worryingly large. I was convinced the map people had got the proportions wrong and expanded Scotland due to widening of the latitude lines when printing a flat map.

I had also run out of food and needed to get up anyway so I went to the local pub to enquire about skippers. I got a few contacts for fishermen and some elderly retired boat owners who might like to help. I sent a few emails and left a few voice messages. I then made the 45-minute walk to the nearest town with a supermarket and bought some food to take back to *Friday*.

The next day I did the same thing in a different town a bit further north. I enquired in pubs, coffee shops, the post office ... anywhere that might be able to help. I sent more emails, made more calls and carried on Tweeting.

I did this for eight days until I was forced to admit to myself that I had run out of options. The closest I got was a guy who charted RIB tours along the coast. He initially said he could do it for £1,000 (£500 for each return leg to the Mull to follow me and then take all our kit to the other side) but he then changed his mind as he wasn't sure about insurance and liability.

With each failed day, the more I came to terms with the fact the swim was over. Em had come back to help me but also to collect her stuff to go home. This was it, my dreams of becoming the first person to swim the length of Britain was all but over, and the most annoying thing was that it was something that was out of my control and not due to my swimming ability. There was no more crying, no more panic attacks, as I pushed everything out my mind to prepare with the inevitable emails I was about to get for not completing the challenge.

My parents were feeling pretty sorry for me and Dad had said he'd buy me a flight back to South Africa to rest up, get away from it all, decide what to do in life and recover from yet another failed attempt at an adventurous challenge.

Em was in the pub already when I went up to join her and get Wi-Fi to email my sponsors to say it was all over. I walked in and she greeted me with a huge smile. Before I could ask her what was going on I received a message on my phone. It was from Jez. It read:

'Mate. I can take this Monday off work and come up and get you to Scotland if you want. Let me know.'

Em started shouting. 'Did you get his message? That's good news Ginge! We can get across the channel!'

She was brimming with excitement. But I wasn't so sure. I had already accepted the swim was over and getting across the channel would just be delaying what seemed to be inevitable failure of Swimming Britain. Land support was a nice idea and doable up the Mull and maybe a bit further on, but once out in the Hebrides it wasn't really a feasible option because of the huge cliffs and lack of roads.

'Yeah, I'm not sure.'

'Come on, Ginge! We can get there and look for a skipper in Scotland when we don't have to make the crossing.'

Em's enthusiasm did help but it was still hard to be positive. I then felt guilty for putting her under the pressure to make me happy. Trying to make a depressed person happy can be very frustrating and I didn't want to be 'that guy'. She had a point though. The crossing seemed to be the one thing deterring skippers and with that out the way we'd possibly have more chance. I knew I had to do everything I could for fear of future regret. I replied to Jez accepting his offer and told Owain to come back too. Opening up my emails, I read a few messages from various people mainly asking about what kit I was swimming in. I worked my way through them until one in particular caught my attention. It was from Lou, from Nomad Sailing, who had helped Jez get *Friday* to Land's End. I hadn't heard from her in a while. I opened it.

Hey Sean

Twitter tells me you need a skipper. I'm in Turkey at the moment but am flying back in four days and can give you ten days of my time if you can cover the cost for me to hire another skipper to run my theory classes while I am away. Should be around £200. If you can do that then I'm yours for ten days.

Hope everything else is well. Hear from you soon.

Lou

xxx

I couldn't believe it. Two days with Jez and then ten days with Lou would not only get me quite far up Scotland but give me more time to find another skipper. Just when all hope was gone, like jump leads to the heart I felt alive again. I also noticed for the first time that Stuart the Scab had almost entirely healed. It's amazing how positivity leads to more positivity. Swimming Britain was on, at least for another 12 days.

*

Jez returned on Friday night but annoyingly we couldn't swim on the Saturday due to gale-force winds. Typical. It had been calm for the past few days. This meant we only had Sunday with Jez and he'd have to leave on the Monday, which was the day Lou was coming. We had to make it over to Scotland by then as that's where Lou was meeting us.

I had mixed emotions leaving Glenarm Harbour, my lonely home for the past 12 days. I was on the one hand happy to see it disappear behind me, as it was associated with so much negativity and broken dreams as I tried to find a new skipper. On the other hand, I was leaving the safety of a harbour to be placed right in the middle of one of Britain's most notoriously dangerous stretches of water, the North Channel. If conditions turned for the worse, neither *Friday* nor myself would be able to cope with the strong currents and potentially huge waves. Luckily, for now, the conditions were near perfect and 12 days' rest had helped me put on some much-needed weight and heal some seriously weak shoulder muscles. Although still not completely recovered I was in a much better position to tackle this stretch of water than I had been two weeks ago.

It was now the 8 September, five days from when I should have finished the swim. If things had gone to plan I should have been along the north coast of Scotland by now. Instead I was yet to even reach Scottish soil. The water temperature wouldn't drop for another few weeks but the weather was going to get progressively worse the further north I went and the closer to October I got.

I figured I'd take another month to finish the swim, if all things went to plan, hoping to finish around the 10 October.

It was exhilarating getting back in the water just south of the Mull of Kintyre.

'You're just at the end of the penis, mate,' Owain laughed and pointed to his groin, which was a little out of character but great to see him in a good mood. He was referring to the Mull of Kintyre Rule, which is an unofficial guideline used by the British Board of Film Classification as the benchmark to decide whether a man's penis could be shown on TV. If the 'angle of dangle' as it is known, is greater than that of the Mull of Kintyre, which, with the Isle of Arran off to the east, looks very much like male genitalia, then the penis could not be shown on TV. It had made us all laugh when we found out about it, and it was nice to see the crew banter back again. What better way to kick off than with some pretty offensive penis jokes, as I swam towards the tip, no pun intended.

The current was so strong I had to swim in a north-easterly direction in order to make any progress into the Mull as the tide whipped me round the south-west corner. If I didn't swim fast enough I wouldn't make the current that goes into the Mull and instead be caught in the current that splits off to America, which would be far from ideal. The tide was the fastest I had ever swam in and at times was pushing seven knots. Not only would I not be able to fight the tide, but *Friday* wasn't powerful enough either. If we did get flung towards America we'd have to just point

Friday north and we'd hopefully find shelter somewhere on Islay, which is west of Kintyre.

Thankfully I made it, and by the end of the session I was firmly inside the Mull of Kintyre's northerly current, so we went ahead and found a safe anchorage to do the skipper swap in the morning. Reaching Scotland felt very different to reaching Ireland. It was more of a sense of relief rather than the celebration we'd previously experienced. I had been staring at Kintyre from Glenarm for weeks and it was nice to know I could finally put it behind me. I was now in Scotland and on my final leg. If I averaged 15 miles per day, nine miles in the first tide and six in the second, in the ten days I had Lou with me, I'd get near Skye and a good way up towards Cape Wrath. From there surely I'd be close enough to the end for a potential skipper to say 'well you've come this far and haven't drowned, so I'll help you'? For now though, it was just good to be making progress again, and a small light of hope started to glow in my heart again.

'It's Lou!' Em shouted as we saw a figure a few hundred metres away, walking along the beach towards where we had come ashore.

Lou was in her late forties and petite in stature. Even though she was small she had a confident swagger, the type that you want from a skipper. She looked ever so cool walking along with her duffel bag and sporty sunglasses casually balanced on top of her short silver hair. We, on the other hand, weren't so cool, and downed our game of cricket and ran around in circles like overexcited puppies, led mainly by Em, whose bounding enthusiasm seemed to be at a whole new level. I think she was just glad to have another girl on the expedition. Living on a 26-foot yacht for the past 70 days with three smelly boys probably wasn't much fun, although she never once complained.

We said our goodbyes to Jez and welcomed Lou to Swimming Britain. It was sad to see Jez walk off down the beach.

We packed everything into the RIB and got the oars out. I offered to row but Em insisted I rest my shoulders and she would do it. Lou looked confused.

'Guys, you have an outboard,' she said.

'Yeah, it broke a long time ago and it's now more of a decoration.' If it was my engine I would have happily left it somewhere in a marina but seeing as it was Arthur's engine, I figured I should keep it.

We hadn't made it more than 10 metres when the first wave crashed over all of us soaking Lou through to the bone. Em continued to struggle on doing a few circles on route.

'I can row quite well. Let me do it,' Lou kept laughingly suggesting as we went in circles with Em's alternate-arm rowing technique, as opposed to both arms together.

It's fair to say that we didn't make a good impression on Lou and the slapstick Swimming Britain Comedy Show was at its peak as we made our way back to *Friday*. Lou sat there quietly in the front of the RIB and I knew exactly what she was thinking: 'What have I got myself into? I could be sunning myself on a beach in Turkey right now.'

We didn't waste any time as Lou and Owain, who seemed a lot chirpier than normal and was really going overly out of his way to help on deck, started the commute back to my swim point. We had missed the morning session to do the swap over and I really needed to make the most of the next ten days.

Luckily, Lou knew how *Friday* worked and within minutes we had her sails out, something that we hadn't done in a while as conditions hadn't been in our favour. Lou just hated the sound of engines and I have to say it brought a calmness to the adventure reaching our start point without the mind-numbing monotone throb of the engine.

That calmness was soon shattered as I got in the water; the waves picked up and were coming in short and sharp from the west. Em was struggling to stay with me and kept getting blown away. I could see she nearly capsized a few times. Progress wasn't bad though and I did seven miles before Lou said we needed to stop the session an hour early. Our only anchorage was seven miles north and once the southerly strong tide started we'd not be able to fight it.

Lou was right and we were still one mile from the safety of a mooring buoy when the tide started to push us backwards. We had no option but to anchor where we were, slightly sheltered by Cara Island, a small privately owned uninhabited island south of Gigha.

At two in the morning, the anchor was dragging so much Lou decided to move us further north again. This meant some disrupted sleep but once in the calmness of Gigha bay I fell into deep sleep.

The following day I was again plagued by nasty side-waves. I soon found myself in a deep mindless wander, the first time I'd let my thoughts go in a while. Normally when I swim or cycle for hours on end I can relax my thoughts and often don't think about anything. It's kind of like driving on the motorway for hours. If someone asks you what you saw or thought about, it's hard to answer. Being able to do this helps pass the time and means you aren't worrying. Too much worry creates stress hormones and therefore you don't operate at your full potential.

During the last few weeks I had most definitely forgotten to live in the moment and enjoy the adventure. I had been overwhelmed by all the things that had gone wrong and wasn't allowing myself to enjoy the scenery and the amazing people I had met along the way. I was also noticing that if I was in a bad mood then the crew seemed to get stressed too. I really needed to be more positive, both for my own sanity and enjoyment, and for the crew's sake. They had done a sterling job so far.

A lone seagull hovered within touching distance of my head, staring down at me in wonderment. I wanted Em to take a picture so stopped swimming and looked back where I thought she was but she wasn't there. *Friday* was a good 50 metres away heading back south and away from me. I looked all around but couldn't see Em. How had she disappeared? I then looked back at *Friday* and noticed

Owain standing on deck, with his life jacket on pointing and shouting. Something was wrong.

I looked to where he was pointing – my heart jumped. There was the bottom of an upturned kayak, and no Em. I started swimming towards the kayak as quickly as I could. I looked up every few breaths but couldn't see her. Eventually I saw her head bobbing on the other side of the kayak. By the time I got there she was very out of breath and shivering.

'You OK, Em?'

'Yeah, fine,' was all she said, holding on to the upturned kayak, which was completely filled with water and extremely heavy. She looked petrified.

'Right, Em, get in the RIB!' said Owain from *Friday*, as they circled around bringing the RIB near Em.

'No, I'm fine. Carry on swimming, we need to make progress, I'll catch up.'

'Em, don't be silly. Get in the RIB, you can't swim with all your winter kit on.' Although she had a life jacket on, all her clothes were now wet and heavy, making swimming virtually impossible.

It was the first time I felt annoyed with Em. She had an amazing can-do attitude and a stubborn streak, which was often good, but this time she needed help. Eventually she listened and climbed into the RIB. I then threw her the rope attached to the kayak and climbed onto the RIB too. It took us at least ten minutes of hauling to eventually get the kayak onto the RIB and empty it of all the water before collapsing, exhausted.

Hauling the kayak took a lot of energy out of me, which made the session pretty slow but we eventually made it to Gigha.

Just before bed Em decided she wanted to share something with all of us.

'Guys. I've been hiding this but I figured we know each other well enough now to mention it,' she said while ringing out her wet clothes. 'I'm petrified of the water.'

'Whatever, Em,' I laughed. This was surely a joke.

'I'm serious. I've cried like almost every day. Petrified! All the time.'

I knew Em had been worried a few times but she never once let it affect her ability.

'So that time the dolphins came?'

'I thought it was a shark and may have weed a little,' she joked.

'Seriously?'

'Yup! It's fine though. I'm not letting it control me but I'm petrified all the time and today's capsize was literally hell. Hell!'

I couldn't quite believe what she was saying. We'd done some pretty crazy sessions and the fact that she had, day after day, faced her fear and performed incredibly was pretty amazing. I only hoped that she carried on being so brave even though she didn't have to pretend any more.

Feeling fresh after a good night's sleep, we got up early and headed back south. It was glass smooth and I was looking forward to a good day after yesterday's drama. About a mile from the start point, *Friday* all of sudden started to splutter and suddenly the engine cut out. We all looked at each other. If the yacht broke, it would definitely be game over for the swim. We sat there in silence as we carried on drifting slowly south.

'When did we last fill up with diesel?' I asked.

'I haven't ever done it,' Owain said. 'Jez was in charge of that.'

We opened the tank to find it completely empty. We laughed at our stupidity. The good news was that it wasn't the engine, but the bad news was that when air gets into the fuel system it creates a bubble and needs bleeding. This is not an easy task and it took some serious Googling to actually find out how to bleed an old 10hp Yanmar marine engine, all the while we were slowly drifting with the tide, which after half an hour was taking us right towards a large RIB with a 'diver down' flag showing. This meant we had to avoid the area around it as there were fishermen underwater near the boat. We shouted our problem to the skipper on the RIB and he slowly moved out the way as we floated past. On deck we could see bags and bags of freshly caught scallops. All our mouths started to water. Owain, who was more chirpy than ever, took a break from manually cranking the engine to get rid of the airlock to chat to the skipper.

'Hello mate, got any scallops to spare?' He laughed jokingly.

'Howzit guys,' said the guy in a heavy South African accent.

Owain launched straight into what I was doing, hoping he might give us some scallops.

'Ya, I saw you guys on the telly, hey. That's epic, bro. Andre. Nice to meet you,' he said while trying to manoeuvre around us while the tide took us wherever it wanted to.

'Are there four of you?' he asked.

'Yes,' replied Owain, who seemed to have now completely forgotten about *Friday*, and the fact that this guy was having to carefully get out of our way while his colleagues were diving underneath. His newfound happiness was a nice change, even if it meant he forgot priority one – boat and crew safety.

'Here, my boss won't notice anyway.' He handed over a sack of 16 large freshly caught Scottish scallops.

'Dude, you legend,' Owain shouted excitedly.

We chatted a bit more before Andre had to head back to where his boss was diving and Owain suddenly remembering he had a job to do and carried on bleeding the engine. It was strange that the second time we had engine problems at sea something good came from it.

I finished my session back at Gigha, again after only doing six miles due to the time wasted with the engine. We went ashore for a quick pint to officially welcome Lou to the expedition and have our first drink on Scottish soil. Within half an hour Lou was on the whisky.

'Sean, you are having this,' Lou presented me with a glass of whisky. I've never been a fan of whisky but really liked the idea of it. I took my first sip half expecting to spit it out but was surprised to find it quite smooth.

'Not bad, actually.'

'Yeah, I told you he'd like that one, Owain,' Lou said, gloating a little.

'OK, OK, Seano, when you're done, try Highland Park. You'll like that one better,' suggested Owain winking at Lou.

I guess they had a little behind the scenes bet going on that I knew nothing about. I could see a competition starting.

I spent the next few hours trying various different whiskies as we chatted with the locals on Gigha. Lou's excitement to be on the trip was rubbing off on Owain. I'd never seen this side of Owain before.

Stumbling back to *Friday* at midnight, I asked Em about Owain's new-found enthusiasm.

'So Owain's a different person of late, isn't he?'

'I know, right!' Em replied.

'Why is that?'

'Well!' Em paused slightly. 'I didn't want to stress you out at the time but basically it's because Owain and Jez didn't get on at all.'

'Shit! Really?' I was surprised that I hadn't picked up on it.

'Yeah, they are just so different and their personalities clashed. Neither of them were in the wrong, they were just very different.'

Of course I'd noticed that they didn't necessarily have that much in common, but I'd never known it was that bad and immediately felt guilty. I can't imagine it was much fun for either of them sitting on the boat all day with only each other to speak to. Part of me wondered if that's why Jez decided to leave. It was a surprise we had all actually got on this well up till now. There were bound to be some differences of opinion when in high stress situations. I'm just surprised that I hadn't noticed.

It took two days to get past Jura and towards the Sound of Luing when it should have only taken a day and a half. This was because I was falling five miles short of my 15-mile daily target. The tide up here wasn't nearly as strong as we had been told it might be, and commuting to and from the start point was taking longer and longer each time due to limited safe anchorages. Lou hated a rough night's sleep and always manage to find us amazing anchorages, even if it was an an hour longer commute. The better sleep, and the improved mood of the crew was so worth it.

When we reached the bottom of the Sound of Jura there was even more bad news. There was a gale storm coming and we needed to find a harbour to sit out the storm, potentially for four days. We only had Lou for another six days and taking four off would mean I wouldn't even make the Isle of Mull.

There was nothing I could do about it though and by that afternoon we were tucked up in Craobh Haven Marina. Strangely enough, the pub next to the marina was having a cowboys and Indians themed party, which felt pretty out of place for a small Scottish harbour town with what seemed like less than a dozen houses around it. Within a few minutes Lou was at the bar chatting to a lady cowboy and had somehow managed to steal someone's Stetson.

Lou was a great addition to the Swimming Britain team and her excitement was rubbing off on all of us. I had been nervous whether Lou would actually fit in and, more importantly, cope with living in *Friday*'s pretty rustic conditions. The fact that Lou hadn't been cramped up like the rest of us certainly explained a large part of her enthusiasm, I'm sure. We were old hags of the sea. She was fresh blood, keen to explore new horizons, with a rose-tinted outlook that the rest of us had lost after months of laboured crossings and sleepless nights.

'Get on it, Owain!' Lou said coming back to the table where we were huddled up and putting four double whiskies down. With potentially four days off ahead a few whiskies were in order. There was definitely a noticeable change in crew morale after a few drinks. Also, if I were to look at the statistics, I'd done some of my biggest days after a few too many beers. Although, admittedly, I'm pretty sure that was pure coincidence. Or maybe it numbed the pain. I know the early Tour de France cyclists used to have wine stops at the top of climbs to help with the final slog to the finish line. I looked around. I felt in no way similar to a Tour de France elite athlete as I sat in a bar surrounded by 50 cowboys and girls signing along to Dolly Parton. Eventually at around midnight we headed back to *Friday* and Owain, who after a few pints has the agility of a baked potato, tripped on the boat hook and fell over one of the

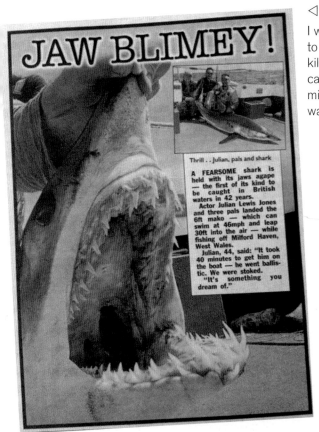

JAW BLIMEY!

Thrill . . Julian, pals and shark

A FEARSOME shark is held with its jaws agape — the first of its kind to be caught in British waters in 42 years.

Actor Julian Lewis Jones and three pals landed the 6ft mako — which can swim at 46mph and leap 30ft into the air — while fishing off Milford Haven, West Wales.

Julian, 44, said: "It took 40 minutes to get him on the boat — he went ballistic. We were stoked.

"It's something you dream of."

◁ I was not thrilled to find out that this killer shark was caught just a few miles from where I was swimming!

Lunch break in the water with my friend Kenton, who joined us for the day
▽

△
Joking with the
team from BBC's
The One Show on
their third trip to
find us

◁
The One Show
sent former
Olympic 400m
sprinter Iwan
Thomas to swim
with me. Having
people from 'the
outside world'
join us, if only for
the day, helped
to keep us sane

△

Owain proudly
displays his catch
of the day

▷

Another amazing
sunset in Scotland.
As we fell further
behind schedule I had
to swim on as many
northerly tides as I
could, no matter what
time of day or night

◁
Night swimming
freaked me
out at first, but
experiencing
incredible
phosphorescence
is something I'll
always remember

Lou and Owain were
heroic in putting in
long hours to and
from anchorages,
getting me to my
start point each day
▽

▷
All that was left
of the kayak
after the Cape
Wrath disaster

◁
More problems.
My toes start to
go black from
lack of circulation

△

The very beautiful but intimidating Hebrides and the choppy water we dealt with most days

▷

It was almost impossible to take on the amount of calories I needed, and the cold water meant I burned body fat quickly. Here I've gone down to 60kg

△

Wishing I'd kept my goggles on as my very excited welcome committee sprays champagne in my eyes as I finally finish

The crew (and mum) all together at John O' Groats
▽

©James Carnegie

©James C

△
Trying to hold it together and say something insightful to the assembled journalists, despite feeling very emotional at the end. Spoiler: I failed

◁
The newspapers that reported on the story the next day, including *The Times* who put my photo on the front page!

stays on *Friday*, thus earning him the new nickname of Twinkle-Toes from Em.

Temperatures plummeted sharply over the next few days and, as we hid from force nine winds, we were happy I wasn't out at sea. *Friday* was becoming unbearably damp and cold so I bought a paraffin heater. It took up most of the floor space in the main cabin but once lit we wondered how we ever survived without it, even if it did cover everything in fine black soot.

Luckily the storm blew over after two days, and not four as the forecast suggested, and I carried on heading up toward Isle of Mull. To make the most of the last few days with Lou, I was swimming at every possible moment, which meant getting in the water at 2am and swimming till sunrise at this time of the month. We were just north of the Sound of Luing and the plan was to head west of a small island.

The night was the darkest it had ever been as I got into the water. I was completely in autopilot mode as I had been over the last few tiring weeks. There were a few lights on the island just ahead of me and the plan was to keep them on my right as we went past. As I approached the island, with Em to my right, and *Friday* to my left and slightly ahead, it started to get really bouncy, waves jumping in all directions. I had reached the rush, the turbulent water often found around headlands as water is redirected or narrowed. This change sends water from the bottom of the ocean upward to the surface creating short sharp waves that have no consistency. I carried on swimming towards the island when I suddenly felt I was being pulled sideways to my right. It was too dark to know for sure but something felt wrong. I then heard a shout and looked up, but I wasn't really able to hear much because of the ear plugs in my ears. I looked to *Friday* who was now quite far away to my left. I turned to Em who was pointing towards me paddling as hard as she could.

'We need to follow *Friday*,' Em shouted with a note of panic in her voice that I'd never heard before. 'She's over there, keep swimming!'

The ferocity of the water was getting worse and even through my ear plugs it sounded like a fast flowing river. Waves crashed into my face and I swallowed an unhealthy amount of seawater, nearly vomiting again. Instantly I became disorientated. The lights on the island were still on my right but it felt like I was swimming against current. Up till now I was looking at *Friday*'s green navigation lights off to my left, but now they were red but still off to my left. This means she was either going backwards or, or … I wasn't actually sure. I was too tired and cold to try and figure out my port from starboard, left from right? I kept repeating, 'Red, port, left. Green, starboard, right.' But it didn't make sense to me. It was too dark to see anything. I felt helpless in this ever-changing ocean and for the first time all swim I actually felt scared.

'Keep swimming,' I heard Em shout and put my head down again.

It seemed fruitless. Did she even know where I was meant to be swimming or were we just swimming for the sake of it? I thought desperately. Moments later I looked up to see *Friday* was now on my right and slightly ahead still with her red navigation light showing. That made no sense at all. Also the island lights were all of a sudden on my left. I was too tired to work out what that meant. With all the disorientation, it honestly felt we were heading back to harbour. Then as quickly as it all started the water went flat again, bringing an eerie sense of calm. Em shouted something. I looked up.

'You're all right, we don't need to push hard now.'

'What happened?' I asked, out of breath and feeling on edge.

'I'm not sure, but I think we got swept east and *Friday*, who got swept west, had to turn around and fight the current to come to us and then we went east after all. We're heading for that island now,' Em pointed to the flickering lights ahead of us.

From the map I seem to remember the only island that big in the area was Easdale. We reached it and there was a nervous silence as Em and I climbed back on board. I think we all knew that it had been a little too close for comfort. The reality was the tide was so strong near that island *Friday* could easily have been swept west and would never have been able to fight the tide. Em and I would have most certainly been on our own in the pitch dark for quite some time as it was fairly unlikely we'd have been able to go ashore due to the sharp rocky cliffs which are characteristic of these parts of the Highlands.

By the time we reached the Sound of Mull it was time to say goodbye to Lou. I still hadn't found another skipper but the Sound of Mull could definitely be swum with land crew as it had a road running all the way down it and was very narrow. In fact we wouldn't even need land support. We could hide the kayak on the shore and hitch a ride to Tobermory as our base each day. From there I'd look for a new skipper.

I woke up after not much sleep during a pretty windy night that required Lou to drop two anchors just in case one slipped. I got up slowly and hit my head on the roof as usual but something was different. I was used to hearing the Da! Da! Da! of *Friday*'s engine, and today especially as Lou was meant to be well underway getting us to Oban, the nearest port for her departure. I entered the main cabin and was surprised to see Lou sitting on the steps eating some cereal.

'Morning, mate,' she said casually, glancing up momentarily before looking back at the charts on the desk.

'Um, morning … aren't we? Why are we?' I was very confused and sounded like Johnny Cash again.

'So, I've spoken to my brother and he's happy to cover the theory course for another two weeks so get your kit on, you've got some swimming to do, boy.'

I couldn't believe it. I felt like crying. In two weeks I'd surely get fairly close to the end.

'Lou, thank you, thank you, thank you.'

'Lou, are you staying?' Em shouted from her bunk.

'Yes!' I replied on her behalf.

There was an eruption of excitement as Em basically fell out of bed to come into the cabin, her sleeping bag still around her ankles. Owain already knew about Lou's decision to stay and had a huge smile on his face.

'Come on!' I shouted, and then felt embarrassed as I'm usually a more of a shout inside type of person rather than public displays of excitement. Now was different. Once in the Sound of Mull we'd be sheltered from most of the bad weather and could really make some good progress, I was sure of it.

11

FRIDAY GOT ILL

As we approached the entrance to the Sound of Mull, the fog set in, reducing visibility to around 100 metres. Ordinarily this is not a problem when going along the coast, but when entering a busy ferry route it's slightly more daunting. Flashbacks of the Belfast crossing coming to mind. Why did the fog come down whenever we were at our highest risk of getting run over?

The tide was good and we were swept into the sound at nearly six knots. It would have been great to carry on in the full rush of the tide, which runs down the middle of the sound, but unfortunately there are a number of ferries which also take the same route. Would a ferry have right of way over a swimmer? There is a sailing rule that states that non-motorised vessels have right of way. I was definitely a non-motorised vessel. I really didn't want to test that theory though and stuck nearer the edge of the sound for peace of mind.

*

After three days of swimming non-stop most of the day and night, we eventually reached Tobermory where we knew we'd have a good night's sleep in the harbour. Tobermory is often used on postcards and in adverts to promote Scotland, and for good reason. The harbour is lined with brightly coloured terraced buildings below picturesque cliffs. When the sun breaks through the clouds, the contrast between the dark sky and the coloured buildings truly is breathtaking. It had been a long few days in the Sound of Mull and nice to finally be on land again for the first time in a while.

BBC Scotland were coming to interview us in the morning, which meant we could all have a much-needed lie-in. The 3am wake-up calls to catch the tide were starting to put a strain on everyone. We also needed to stock up on various essentials like toilet paper. I'd hate to think what we'd do if we ran out of toilet paper. Owain came up with the only plausible solution, which was using socks! Luckily we had always managed to get to land before ever needing to use our socks.

We had a welcome evening in the pub trying yet more whisky before retiring to the flattest night's sleep we'd had in ages. The next morning we got an email from BBC Scotland saying they couldn't come anymore as the panda in Edinburgh Zoo might be pregnant and they needed to go there instead. Trumped by a potentially pregnant panda – brilliant. (It turned out the panda wasn't pregnant after all.)

We did errands before heading out to my start point, parallel with Tobermory. As we approached the GPS point, we noticed a kayaker just hanging around right where I was to start. On arriving he came over to us.

'Are you the swimmer?' he said to Lou.

'Ha ha,' Lou laughed. 'Not me but Sean is the swimmer and he's below.'

I came out and prepared to get in the water.

'Hey Sean. I'm Anthony. I've been following your tracker online so thought I'd come and kayak with you for a few hours, if that is OK?'

'Of course it is, mate. I'm sure Em would love the company.'

The smile on Em's face seemed to confirm that. Following a cold, miserable swimmer for the last 86 days wasn't much fun for her, especially when I couldn't really even talk to her because of the plugs in my ears. She immediately started to chat to Anthony about, well, I have no idea, although I was getting fairly good a lip reading, I still wasn't up to scratch.

I jumped in and carried on as usual while Em and Anthony kayaked next to me. It was nice to know people were following me online. My online audience were like the crowd cheering me on in a marathon. The closer you get to the end the more they cheered and it was nice to get more support the closer and closer I got to John O'Groats, the point on the map I had been staring at for nearly three months now. I had even downloaded a picture of John O'Groats Harbour onto my laptop and would visualise getting out of the water knowing I'd never have to swim in the cold Atlantic ever again. In some ways that picture and that little 'END' mark on the map on the toilet door really did help me. Keep the end in sight but take each day as it comes, I thought. In theory this is good but the constant chasing of the weather was physiologically demanding. Once winter set in then it was all over. Although I had had a good stretch in the last few days it was ever present in the back of my mind that I was still a month behind schedule. The inner whisper of 'it's too late, you're not going to make it' stayed with me. I dared not talk about it with the crew, for verbalising it was realising the reality. Blind naïvety and stubbornness seemed a better approach.

Anthony stayed with us for a few hours and then had to turn around to head back to wherever he came from, a small town on Mull as far as I could make out through my ear plugs.

By late afternoon, I had come out of the Sound of Mull and had just reached Ardnamurchan Point, the most westerly point of UK mainland and an important milestone, from a yachting point of view anyway. Rounding Ardnamurchan Point allows sailors to put a bunch of heather on the front pulpit of their boat, normally for boats heading north showing they were not hostile. Naturally Lou had some heather ready and waiting, and took great pleasure photographing it and sending it to Jim, her brother who was running their sailing school all on his own. Although I was covering freelancers to run their theory courses, it was a small price to pay to have a yacht master instructor with us, and particularly one that dislikes rough anchorages and loves whisky even more.

We finished the session just as it was getting dark and headed further around to the nearest bay. We found the best anchorage possible and set up for the night. As we were dropping anchor (and two anchors again, which now gave Lou the nickname Two-Anchor Lou) three kayakers came up to us.

'Hey guys. Where are you off to?' they asked.

'Just up to John O'Groats,' replied Em. 'We're with the guy swimming.'

'Really?' replied one of them. 'I heard about him a while back, and don't take this the wrong way, but I thought he gave up long ago.'

I was inside listening in to the chat and laughing to myself. Had people really thought I had given up? Giving up due to being tired or cold was not an option at all. If we could make progress we needed to make the most of it. I was yet to actually succeed in any major adventure and right now the risk of failing again was increasing every day the nearer we got to winter and the dreaded Cape Wrath, which was our final obstacle.

'Is he here?' they asked.

Em shouted down to me and I came up to say hi.

'There's the bearded man himself. Is it true about the jellyfish and the beard?'

This seemed to be the main thing most of the media had picked up on after the seasickness and the one thing people seemed to remember. The fact I used a beard for jellyfish protection seemed far more interesting than swimming 900 miles in 12 degree water for months on end.

'Yes, it's true.'

'Fair play. Well done. You're not far now.'

The three of them then disappeared into the night with their head torches on. It was nice that people were coming to find us and today was the day for kayakers.

Dinner was steak, mash and broccoli. The evening was clear so we had dinner on deck and were just retiring when Two-Anchor Lou decided she wanted to move *Friday* about 100 metres further north to get out the waves which had turned bigger with the change in tide direction. She went to switch the engine on but nothing happened. There was just a small clicking sound. We all looked at each other. Owain, being the only one who knew anything about engines now that Jez was gone, took the floorboards up and moved the stairs out of the way get at the engine. Nothing looked out the ordinary and after much more faffing he figured it was probably the starter motor. I hadn't really paid much attention to boat maintenance in all my preparation, which was a huge oversight. If *Friday*'s engine broke then it would definitely be the end of the swim. I would never be able to afford a replacement engine. I suddenly realised that we hadn't even changed the oil on *Friday*. How could I have been so stupid?

Being anchored and not on a mooring buoy without a working engine is apparently good enough of a reason to call a mayday to the coastguard. My heart raced. The word 'mayday' sends shivers down my spine as calling one usually meant your boat was sinking or there was serious concern for a man overboard or something equally dangerous. It was the phrase that I associated with the swim probably being over. The other option is make a call on Channel 16 (the international distress channel that all sailors have their radios tuned to at all times) out to other boats who might be able to help.

Lou was just about to radio for someone when Owain remembered that we could manually crank the engine. He found the crank arm and attached it. There was a little lever which effectively puts the engine in neutral and allowed the engine to turn. You then needed to crank the engine as fast as possible, like you would an old car. When at full speed, you dropped the lever, and pulled it off as quickly as possible. If you didn't then the crank would spin so fast it could break your wrist. The other problem was that the crank arm, when at the upper right section of its rotation, was very close to the side of the galley wall, which meant you inevitably smashed your knuckles every time you went round.

Owain tried a few times but just couldn't get it going fast enough and wore all the skin off his knuckles, which began to bleed. The only time he did get it going he didn't manage to detach the crank and it stayed on the engine spinning around, which was not safe. If it flew off it could break something, or someone.

We had to cut the engine and try again but it seemed Owain had used all his energy on that one good spin. After ten minutes he gave up, too fatigued to carry on. I offered to give it a go but Em and Lou said they'd try first. The last thing I needed was a broken wrist. Also, after a long day swimming, my arms were feeling very tired. Lou and Em didn't have much luck either and eventually there was no option but for me to try. I braced myself and started slowly, increasing my speed gradually with each turn until I thought I was at my fastest.

'Go!' I shouted and pulled the crank off. The timing was perfect and *Friday*'s engine banged and spluttered into action.

'Yes, Sean!' Lou shouted.

I guess after swimming for three months my arms were relatively strong. Now that the engine was working our only option was to head back to Tobermory and see if we could find someone to fix it. If it was in fact a starter motor it could be days before we could get a new one from somewhere, probably eBay!

It was 3am before we finally made it into Tobermory. It had been a good day swimming but we now had the huge task of trying to fix *Friday*'s engine. Cranking it every day was not an option.

'Ah bonjour, monsieur.' A tall Frenchman approached *Friday* pushing a cart full of tools. It was Philippe, the only boat electrician on the island.

'What is zi problem?' he asked still with a heavy French accent, even though he had lived in Scotland for 'many many year' as he put it.

Philippe got to work straight away while we all crowded around, probably making his life worse. I'm sure he'd have preferred to do it alone but we were all on tenterhooks, waiting for good or bad news.

'Ah, I see!' he said.

My heart skipped a beat.

'It is a fuse. Easy fix, no problem.'

We couldn't have got better news. You could instantly feel the relief run through all of us as Lou offered to do a coffee run. Even though Philippe would be done in ten minutes we still had to wait out the tide for another half hour before heading out again. We may have lost a session but at least it wasn't serious. *Friday* really was an incredible boat.

We somehow always manage to miss something for *Friday* and even though we did a big shop the day before, we forgot to restock on butter and nut oil – the two things I needed the most to increase the fat content in my diet. I was now going through half a tub of butter a day and adding around 500kcal extra of various nut oils in with each meal too. We had enough to last a few more days but I felt we needed more so went off and left Philippe to do his work.

By that afternoon, we were back out on the water heading back to Ardnamurchan Point where I stopped the night before.

It was perfectly calm and I was getting into the swing of things when all of a sudden there were loads of jellyfish again. I hadn't seen any in a while but they tend to come to the surface when it is calm. This slowed my pace a lot but still I felt good. Halfway through the session we were also pounced upon by a pod of dolphins that came up right near us. Em gave an uncharacteristic shriek as a fin came out the water next to her. It still made my heart jump whenever I saw a fin in the water. Thoughts about the mako shark they caught while we were in Pembrokeshire were still present. I'm not sure I'll ever be completely comfortable in the water but instead have just learned to deal with it. You may hate it but you just get on with it.

I was consciously eating more during each session and ate two full Stowaways meals in four hours. With the extra fat that was a total of nearly 3000kcal. If I did that again in the second session, plus dinner and breakfast, my daily intake was around 8000kcal, which was about right. I was still somehow losing weight but I literally couldn't fit more in my stomach.

Although it was calm I somehow only managed three miles in three hours as we got the last of the morning tide. I was steadily getting slower and slower each day, which was partly due to the weather and water getting colder, but mainly because I had now been at sea for 88 days and was the most fatigued I have been in my entire life. I had dropped below ten stone and had no body fat left. I couldn't get enough food in me and with every session I was starting to break down vital muscle tissue for energy. This can become a downhill spiral, but no matter how much I ate nothing was working. In an ideal world I would take two to three weeks off and then carry on. I had no such luxury. Winter was fast approaching, which was actually sending both physical and mental shivers down my spine. I should have been finished two weeks ago and I wasn't even past Skye yet.

We went back to Muck to sit out the southerly tide and then headed back for the evening session. The wind picked up and small sharp waves started to slap the side of my face knocking my goggles off every few minutes. I only managed three miles in the evening session, which meant I probably wasn't actually doing much more than floating with the tide. I didn't really know what to do. I had given it my all. The date was the 25 September and if I carried on at this rate I'd only get to John O'Groats by Christmas, but before that the crew would definitely leave me. I suddenly felt, for the first time since losing Jez, that maybe I wouldn't be able to finish the swim and this time it was all my own fault for not being a strong enough swimmer. I finished the session and we went to Isle of Eigg for anchorage. I confided in Em in the cabin.

'I'm not sure I can carry on like this. I'm just too slow.'

'Don't worry, Ginge. You're doing amazing,' Em replied, always positive.

'I'm not and I hate it. At this rate I'll lake another two months or more. You guys won't stay that long.'

'Ginge. Don't worry about us. I'm with you till the end and so is Owain. We'll just tie Lou to *Friday* so she can't leave,' she joked.

I guess knowing for certain I'd have the crew till the end would make a lot of difference. I hadn't really voiced it from fear of hearing the worst. Em and Owain only signed up for a two-and-a-half month adventure. I didn't know what other commitments they had. It just didn't seem fair on them to keep them here when at this point it seemed the most likely I wouldn't finish.

'Also,' Em continued. 'Please, Ginge, can you be more positive? I know it's hard but if you're down then we're all down.'

She was right. I needed to be more upbeat. Things in Scotland hadn't gone at all to plan but I needed to be more positive, even for my own sanity.

'What if we only did one session a day?' Em suggested. 'We can then kill that session and have the rest of the day to recover and explore and it means Owain and Lou won't have to do two long commutes each day. Remember why you wanted to do this swim in the first place? To explore Great Britain.'

She was right. It seemed since Cornwall we were either doing a huge crossings or fighting bad weather. I had forgotten why I wanted to do this swim.

'But it'll take a week longer. Will Owain stay? And what about Lou?'

'Owain will stay. I've chatted to him and he's here till the end. Lou, I don't know. We'll just have to play it by ear.'

'Let's take the day off tomorrow on Eigg and decide.'

'OK,' I agreed, and Em went through to tell Owain and Lou the plan.

'Great,' Said Lou. 'Now I can get some balsamic vinegar for our salad. I bloody love balsamic vinegar.'

'There is no way they have balsamic vinegar on Eigg,' said Owain.

'Of course they do!' replied Lou.

'If they have balsamic vinegar, I'll swim naked,' said Owain, confidently.

'Deal!' said Em and Lou at the same time.

I didn't fancy Owain's chances, if I was honest.

The next day we went ashore at around midday. Eigg was a very small island, at five and a half miles long and just three miles wide. The island was once privately owned but the community got together and bought it from the landlord in 1997. There are now about 100 people on the island, including the lady who has the ice cream shop and B&B who is also the paramedic. There was a large gathering of people all outside the café/bar right by the harbour. Even though it was only midday on a Thursday quite a few of them were already completely smashed. As we walked up the slipway a very friendly lady called Maggie, who wasn't one of the drunk ones, came towards us with huge smile on her face and a pot of money.

'Swimmer! We've been following your tracker online and have been asking people to donate. We raised £80 so far. Here you go.' Maggie gave us the pot. How incredibly kind she, and the rest of Eigg, were.

'Come now. Have a dram!' She dragged us into the bar, where we sat down and were presented with a whisky each. What a reception. Normally we sneak into a pub unannounced. Eigg had different ideas for us.

'Oh well, when on Eigg!' said Owain referencing the few intoxicated people outside the café.

Lou disappeared and came back a few minutes later with the biggest smile on her face looking straight at Owain.

'Guess what, Owain?'

'No?'

'Yes. Owain. Get your kit off!' shouted Em excitedly as Lou waved a bottle of balsamic vinegar in his face.

Owain just put his head in his hands. At least someone would join me in the water to appreciate how cold it was.

The rest of the afternoon was spent in the bar chatting to various people who live on Eigg. One young fellow we met kayaked to Eigg five years previously and never left. His kayak was still there next to the harbour wall, filled with water and overgrown weeds.

After a few too many pints he staggered over to me at one point and said, 'Mate. You've lost your marbles haven't you? Look I found them. They're all shrivelled and small like, from the cold, look!'

He proceeded to take three small metal marbles or ball bearings out his pocket. Who keeps ball bearings in their pocket? Someone who started drinking at 9am I guess? They were all incredibly friendly though and were by far the most interested in the swim to date, asking millions of questions. In the afternoon we walked to the ice cream shop and then back to *Friday* for dinner, and then decided to go back to the bar for one more drink before retiring. The bar was bustling with people and Lou was in her element showing everyone our route north on the new charts we got in Tobermory.

By the time we left, the bar was getting quite rowdy, but in a friendly way. As we left we were promised that someone would pipe us away in the morning. Someone with bagpipes on the harbour wall as I swam away from Eigg. That would be incredible. Also the kayaker had promised to come and kayak with Em and they should carry on round the world. Judging by the state of him, I figured we wouldn't have another kayak buddy tomorrow. I'm sure not everyone on Eigg drinks heavily but the ones hanging around the harbour certainly know how to let their hair down.

There wasn't a soul to be seen when we woke up and, even after waiting an hour just in case they were getting ready, we came to the conclusion that our bagpiper was probably passed out in a bush somewhere and not going to pipe us out. Less surprisingly, the kayaker was nowhere to be seen either.

I had spoken to Lou and Owain who agreed with our 'one tide a day' strategy from now on even if it meant taking a week longer. Em and Owain assured me they were there till the end, which was a great relief, and Lou also hinted that she might be able to stay longer as Jim, who was now pretty much a living legend in my books, was managing to cover everything for her. I could also see Lou was really enjoying the sailing side of things, always looking at navigation points with her binoculars and taking photos of harbour entrances, which was nice to see. It'd kill me if any of the crew were hating it.

I hadn't quite appreciated how much pressure I was putting myself through not knowing if I'd have crew till the end considering I was so far behind. Having Em and Owain's word really was a weight off my shoulders.

I felt a lot better and after one of the flattest days almost all swim, we anchored off a picturesque beach and had some fresh vegetables we'd got from a guy called Chris on Eigg. Fresh fruit and veg was always welcomed as it was something we couldn't keep for long on the boat due to not having a fridge.

I was feeling positive and, besides two sore toes from where I must have bumped them when my feet were numb at the end of each session, I went to bed happy knowing we didn't have to get up early for the first tide and instead would only do the early afternoon one.

I woke up to a strange purring sound followed by a splutter. I knew exactly what it was. The engine again. I went to the saloon to see Owain cranking away, every now and then swearing from banging his knuckles on the galley wall. It really did seem dead this time. I too gave it a go but this time had no luck. *Friday* really was not willing to start.

'Sean, I'll tell you what,' Lou said, now in captain mode. 'We can sail off this spot and get you back to the start point and the wind is good enough to sail with you all day. There is a harbour in Mallaig just further north of where you will get to this eve. At least we're making progress and Owain can sort a mechanic while we're on the move.'

It was a slow commute back and I was eventually back in the water as the tide turned. I set off swimming and soon left *Friday* way behind me, who would periodically come to a near stop when the wind died down. Eventually we reached Mallaig and I got back on board. This plan, however, meant that we would need to sail into the busy harbour and onto the pontoon. Coming into a harbour under sail is very much frowned upon in yachting communities, as you don't have much control, and you risk smashing into other boats.

'Unless you pull it off, then you're a hero,' said Lou, with a smile on her face. We tried calling the harbour master for ages trying to tell him our intentions but no one was answering.

Steadily we made our way into the harbour with not much issue. The next difficulty was to get onto the pontoon. The only way we could slow *Friday* down was to manually drop the sails. If we did this too early we wouldn't make the pontoon and be drifting around the harbour helplessly. Too late and we'd crash right into the pontoon and almost definitely put a hole in *Friday*. Owain was steering. Em was in charge of putting a fender between *Friday* and the pontoon, I was in charge of dropping the sail when Lou told me to, and Lou was ready to jump off and tie us down before we hit the pontoon. I was slightly worried about Owain's steering ability but Twinkle-Toes' lack of agility and knot-tying ability meant Lou had to do that.

As we started to approach the pontoon, a gust of wind picked up right as the harbour narrowed, increasing our speed a little beyond comfort.

'Drop half the sail,' Lou shouted.

I did so but *Friday* didn't seem to slow down much.

'More, more. Drop it more.'

I pulled more of the sail down as quickly as I could and *Friday* slowed down slightly. We were now a good 20 metres from the pontoon and still at quite a speed.

'Go, drop all of it.'

I did so. There was nothing left to do. Lou was ready and we came careering into the space. Lou jumped off and tied off the stern of *Friday* to the pontoon while Em held the fender against the bow. We came to a screeching halt and banged into the front of the pontoon, nearly sending Em overboard. But *Friday* was OK, we were in the harbour, and we breathed a huge sigh of relief.

'Yeah man. That's how it's done!' Lou cheered. 'Well done, Owain!'

Our success momentarily overshadowed the fact that *Friday* was broken, but Owain said a mechanic would come in the morning. We all went to the pub.

The mechanic turned up an hour late and didn't even try to disguise the fact he was late because he had 'the world's biggest hangover'. He must have been on Eigg, I guess.

It took him a good hour looking for the fault and he was just about to say it was the starter motor when he noticed some frayed wires touching the side of the hull. This was causing the short circuit and blowing the fuse. What a simple fix. Thankfully it wasn't serious. Google did say these Yanmar engines were indestructible. We sure had put this one through its paces.

12

WHEN THE GOING GETS TOUGH

Subject: Do NOT swim through Sound of Sleat.

My name is ········· and I see you are planning to swim through the Sound of Sleat. I highly recommend you skip this section and start again after it. I have over 20 years of experience in these waters and in my opinion if you swim that section you will not survive. This is a nasty stretch of water I've seen boats struggle in the sound. There are underwater whirlpools that you will get sucked into and a boat will not be able to save you.

Please seriously consider my advice.

The email had come from a gentleman who had filled in the form on the Swimming Britain website. I was slightly taken aback. I hadn't received a negative email in a while. He was talking about the Sound of Sleat just north of us and would to be the next section of the swim. It is an extremely narrow channel, the narrowest I'd have to swim through, and by quite a margin, connecting Kyle Rhea and Loch Alsh. It's about two miles long and funnels into a passage no more than 500 metres wide. The tide at full rush can reach speeds of ten knots. We knew this would be a tricky section to navigate but we'd decided it was nothing we couldn't deal with as long as we did it at slack water.

Even though I was confident in dealing with Sleat, I now had a huge feeling of doubt, much like when Bob the fisherman at Sennen Cove said he wouldn't take me to Land's End. I was worried.

'Lou, check this out,' I showed her the email.

'Don't listen to him, at slack water we'll be fine. He's just trying to cover himself I think, for his own conscience.'

'Owain, can you email him back to ask advice and just tell him skipping it is not an option for us and what's the best advice he has for us.'

Owain was good at wording emails. An email from me might have been along the lines of, 'Stop stressing us out and bugger off.' Owain was more diplomatic.

I didn't swim the next day due to ever-stronger winds that even made even the harbour rough. The next morning we got a reply from 'The Naysayer' (as we now called him), which went along the lines of, 'I won't give you any advice except do NOT swim.' He even said if he had the power he'd try come and physically stop us but he couldn't. The sea is free after all.

After reading his email a few times, I began to feel genuinely worried for the first time. I wasn't even this worried when swimming across the Irish Sea. Yes, many, many people had told me this swim wasn't possible, but those people generally sent one email and then I never heard from them again. No one had gone so far out their way as to want to come and physically stop me with their boat.

By the afternoon, the wind had died right down and I carried on north towards the Sound of Sleat. Mr Naysayer had put the fear of God in us. By all accounts this time there seemed a real risk of something going horribly wrong.

'Morning mate!' shouted Iwan from a motorboat alongside me.

The One Show had come to film me again and sent none other than sporting royalty Iwan Thomas, the famous 400 metre Olympic runner. By a strange coincidence Owain's wife had met him only the week before at some event too.

The crew were buzzing again, as was I. It was, however, slightly annoying that the day they came to film was one of the flattest days we'd had in weeks. If they had come yesterday they'd have had a true representation of what the swim was really like, with choppy waves and strong winds. Today it looked like I was taking a casual swim up a pond, which was really misrepresentative of what it's actually been like. Maybe Iwan will get stung by a jellyfish. I wouldn't wish that on anyone but it would make good telly. (OK, I'm going to hell.)

'Sean, come aboard,' Iwan shouted.

I climbed up the ladder and nearly fell off as I had no feeling in my feet. We chatted for a while about everything that had happened since we last saw them and what I was to expect in the next few weeks, including the dreaded Sound of Sleat. Iwan was fantastically excitable and every now and then would interrupt me, shout, 'there's a dolphin', and grab the cameraman to film it. It was great to have people from 'the outside world' come and visit us. It momentarily brought us back to normality.

Months on a small, damp 26-foot yacht and our grasp on reality had become warped. For example, if Owain or I needed a pee, it was normal just to piss over the edge of the boat. Even during conversation. They call it adventurer's bladder when you never have to hold your pee so just go whenever you need to. Initially we'd go all the way up the front of *Friday* but now we barely left where we were and just turned around. It took at least a month before we were comfortable enough to do this around the girls but there was literally nothing we didn't know about each other after months at sea. I'm not sure Lou and Em were ever consulted on our new toilet regime, which always sparked some childish banter whenever we did it. This was normal for us, but very much frowned upon if you did it in the real world, I remembered.

'Right, mate. I'm coming to swim with you. Let's go.'

'Hope you're not scared of jellyfish,' I joked.

'Really? Are there any here?'

'I haven't seen any all morning but they are about. Especially when it's flat like this.'

'Ah, I hope not. Bloody hate them jellies.'

Iwan swam with me for as long as he was allowed to before the production team made him to stop as they needed to get back to shore to do the edit. He was genuinely gutted but we had a manly hug in the water – which is not as easy as it sounds – before he clambered back on board and they zoomed off, leaving us all alone in an eerily calm and quiet bay.

'Sean,' Lou shouted. 'You drifted 200 metres while doing the interview on their boat so we need to go back and cover that distance again.'

I got out of the water and we went back 200 metres and I jumped back in and headed for the dreaded Sound of Sleat. We'd get as close as possible to it this evening and then assess the situation before attempting it at slack water in the morning.

Finally we could see it. The closer I got to it the faster I was moving. Even 100 metres before the entrance I was doing five knots and we weren't even at full flood. At around 50 metres before the entrance Lou shouted.

'Get in.'

I swam to the RIB and jumped in. Lou did a sharp U-turn and started to head away but we had pushed it a little too far. I looked up to see that we were going backwards, getting sucked into the sound. I clambered from the RIB and onto *Friday*. Lou was as calm as ever and didn't seem worried at all.

'Lou, I don't know if you've noticed. We're going backward.'

'If you're not going backward you didn't try hard enough,' she joked and put *Friday* into full throttle.

We slowly started to move forward and when I say slowly, I mean slowly. The GPS said our speed was 0.01 knots. *Friday*'s poor engine felt like it was coming through the floorboards. It took a good 15 minutes to get away from the jaws of Sleat. I'm glad Lou was so calm because it sure looked like we'd get sucked in. I could see what The Naysayer was talking about. The flow of water really was strong and we weren't even at full flood. This didn't help our nerves whatsoever as the mist settled in for a damp and cramped night stuck inside *Friday*.

This was it. The sound looked eerily calm as we headed back to the entrance. My heart was racing. Yesterday's close shave and Mr Naysayer's emails were at the forefront of my mind. I jumped in and for the first time in a while didn't feel cold at all, my body was full of adrenalin. I put my face down and made sure Em was right next to me the whole time. If I did get sucked into a whirlpool at least I had the option of hanging on to the kayak, although I could see Em's fear of the ocean fuelling imagined disasters where we both get sucked into the depths, never to return. I decided not to talk about it with her in an effort not to spark panic.

I steadily started to make my way into the sound, putting more effort into each hand movement than I had ever done, my heart still racing. I suddenly heard Em shout something. I looked up expecting to be told to get out or swim to the left to avoid a whirlpool. Instead she pointed to the shore where there was a family of four waving at me. The young kids were shouting, 'Good luck.' I waved back. I put my head down trying not to overanalyse the meaning of a family coming down to see me swim down potentially the most dangerous stretch of water in the UK. If I was at risk of dying then surely you wouldn't bring your kids to see it. Or was this like car crash ... I stopped myself from carrying on. My thoughts made no sense. I was in it now and needed to concentrate on my style rather than feed my overactive imagination.

I pushed on for another ten minutes, entirely fuelled by adrenalin, waiting for a huge whirlpool to appear from nowhere but one never came. By the halfway point I stopped swimming and looked at Em. I didn't even have to say anything and she replied.

'I know. This is easy. What was The Naysayer on about?'

It was so easy there was even seals bobbing up and down behind us, following me the whole way. Eventually I popped out the other side and into Loch Alsh and Lou came alongside me. Owain was on deck and looked furious.

'I really want to phone that idiot and tell him what a twat he was. That was pretty much the easiest section we've done.'

Owain was right. I too wanted to phone him to say that he needlessly put us all under a lot of stress for no reason whatsoever. It wasn't worth it though. We were through it and could see the Skye Bridge ahead, the next milestone. It was better to put our energies to good use, like fishing.

'Fish for dinner, Owain?' I shouted.

'OK then,' he said and sat down and let out some line.

We were delighted to have made it through safely but we all knew my biggest hurdle was still 104 miles away in the form of Cape Wrath, arguably Britain's most notorious stretches of coastline. There was a real chance of something going seriously wrong if we didn't plan that section well.

Conditions over the next few days had somewhat eased and my progress was back to around ten miles per day again. Every few days I'd suggest doing double tides but then realised I'd fall back into that long-term fatigue I was desperately trying to avoid. I was just about balancing recovery with progress on one tide a day and we were all in a better state of mind for it.

We were just nearing Applecross when, during one of my feeds in the water, Owain informed me that the cooker had stopped working. He had taken it completely apart to no avail. It was a very old paraffin cooker and it was likely the injectors had been clogged up and without the proper cleaning kit, which we obviously didn't have, there was nothing we could do. I was struggling to get food down anyway and on the one occasion when I had tried cold food I threw it up. Having a working stove was integral. The sea temperature had dropped to around 12 degrees but more importantly the air temperature was around ten degrees in the day and nearly freezing at night. To make matters worse, he had called every shop in Applecross to find a camping stove but no one had any. We had only one option and that was to head all the way back to Skye.

It was 5pm when we turned around and were immediately faced with a mind-numbingly cold headwind and waves to match. Lou and Owain pushed hard well into the night and eventually at around 2am decided to drop anchor as they weren't making much progress. They then got up at 5am to do the final nine miles back to Skye. Long commutes are always stressful but eventually, after 23 hours, we made it back to Skye, exhausted and cold.

'Guess what today is?' Em shouted from her bunk.

'Miserable!' Owain replied, looking pretty tired.

'It's Day 100!'

Shit. It was Day 100 of the swim and I still wasn't anywhere near the end. I had already surpassed the longest swimming-based adventure in history, from a time point of view, which as far as I was aware was held by Ben Lecomte who controversially swam the Atlantic in 73 days but couldn't account for drifting on the boat at night. Even Martin Strel's Amazon swim, although much further in distance, took him 66 days. It was likely I still had another two weeks to go, at the very least, and that was if I had no bad weather days, which let's be honest, in October in Scotland was not going to happen. It was also slightly disappointing that Day 100 was an irrelevant day trying to find a camping stove in Skye as opposed to swimming somewhere noteworthy. Nevertheless, it was Day 100 and seeing as it was a land day I figured I'd treat the crew to a proper pub meal. They certainly deserved it after a 23-hour commute.

We bought two stoves and 15 gas canisters and started the long journey back towards Applecross. We had the wind behind us this time and it took us only six hours. I managed six miles in the evening session before we needed to take cover in Loch Torridon for some potentially bad weather coming.

We spent the best part of two days in a little bay getting bombarded by heavy winds and the occasional hailstorm. Cabin fever was at an all-time high. It was almost impossible to go to shore as we were flanked by huge cliffs and the wind was so strong it made rowing against it fruitless. Eventually at the end of the second day, we had all had enough and decided to try and clamber up the cliffs just to be on land and out of each other's faces.

Owain stayed on *Friday* to do some fishing while Em, Lou and I went foraging for limpets as a starter to our fishcake dinner that Lou was going to make. There is something special about a dinner that you have caught or foraged yourself. You appreciate it more, even though we all agreed afterwards limpets tasted like dirt. Lou was somehow in the party mood and whipped out a bottle of whisky that she had bought. The deal was that I provided everything including beverages for the crew but Lou insisted she wanted to contribute. Within an hour, Lou was dancing on the stairs listening to Pink on loudspeaker and shouting at Owain.

'Get on it, Owain. Come on. Get on it.'

Owain wasn't budging. *Friday* definitely wasn't big enough for Twinkle-Toes to do any dancing, although I would have paid to see that. The whole scenario was hilarious and a much-needed mood lifter. It's amazing how infectious someone in a good mood can be and Lou was certainly helping us all through it, and her fishcakes were out of this world.

Just before bed, I noticed the two toes that were sore a few days previously were starting to swell a little and felt quite warm to touch. The strange thing was that it was the same toe on each foot, one in from my pinkie toe. I couldn't recall bumping them but my feet were so numb most of the time I wasn't surprised it had happened while trying to get in and out of the RIB each session.

Also my wetsuits were really starting to smell of piss. In each session I peed around three litres and it all stayed around my midriff. When I got out the water, I pulled the front of my suit open to let a rush of cold water in to flush out most of the pee but it didn't really work. They really needed a wash.

Over the next four days, my toes got increasingly worse and slowly started to turn black. I decided that I should probably see a doctor, so we went ashore at the nearest possible place that seemed remotely likely to have a doctor. We were in luck. There was one a few miles up the road so we all walked up and sat in the waiting room looking quite tattered and smelly, quite the sight for some of the other patients in the waiting room. I was quite nervous about seeing a doctor because I was worried they'd tell me not to swim for a few weeks. That would be the worst result because I obviously wouldn't listen, or couldn't afford to listen as winter was already fast approaching and I needed to swim at every possible opportunity. I guess I just wanted some peace of mind.

I was called in to see the first doctor. After studying my toes for a while, he said he needed to get another doctor's opinion. Brilliant. That's what happens when something is properly wrong with you. Moments later another doctor came in. He had a strong Scottish accent.

'You're the swimmer aren't you? I noticed from the beard.'

'Yes, that's me, doc. You obviously know then that I need to carry on. I just want to know if this is something serious. I can deal with the pain but some people online have mentioned frost bite, which worries me.'

The doctor examined my toes closer.

'Right, Mr Conway. It's kind of like frost bite but not frost bite. Basically, the lack of blood to your extremities for a long period of time has caused tissue damage and now there's an infection. Now I know that no matter what I say you're going to continue and to be honest, you should be fine. You shouldn't lose the toe. And if you do, you become a real adventurer right? You don't really need that toe anyway,' he said jokingly. I couldn't quite believe it. I was honestly expecting the 'health and safety' part of his brain to give me the answers he should have, but instead he was refreshingly open to my situation.

'Take some antibiotics over the next week to reduce the swelling and if the black starts going further up your leg then come back and see us.'

A black leg! There was no way I'd let it get that far but I said my thank yous and left feeling a lot more positive now that I had advice that I wasn't going to die or lose my leg. As an added bonus I didn't even have to pay for the medicine as prescriptions are free in Scotland.

We got back to the RIB and decided to check on some emails in the pub nearby. We went in and ordered some tea and Em, who still was in charge of money despite dropping the wallet, came back looking perturbed.

'Ginge, can I have a word?' she asked.

'Sure,' I said and we went to another room.

'Your card has failed and we only have £100 left in the wallet.'

'Shit, really? How have we spanked all the money?'

'Dunno, Ginge.' Em replied.

I went to my laptop and logged on to internet banking and sure enough I was £1,523 overdrawn, which was £23 over my overdraft limit. I sat back in complete despair. I had basically taken too long and now completely run out of money. I had been so caught up in the mental and physical daily battle I had completely overlooked the finances. I really thought I had enough. Not only did I need to buy food for the crew for the next two to three weeks, I also need to pay the replacement skipper Lou was hiring to run courses on her behalf. I did some quick sums and worked out I needed about another £4,000 to get me to the end, or £5,500 if I wanted to pay back my overdraft. Considering the swim was looking like it might take twice as long as I thought, I'm surprised we got this far. Thank you Stowaways for giving us meals otherwise I'd have been out a long time ago.

How could I have left it this late? It was a bit like *Friday*'s engine, something I hadn't even thought about. I sat back and started to rack my brain for a solution. I could ask my dad for some more money, which I hated doing as he had already given me some money at the start. I could ask Speedo for some money. It had been so hard to get sponsorship funding in the first place I knew it'd be difficult to ask for more, especially as I was so far behind and the risk of not finishing growing stronger every day. Thirdly, I could do some crowdfunding and pre-sell a book about the swim. The problem with crowdfunding is if you don't reach the amount you asked for then you don't get any of the money. The last option was I could sell *Friday* and ask the buyer if I could borrow her for another two weeks. That was the last resort so I decided to try the first three options and if none of them worked then I'd look to sell *Friday*, which hurt me to even think about. She had done us proud and I didn't want to see her go.

Firstly I emailed Dad and asked for a loan of £1,000. I then emailed Sal at Speedo and offered my time after the swim. I said I'd do free talks for them, go to trade shows, even work in their store, anything really. For this I asked them for £2,500. With this approach I figured the money wouldn't be coming out of their marketing budget, which I already knew was stretched, but rather their entertainment, or staff salary budget or something. I had no idea if it would work but Sal at Speedo had been very supportive so far. Lastly, after doing a lot of research, I found a crowdfunding platform that paid money directly into your account even if you didn't make the final target, which I had set at £4,000, in case nothing else worked. I now needed to sell stuff. Crowdfunding isn't all about just getting handouts. You need to give the 'backers' something. I came up with the following products.

1 of 100 signed copies of the book
when it comes out – £15

1 of 15 goggles that I wore during the swim – £30

1 of 20 signed swim caps that I got given
from Speedo – £25

1 of 2 of the larger wetsuits I wore
at the beginning – £350

1 of 10 talks about my swim – £400

It took me an hour to set up the page and I then Tweeted my plea before heading back to *Friday* for an early night. All I needed was to sell five books a day and I'd be able to buy the crew food. That didn't seem all that hard to do but it relied heavily on people believing I was going to complete the swim otherwise there was no book to write.

I didn't need to start the day's swim until 5pm, so we had all day to do some chores and most importantly head to Wi-Fi in the hotel to see if I indeed had enough money to get food for the next two days. In case we didn't Lou and Owain went foraging for some mussels and limpets they had spotted on the other side of the bay. Limpets tasted like shite but might be the only thing we'd have for lunch.

I took a deep breath and logged in to my email and an influx of emails clogged up my inbox.

Sarah Jones has backed your project
Anthony Riches has backed your project

And so on. There must have been nearly 50 emails. I logged in to the crowdfunding page to see a grand total of £2,000 raised overnight. I had basically sold half the caps and goggles, a load of books and a talk. No one bought any of my pissy wetsuits though, which wasn't all that surprising. I couldn't believe it. How was that possible? I only tweeted it late last night. It turned out that the *Independent* and the *Daily Telegraph* had seen my Tweet about it and run it in the paper.

To make things better, Dad said I could have the money as an early Christmas and birthday present. That would look after some of my overdraft so was a huge help. Then there was an email from Sal at Speedo also agreeing to buying days from me after the swim.

Things couldn't have gone any better. Em and I ran back to tell Lou and Owain the news. I had this huge weight off my shoulder, much like when I got that email from Lou saying she would skipper us. There was nothing worse than potentially being told that your dream was over due to something out of your control. That had happened to me when I got run over in America and every time something similar happens I get scared. Scared of failing. Scared of not achieving my dream. It's a horribly lonely place to be when everything hangs in the decisions or actions of other people. Luckily both times on this swim people had pulled through for me, Lou and now the Great British public. Not only was it a huge relief but I also felt incredibly motivated to now finish the swim as a thank you to everyone who helped me out.

'We've got money for food now guys,' Em shouted.

'Well we won't need these then,' said Lou, cheerfully tipping out all the shitty limpets back into the sea. Not only did I have enough money for food and diesel, I now also had enough to keep Lou for the rest of the swim. Now there was just the small task of finishing the swim. No pressure at all.

The day got even better when Lou presented us with a huge bucket of freshly caught mussels. The mood was at an all-time high.

'Owain, haven't you forgotten something?' said Lou while preparing the mussels.

'Um? No!' replied Owain, looking slightly worried.

'Come on! Get your kit off lad!'

The balsamic naked swim bet. I had totally forgotten.

'Not today! I'll do it I promise, but not today,' Owain replied.

'Owain. Look, the sun is out, which it hasn't been in days. This bay is the cleanest bay we've been in and we are far enough from shore not to offend anyone. If I were you I'd get it over and done with now.'

You could see the cogs in Owain's brain working away. There was a moment of silence before he started to give in.

'Right! I'll do it.'

Owain disappeared below and came out a few moments later in his speedos and a towel. We were all sitting in the cockpit as he walked to the middle of *Friday*. I really didn't want to see Owain naked but did want to see him experience the cold water like I had over the last 108 days.

He slowly took off his Speedos, revealing his pasty white buttocks while clutching his man bits with both hands.

'O-wain! O-wain! O-wain!' Em chanted.

'Damn you balsamic vinegar!' he shouted, and launched himself into the air. Then, instead of doing a good old-fashioned British bomb, he did a flip and decided to dive in which meant, without any warning whatsoever, we all got an upside-down full frontal view of Owain in all his glory.

'Oooooowain! Why did you dive? I can't un-see that,' Em shouted covering her eyes.

Owain came up spluttering and swearing.

'Shit it's cold! Shit! Shit!' as he doggy-paddled round to the RIB.

'How do I get in without injuring my johnson?'

He had the task of trying to get out the water and into the RIB, which usually involves pulling yourself up with both hands and balancing your torso on the edge of the RIB. This can be painful with clothes on. Naked was definitely going to hurt. Owain struggled a few times while we all sat there and laughed and in no way offered to help. He was trying to pull himself up with one hand while holding his man bits with the other. After five attempts he eventually flopped into the RIB in the twinkle-toed fashion we'd come to expect, still clutching his jewels. It sure was one of the funniest things we'd all seen in a while and fair play to him for doing it. I only wish he had done a British bomb.

I had arranged for a friend, who happened to be up in Scotland that week, to take Arthur's engine back to London. I had spent well over £500 in fixing it and had only used it for the first few weeks. Since then it had been nothing more than an ornament weighing the RIB down while we rowed to shore each day. It was strangely comforting taking it off the RIB and sending it away. Part of me wanted to give Arthur a piece of my mind lending me an engine that was pretty much broken, but I knew he had his best intentions so just sent a thank you message.

John O'Groats really was in sight now. The last hurdle was Cape Wrath, which seemed to get more daunting the more we mentioned it. Just the word Wrath made it all the worse. If it had been called Cape Sunflower or something equally pleasing I'm sure we wouldn't have been stressing as much, but it wasn't. It was Wrath and certainly needed to be taken seriously.

The reason it was such a difficult section was because it lay open to the full force of the Atlantic Ocean. Up till now we'd been sheltered by the Outer Hebrides but at

Cape Wrath there was no such shelter. Those waves can start hundreds of miles away, slowly building in speed and strength before smashing against the towering 200-foot cliffs with the force of 1,000 oxen. Not only was it a difficult section to swim but *Friday* was certainly in the 'far too small' side of the scale to attempt unless conditions were perfect. An unlikely scenario now that it was nearly November.

It was tide switchover time, which meant I went from doing late-night sessions to early-morning sessions, which was a real shock to the system. Getting in the water at 5am when it's dark and cold seemed way worse that getting in at sunset. The switchover meant I was spending more time swimming at night and again the phosphorescence were out in full force. There weren't as many of them as back in Ireland but they were considerably bigger in size. So big in fact that when I came up they'd be all caught up in my beard. I looked like a Christmas tree, which was entertaining for everyone and sparked a few jokes about us still being on this adventure and all spending Christmas together on *Friday* while still somewhere in the Hebrides. If all things went to plan we were about three or four days from Cape Wrath, and then four or five days from the end. So in the best case scenario I'd be done in a week, or worst case ten days. Only ten more days in the actual water (excluding bad weather days where I couldn't swim) till I never have to put on a stinking cold wetsuit that smelled of pee ever again. That in itself was enough of a motivator to swim faster.

The very next day we had to take cover in Lochinver as some pretty bad weather was fast approaching. This would add two more days to the potential ten, but as usual there was nothing we could do about it. We sat out the storm taking the opportunity to invite BBC Scotland to come and interview us now that they knew the panda definitely wasn't pregnant. I had set myself a £10,000 target for War Child and I was only halfway, so I really wanted to push the fundraising in the last few weeks and publicity helped.

Bad weather days, although welcomed by my fatigued body, were getting more and more frustrating. The one-week forecast on XC Weather was becoming increasingly orange or red, which meant we couldn't go out. We needed blue or green, which were certainly becoming more infrequent as winter crept worryingly fast towards us.

With two days off and access to a shower, I decided to go for my second shower in nearly two months, my fourth shower since the start of the swim 112 days ago. My shower up till now had consisted of Em boiling the kettle after each session and pouring it onto one of my t-shirts I wasn't using. I'd then wipe myself down, mainly to get the piss off me, before drying myself and getting into my tracksuit. It was also the first time I shampooed my hair and my beard, which uncovered all sorts of weird bits of dirt and grime that had been caught in there for the last three and a half months. I had forgotten just how energising a shower can be and came out feeling a new man.

*

After two bad weather days, we got up at 4am to head back out to sea. The waves were big but nicely formed coming in from slightly behind me and from my left, lifting me a few feet in the air. This was my favourite condition to swim in as I almost felt I was surfing down them.

In an effort to keep Lou and Owain entertained while I was in the water I had offered a bottle of whisky to the person who caught the most fish over a period of three days. It was day two and it's fair to say it was a killing spree out there. They both had lines out with five hooks each. There was one point, when we must have gone through a huge shoal, when they both brought up five fish each at the same time. *Friday* veered off to the left as they both were more interested in getting the fish off the line so that they could get the hooks back in the water. It was a race as the person whose line went back in first had much more chance of getting another batch from the shoal. It was good to hear the cheers from the water every time either of them had a fish. With a bottle of Scotland's finest at stake, it was serious business.

By the end of the day, Lou had caught 22 and Owain 19. The cockpit looked like the scene of a massacre with a bucket of the best six in the middle – the rest they had thrown back. I guess dinner was fish then, a nice change from some of the monotony of the Stowaways. We were down to our least favourite flavours. It's a wonder we could even stomach them at all after this long. I guess that is a testament of actually how good they were but anything after nearly four months is going to become tasteless. A few of my Atlantic Rowing friends said they got sick of their meals after a week, so we had done well all things considered.

I finished my session just shy of ten miles and the nearest safe anchor was behind a small island three hours away. It was days like this that reinforced our decision to only do one tide a day. The commutes to and from anchorages were getting longer and longer the closer we got to Cape Wrath, with safe places to moor up few and far between. It was worth pushing the extra hours to a good anchorage as the safety and better sleep far outweighed the journey.

Two days later and we could finally see Cape Wrath in the distance. If all went to plan, I'd reach it tomorrow. It was a huge moment in the swim because once round the corner we really were on the home straight. I felt a mixture of excitement and nerves every time I stopped to look ahead towards those distinctive towering cliffs. A few times while deep in thought I'd get a live fish flying through the air and land next to me.

'Keep swimming,' Owain would shout and then launch another fish he had just caught into the air. You could almost see the fish trying to swim even before it hit the water. A slightly odd sight to be awakened to after daydreaming of biblical wrath that lay ahead of me. Besides its daunting name, Cape Wrath was going to be the trickiest section of the swim. The tide was so strong I had no option but to try and swim the 20-mile section between Kinlochbervie and Kyle of Durness, the first safe anchorage on the north coast, in one go. There was nothing but towering cliffs in-between the two anchorages and not a place we wanted to hang around. Also with the strong tide it made logistics extremely difficult too. If the tide turned before we made anchorage we'd land up getting flung all the way back out to sea in the wrong direction. Conditions needed to be perfect and I needed to give it my all and not hold anything back.

By the end of the day I had reached Kinlochbervie, the final port of call. We went into the harbour to make sure we got a good night's sleep before attempting Cape Wrath. Ideally I would have liked to take a day off to prepare but Lou said we needed to go tomorrow as the weather was looking bad for the few days after. It was a case of take any weather window we could and tomorrow was looking to be that window. I went to bed feeling quite nervous but prepared. We'd had 115 days to prepare for tomorrow's swim and were as ready as we'd ever be. Cape Wrath was ours to be conquered.

13

DISASTER

As the forecast predicted, the weather was ideal as I got in the water just north of Kinlochbervie. This was the closest I had swum to the shore since Cornwall and it certainly added a sense of grandeur as I looked up to the high cliffs above me.

'Ready for this, Em?'

'Yes, Ginge. Once we're there we're practically done! Big day today. Day 116. Come on.'

It was time to give it everything. I put my face down and did what I had been doing for the last 116 days. Stroke, stroke, breath! Stroke, stroke, breath! Only this time with more urgency and determination than ever.

We slowly worked our way towards Cape Wrath, whose cliffs were getting bigger and more *Lord of the Rings*-like the closer we got. My mind was in a new place, a place it hadn't been before. I had been staring at Cape Wrath on the toilet door map for the best part of 4 months and now I was here. In my mind, once I rounded that corner the swim was as good as done. I was mixed with nerves, excitement and relief.

I was lost in my thoughts when suddenly, about 3 feet below me I saw a bird flying, in the water. I stopped swimming wondering if I had in fact gone mad. I stared at the little creature swimming next to me. It then looked over and winked at me. This was surely a dream. The little bird then darted off, swam up to the surface, and took off, flying high into the sky and over the cliffs. Did that just happen?

'Em, did you see the bird?'

'Yeah, it took off and flew away.'

'It was swimming with me and winked at me.'

'I'm sure it did, Ginge. Now come on, keep swimming.'

To this day, I'm not sure if I dreamt it but that little bird winking at me gave me a strange sense of comfort for what lay ahead. I put my face back in the water and continued north.

I must have zoned out because when I next came up, Em wasn't next to me as she normally was and the waves were all of a sudden much, much bigger. Panicking that she might have capsized again, I quickly looked back towards *Friday* to see her next to the RIB. Just then a small side-wave crashed over my head. I looked out to see millions of white horses (the name for the white bit of foam on the top of a cresting wave) all the way out to sea. The weather had changed quite dramatically in a short space of time. I swam back to *Friday*.

'Everything OK, Em?'

'I'm nearly cap … ' I didn't hear the rest of the sentence as a wave crashed over my head.

'Capsizing!' Em shouted.

The short sharp side-waves were constantly pushing Em to the tipping point. This was less than ideal. If there was ever a time I needed a kayak this was it.

'Are we OK to continue?' I shouted

'Yes, we'll come close, keep going,' Lou shouted as Em clambered aboard. I was now alone at sea. I was about 500 metres from Cape Wrath and could feel the tide pushing me forward. All I needed to do was get past the top and I knew the tide would push me round the corner.

'OK!' I shouted, and carried on swimming. Lou and *Friday* came round the inside of me and we pushed north. It seemed with every stroke the wind and the waves were getting stronger. This was definitely not in the forecast at all.

I was about 100 metres from Cape Wrath when I looked across to *Friday* and noticed the kayak wasn't anywhere to be seen.

'Kayak!' I shouted and pointed.

Em turned around and looked towards the rocks, then bent over to Lou who then looked in the direction she was pointing. In the distance about 30 metres from *Friday* was the kayak, floating upside down and drifting towards the rocks. It had broken free from *Friday*, because of a frayed rope. Shit. It was Jez's kayak. He'd kill me if I lost it. Also, Em had kayaked the entire way from Land's End and needed to complete her adventure. In some small way that kayak had become part of the crew. It needed saving. I started swimming past *Friday* and towards the kayak, which was drifting dangerously close to the cliffs. I was about ten metres from it when I saw the kayak rope in the water. I grabbed it and pulled as hard as I could and started dragging it back to *Friday*. Em had already jumped into the RIB and was waiting for me. Eventually I got there and threw Em the line. I needed to rest a moment as I had no energy to climb into the RIB. The waves were now getting bigger and bigger. When I could I climbed into the RIB and Em and I struggled to pull the kayak on board to empty it. It took the last bit of energy we had.

'Guys. We're getting pushed into the rocks,' Lou shouted.

Friday was facing east and even at full throttle we were still going west, directly towards the towering cliffs.

'I need to get out of here. It's too dangerous.'

'Lou. Can we hold position?' I shouted.

'Only just. Why?'

'I think I need to get back in and swim out of here. The tide will push me north. Let's just get along the top and we can then make for Durness.'

'You sure?' Lou looked worried.

'I think so.'

It seemed the most ridiculous decision ever but the reality was that getting back to this point again tomorrow would be near impossible. With the counter tides and waves I knew I had to finish my swim at least a few miles along the north coast.

'OK. But hurry!'

Em and I tied the kayak down and I put my goggles back on to prepare to get back in the water. Time stood still for a moment and everything went silent. Huge waves were crashing against the wrath-like cliffs about 20 metres to the left. Seagulls were hovering above, gathering in groups, waiting for disaster. The crew were all soaked and getting bashed from left to right. This was it, a moment in life when you're just about to do something and honestly have no idea how it's going to end. I fell backwards into a wave and the serenity turned to immediate chaos as waves crashed over my head and reverberated around my skull. Both *Friday* and I turned north.

'Just swim towards us,' Lou shouted as *Friday* bobbed from side to side and slowly moved away from the dangerous rocks.

I put my head down and faced north, and swam like I have never swum before. Every hand position, every kick, every breath needed to be perfect.

It wasn't long before *Friday* had been swept a few hundred metres from me. I could see *Friday* but judging by Em and Owain looking in all directions they had lost sight of me. I was now truly alone in one of the most inhospitable stretches of the swim. I began to wave. I waved for a good minute but the times when both *Friday* and I were at the crest of a wave at the same time were almost never. It was useless. I began to hyperventilate. What if they never see me? What if they thought I was further ahead? Alone at sea in these waters would most definitely result in my death. I needed to get closer. I started swimming towards them but for every 20 metres I swam the tide and wind was pushing *Friday* 15 metres away from me. Progress was slow. I'd stop swimming every minute and wave but they still couldn't see me. I was knackered. I lay on my back for a moment floating in the sea, letting the now 20 foot waves crash over me. In theory this tide could float me all the way to Durness but it was likely the tide would turn before I reached the Loch and I'd float all the way back to Cape Wrath.

I looked up again and gave another desperate wave. Thankfully this time Em saw me and signalled to Lou and Owain. They turned around and held position as I made my way towards them.

'Seano. That was insane, man. You OK?' Owain shouted as I clambered onto the RIB.

'I'm OK!' was all I could say.

Normally getting back on *Friday* was my safety but the reality was we were still pretty vulnerable. The waves were getting bigger and bigger, and we still needed to do the two-hour journey to Durness. I clambered onto the yacht and we all sat there in silence for moment as we all tried to make sense of what had happened.

'Owain! Steer,' Lou shouted. 'You guys are shit at knots!'

The kayak had fallen off the RIB and was now upside down causing drag. We needed to tie it on better and Lou was certainly the best at knots. Lou and I jumped into the RIB and slowly pulled the kayak back. The waves were too big. The line from the RIB to *Friday* would slacken on the down waves, and then as *Friday* went over the crest of another wave the rope would tighten and like a bucking bronco send me and Lou flying. On the fourth occasion a huge wave crashed over the back of the RIB and Lou's automatically inflatable life jacket blew up in her face knocking her jaw backwards, the line between the RIB and *Friday* then jerked catching underneath her arm.

'Shit, shit,' Lou screamed, before just about managing to get her arm free when the line slackened again. We had just about got the kayak on board and Lou started tying it on properly.

We both then clambered back onto *Friday* and sat down in silence. Everything was wet. Water was pouring through a hole in the side of *Friday* and waves kept crashing over the back of the RIB and into the cockpit. We needed to make Durness as soon as possible and before the tide changed. It was a race against time and the elements and from where we stood, the elements looked like they would win.

Ten minutes later …

'The RIB!' Owain shouted.

The RIB had completely flipped upside down and was now being dragged with its nose digging deep into the water.

'What about the kayak?'

'Dunno, must be underneath.'

We looked around and then about 20 metres behind us we saw the nose of the kayak slowly floating further and further away. My heart sank.

'We got to leave it Sean, we can't turn around,' Lou said.

I knew she was right. I stood there watching the tip of the kayak rise up and then disappear below the crest of a wave, getting further and further away from us. I felt bad for Em who had done so much in the kayak. She had formed a special bond with it. It had helped me swim in the right direction, provided me with food and most of all was the reason I had Em, whose charisma and enthusiasm had saved me from the brink of giving up many times. The expedition wouldn't be the same without it.

It wasn't long before the kayak had totally disappeared from view and we continued to drag the upside-down RIB towards Durness. Good thing I had sent Arthur's engine back when I did otherwise we'd be dragging that under the water too. Lou radioed the coastguard to inform them that we had lost a red Prijon kayak and if anyone found it they need not to worry about a missing person. An hour later we got a call from the coastguard informing us they found a kayak, but a yellow one. I guess it wasn't just us having issues at sea. Sailing a 26-foot, old wooden yacht in waves nearly as high as she was long was both physically and mentally demanding. *Friday* didn't have a helm wheel and operating a tiller arm was excruciating. Every time a wave hit us from the side it would push the rudder sending the tiller arm shooting left and right. No matter how strong you were you couldn't fight half a ton of water against the rudder. Lou and Owain would take it in turns swapping sides to give each arm a rest as we battled through the waves doing not much more than three miles per hour.

It took almost two hours to reach the safety of Durness and out of the way of the huge Atlantic rollers. The loch was still very choppy but we managed to find a tiny corner to drop two anchors and assess the damage. The first job was to flip the RIB over. We hauled it up on its side and let it fall upright. Everything that was in the RIB was gone, including two oars, an anchor and chain, a jerrycan and spare line. Two of the four bolts on the hull of the RIB used to attach the drag line had completely broken off leaving a gaping hole in the RIB floor, meaning we'd been two bolts away from losing the RIB altogether. The only thing left was Em's paddle. It had somehow bent completely in half, which was a frightening sight that showed just how much force those waves had.

The mood was very tense as we all sat there in silence trying to make sense of what just happened. Cape Wrath had lived up to its name and it's a wonder how we came out the other side without any major injuries. I then thought of the kayak, floating aimlessly around Cape Wrath. It would probably be stuck in tidal limbo for weeks or months, alone with just enough buoyancy to stop it from sinking, putting it out of its misery. I suddenly felt sad again for Em, who now had no kayak to complete her epic adventure. This swim was a challenge for all of us and Em's had come to a premature end. The worst bit was that I could tell Em was disappointed but she never said anything, instead deciding to retire to the front cabin. As tired as I was, I thought I'd give her some space.

The next issue was to see about the leak in the side of *Friday*. Luckily it was just a plug stopper that had come loose and after some hammering we were able to put it back.

Although in the safety of Durness, there was no way we would be able to stay here. It was just way too rough, we couldn't get to shore as we had no oars and, even if we did make it, there was nothing around for miles. If the weather eased up we could head back to Cape Wrath from here, if not then we really needed to get to the safety of Loch Eriboll, a further two or three hours away. One thing was for certain, we weren't going to do either of those today as the idea of going back out to that sea frightened all of us. We had no choice but to try stick it out here for the night and see what tomorrow would bring.

None of us got any sleep at all as we heaved from left to right all night, being thrown around the cabin as we tried to sleep. It was pouring with rain and everything was wet. The weather, although slightly improved, was not good enough for us to attempt Cape Wrath again, so we decided to fight the waves and head to Eriboll. The journey was a lot like yesterday. The RIB flipped over again and, although Owain managed to get it back upright from *Friday*, which to this day defies human power, it was only a matter of time before it was upside down again.

We reached Eriboll three hours later and headed far down the loch towards a mooring buoy that Lou spotted on Google Earth. We arrived at the buoy and all let out a sigh as we hooked up to it, knowing we were finally safe and could actually let go of all the tension built up over the last few days. The weather forecast suggested gale force eight winds for the next four days so it looked like we were here for a while.

Eriboll was a beautiful loch and our mooring buoy was just below an idyllic white stone cottage tucked into some trees. It took us about an hour to spot it but there, below the house and under a tree, was a very old kayak that looked like it hadn't been used for years.

'Lou, look,' Em shouted and pointed. We all knew what she was thinking. 'I wonder if they would let me use it to carry on?'

'I can't see why not. Doesn't look like anyone uses it.'

'Right! I'm going to ask!'

'Hold fire, I'm coming to shore too. I got a serious case of cabin fever.' Owain shouted.

Owain was right. We really needed to get to land for the sake of our sanity.

We all climbed into the RIB and then stopped and looked at each other. We had no way of paddling. I jumped back into *Friday* to get Em's broken paddle and we snapped it completely. The plan was to use it like an Indian canoe paddle, with one person paddling on each side. Owain and Lou took up the task.

In theory this should be easy, but with tired arms and one person inevitably rowing harder than the other we were just going in circles. Em and I were in stitches at the thought of someone watching us. It took about ten minutes to paddle the 50 metre stretch to land and by the time we landed, Owain had given up, Lou was using one paddle in the front of the boat by herself and Em and I were crying with laughter. It was exactly what we needed. A bit of team spirit to make us forget about Cape Wrath.

While we tied up the RIB, Em went off on her own to knock on the cottage door. We figured a girl by herself was far less intimidating than four dirty grubby people might have been.

Moments later, Em waved to us from the porch so we went up to the cottage.

We were greeted at the door by a very friendly woman. I was half expecting an old lady to be living out here but she was young, in her late thirties.

'Helloo there, come in, come in. I'm Fiona. Tea anyone?' She said.

We all sat around the kitchen counter telling her about what had just happened to us while Fiona just kept repeating, 'You're mad, you're all mad, you are,' and then laughing.

Fiona had heard something about the swim but didn't really know much and was very interested in everything we had done.

It couldn't have been five minutes before the phone rang.

'Hello?' Fiona answered. 'Oh no! It wasn't four men. Two guys and two girls. It's that swimmer guy. Remember from the news. And his crew. We just having tea. When are you back? ... OK, see you soon.' And she put the phone down.

'This is what happens up here. A fisherman out in the bay saw the four of you coming up to the cottage and was worried so phoned John, my husband, to tell him so that was him calling in. Word spreads fast around here doesn't it?'

That was hilarious. I kind of liked that they were all looking out for each other though.

Half an hour later, John arrived.

'What's this? Tea? Come one. You folk need a dram.'

And he went to the cupboard and whipped out a bottle of good single malt.

We spent a wonderful afternoon chatting, drinking tea and whisky, and learning all about the clans and landowners in northern Scotland. By the time we had to head back to *Friday* we had already been invited for breakfast. Fiona and John had taken the notion of hospitality to a whole new level. Em didn't think it was the right time to ask for their kayak so decided to leave it for now. They were so accommodating we didn't want to be seen to take advantage of that.

The next morning, with a slightly heavy head after too many whiskies, we rowed in circles to shore and had a delicious scrambled egg breakfast. After an hour, Em hesitantly asked if we could borrow that kayak. Without even a flinch John was up and went to the shed and brought out another kayak.

'This one is better if you want this one instead, but it needs a few holes fixed, which I can do for you.'

'Wow, thanks John but honestly, the one on the beach is fine.'

'Are you sure. It's nay bother.'

'No, honestly John,' Em insisted. 'You've done enough.'

'OK, then. I guess you'll need a paddle too. I seen you guys going in circles this morning,' John laughed. 'What else you need? I have loads of shite here.'

I'd never met such a hospitable and giving family before. They were up there with Steve and Kate from Cornwall. Such generosity. Em now had a kayak and a paddle and could continue her own adventure.

That afternoon, we headed back to Cape Wrath. We wouldn't be able to do it in one go so would stay in Durness for the night and then make our way to my start point tomorrow. John and Fiona and their kids came out to *Friday* with us, which was a nice send-off as we sailed away to their cheers. After a few days where all hope was lost, or broken, John and Fiona had come to the rescue. We owed them a lot.

We found the same little bay in Durness and dropped two anchors again, and had Stowaways and wine for dinner. Tomorrow we'd go back to where it all went horribly wrong. To say we were nervous was an understatement. Our few days in Eriboll with John and Fiona had been good for us, but it had meant we pushed from our minds the reality of the situation, from fear more than anything. Even though conditions we better they still weren't ideal. Tonight the clocks were going back, which meant winter really was just about upon us. I couldn't believe that it had been a month since we were on Eigg. It felt like yesterday.

We were all on edge as we headed out of Durness and back into hell. By the time we reached my GPS point, the waves were way too big for Em to kayak so it looked like I'd be on my own again. Rain started pelting down as each wave crested and crashed, often coming right over the back of the cockpit and into the main cabin. We needed to get on with it. I jumped in and started swimming. The waves were around 30 feet high as the wind pushed *Friday* away from me. It was too windy for them to stay near me so the strategy was to get pushed ahead 100 metres and then turn around, hold position till I arrived and then do the same. Those times when they went ahead were the most nerve-racking. If they had engine failure, or lost my location in the water, they'd get swept away from me and I'd definitely not survive being alone on this section as there was nowhere to go ashore.

I carried on pushing through, almost surfing down the huge waves, my heart racing every time *Friday* got more than 100 metres from me. Sometimes when she went into the trough of a wave even her mast would disappear from sight. When *Friday* was at the crest of a wave and I was in the trough of the wave, I'd be looking right up into the heavens at her silhouette, sharp and dramatic against a dark and moody sky. At times she was heeling over at such an angle I could see most of the one side of her hull out of the water. The first thing I thought was she needed a clean. There was a lot of seaweed growing on her.

I swam for three hours, covering seven miles, and made it just past the entrance to Durness before Lou decided we need to make for shelter. To this day I'll never forget swimming in those monstrous waves, feeling alone and helpless in an ever-changing sea. I had, however, done it and survived. Now at least, even if we were faced with similar waves tomorrow, we knew we could deal with them. In a weird way I wish we had attempted to swim in big waves like this before but, on thinking back, there wasn't a time when they were ever this huge. Did we miss some potential swimming days for no reason? If I managed to swim today then surely I'd have been able to swim in most of the last bad weather days and therefore probably have completed the swim already. But then, although nothing major had gone wrong, I felt both *Friday* and I were operating at the brink of our capabilities in these big waves, pushing ourselves to the very edge. I couldn't help but think that if we kept doing that, sooner or later something was going to break. Either me or *Friday*, either of which would result in the swim coming to a premature and possibly disastrous end.

An hour later we were in a small bay between Eriboll and Durness tucked up ready for what the morning would bring us.

Just before heading out, a fisherman came over to us and said he'd caught too many crabs and lobster and wanted to know if we wanted any. We laughed as that's not a question you get asked often. We were then presented with two lobsters and five crabs.

'I've always wanted crabs from a fisherman,' joked Owain.

Tonight's dinner was going to be amazing and my mouth was watering already. The same fisherman also offered to give us some diesel and he'd drop it off in the morning at our next anchorage, which Lou pointed out a few miles away. People up here took the concept of friendliness to a whole new level.

I managed only four and a half miles in the afternoon session before the waves really were too high and the RIB kept capsizing. John's kayak was now on the deck of *Friday* as we didn't want to risk losing it too. Em really did not want to get back in the water and I think had come to terms with her adventure ending at Cape Wrath, which is still technically the length of Britain, I guess.

That night we spent a good hour trying to download cooking instructions for crab and lobster with only GPRS internet, and then another two hours trying to break and eat crab without the proper tools. Luckily we had a hammer, which was doing a good job even if most of the crab landed up on the manky floor.

When we awoke the next day, there were two cans of diesel on the deck of *Friday*. The fisherman had come early and dropped them off. I felt bad for not being awake to say thanks.

Progress was slow again as huge waves crashed over me and often right over *Friday* too. For some reason Em and Owain were starting to get really seasick again, their bodies just not used to dealing with this level of wave-battering. The coastguard kept calling us too as apparently people along the shore were calling in a boat doing circles in pretty big waves. Good to know there were people out there looking out for us. I really was pushing the line of safety versus determination but had every faith in Lou. If something did however go wrong, people would have every right to say, 'well, you deserved it for being so stupid'. I'd like to think we were being bold and charting new ground. Nothing worth achieving is ever easy.

That evening we made it to the Kyle of Tongue and the final safe anchorage till Thurso a good 30 miles away. In order to make the next section we'd need three days of good weather. Instead, as fate would have it, Lou informed us that we had four days of gale-force winds. What were the chances of getting three good weather days along the north coast of Scotland? It was the 29 October. Soon it would be November. NOVEMBER!! If, two months ago when Lou joined, I had thought I'd still be swimming in November, would I have continued? It's impossible to know the answer to that, but I think ignorance certainly helped us all take one day at a time.

Luckily we found a small hotel, the only one still open around there, that had Wi-Fi so decided to make camp there for four days. After the second day, the landlady asked me to sign the visitors book and there, a few spaces above my name, was Usain Bolt's. God only know what the world's fastest runner was doing up here in the middle of winter. Now they had the world's slowest swimmer to add to their list of athletes who'd stayed in the hotel.

It was a tough four days constantly looking out to sea wondering if in fact I could be swimming. My mind was going crazy thinking of all the times I hadn't swum when I might have been able to. The time I spent looking for a skipper, the times we missed the tide, the times I skipped a session to do errands. All these things meant I was in Scotland in November and had surely missed my weather window. Would I have to come back next year and complete the swim? That would be pointless.

The problem was there were no safe anchorages if the wind was more than force three or four, and it had been five or six for weeks now. The ten-day forecast didn't look any better. I was thinking of every possible option and one even included swimming on my own. There was a beach every seven miles or so along the coast so technically I could do that with land support. I was also feeling guilty for keeping the crew away from their families and businesses. Lou was only meant to stay with us for ten days. She had now been here for over 60 days, not what she was expecting when she tweeted me from sunny Turkey all that time ago.

On day three, while in the hotel, we got a call from a fisherman saying our RIB had sunk. We ran down to the harbour wall where we had tied the RIB up and it was upside down, one of the sides completely deflated and sinking. The waves had picked up and the rope had snapped, and the RIB had been trashed around against the wall for the past few hours. Now I owed Jez a kayak and Arthur a RIB. We sat there wondering what to do as we now had no way of getting back to *Friday*, anchored about 60 metres offshore. Lou went off and came back a few moments later.

'Right guys. I've spoken to my brother and Nomad Sailing is paying for a night in the hotel for us.'

What legends Lou and her brother where. This would give us the night to find another RIB. Maybe there was one on eBay?

There weren't any RIBs on eBay so we racked our brains for ages about what to do and the only option we kept coming back to was to ask John if he had one. I hated that they had done so much for us yet we were still asking for more help, but it really was our only option. John and Fiona were all too welcoming, and later that evening they came round and brought us their small inflatable RIB. It wouldn't fit all four of us but we could take it in turns ferrying back and forth to *Friday*.

14

GETTING TO THE START LINE IS HARD, BUT THE FINISH LINE, EVEN HARDER

It was time to go back out and try to push at least a few miles to get as far past Tongue as possible. The plan was to get about four miles east of Tongue and then come back for safe anchoring. It was unlikely I'd be able to do this in one session so we set our alarms at 4.30am and started the commute. For some reason, I started to feel a strange sense of panic. This was the first time I had felt this way. I really, really, did not want to get back in that water.

At 6am, however, I had to get back in and started making progress east. Because of commute logistics, I only had three hours to do my best. I managed six miles in those three hours before the tide started to turn, so we went to the nearest anchorage, which was a mooring buoy in a little cove off Neave Island. The island was idyllic, although none of us were in the mood to explore. Instead we sat out the tide, keeping to ourselves. I spent most of the time lying on my bunk wondering how on earth I was going to make it to Thurso if I was only managing six miles a day.

We set out for the evening session just to see if we could do some mileage, anything to get us closer to Thurso. It had a safe harbour and was also so close to John O'Groats it certainly gave us the sense that the swim was almost done. Surely nothing could stop us once we were there?

The days were quite short now, which meant it was dark almost as soon as I got in the water. I swam for about an hour, but because of a heavy headwind I was out-swimming *Friday* and the waves were too big for Em to kayak with me. I decided that night swimming with these waves was just not sensible so decided to stop there. Feeling pretty deflated, we headed back to Neave Island to the safety of the mooring buoy. The weather had drastically changed, rain was coming in at right angles. By the time we got back to the buoy it was high water, so the buoy was a foot below the surface, which made hooking up to it impossible. It was pitch black and Lou kept trying to get as close as possible for Owain to grab the buoy with the boat hook, but we kept getting blown off it. Eventually he managed to grab the buoy but a huge wave hit us, ripping the boat hook from Owain's hands.

'Let's drop the anchors,' Lou shouted over the sound of crashing waves and hard rain.

'OK,' Owain replied, jumping into action and dropped both anchors near the buoy. It wasn't by any means ideal but we had no option.

It was 9pm and this was possibly the roughest we had ever anchored. *Friday* kept swirling around in all directions as waves whirlpooled in the small bay. At 2am, after no sleep at all, we heard the anchor dragging quite significantly. This was not a good sign. We really needed to get on the mooring buoy.

'Right guys. The tide is lower, we should be able to get on the buoy,' Lou suggested. Owain and I got up, put on our life jackets and waterproofs, and went outside. Em took the torch to shine on the buoy.

The idea was to try to lasso the buoy with a smaller line, then bring it towards us and attach it to a stronger line. It took Lou about 15 attempts as *Friday* heaved from left to right but she eventually got the rope around it.

'Sean, hold this and try to bring the buoy up a bit so I can get the bigger line under it.'

She gave me the rope and without thinking I did something very stupid. Instead of just holding the rope with my fingers, I wrapped it around my knuckles. About ten seconds later, while pulling as hard as I could, my knuckles white, *Friday* was hit by a huge wave and heaved a few feet away from the buoy. If I had just been holding the rope it would have been pulled from my hands and I'd have suffered rope burn at worst. With the rope around my knuckles I was pulled across the deck and my hand got jammed between the rope and the pulpit. I wanted to scream but kept my nerve so as not to distract Lou from getting the buoy hooked up. I was pinned down and unable to move my hand. I thought my knuckles were going to explode, pop right out the top of my hand. Luckily *Friday* then pitched back towards the buoy, slackening the line a bit and I was able to free myself. Shafts of pain shot up my arm. I couldn't move my fingers. At that moment, Lou was able to attach the line to the buoy and rejoiced.

'Come on boys. We can sleep now. Two anchors and a mooring buoy. We're not going anywhere.'

I got back into bed clutching my hand. I didn't want to tell anyone so just took some painkillers and hoped it would be better in the morning.

None of us had any sleep as the weather got progressively worse all night. My hand seemed to be OK and looked like just a bruise, which was a relief. We didn't have much internet but just managed to get a forecast, which suggested bad weather for another four days. The problem was we were now stuck on Neave Island. It was too rough to leave the bay or go to shore. Instead we were confined to *Friday* all day, bobbing from side to side, slowly going mad.

The next day we decided to attempt to go back to the safety of Tongue. Lou and Owain got up early and prepared to pull anchor. One anchor came up but the second one was truly stuck. After two hours of trying everything, including starting the engine and trying to free it by going back and forth, nothing was working.

'We're gonna have to cut it unfortunately,' Lou said, quite annoyed. 'I've never lost an anchor and was hoping I never would.'

Cutting an anchor is cause for ridicule in the sailing world, mostly friendly banter, but Lou knew her brother would never let this one go.

'Um Lou, we don't have a hacksaw,' Owain said.

'Really! What do we have?'

'Nothing. A steak knife is all I can find.'

I remembered I had a Leatherman, which had a small metal file on it.

'Try this, Owain,' I said handing him the file.

It wasn't ideal but it was our only option.

It took two hours to file down the anchor chain as we all took 20-minute shifts giving it a go. Eventually we got it free and let the chain slip over the edge and disappear into the depths. We now only had one anchor and it wasn't a good one either. We really did need some good weather to get to Thurso as anchoring safely just got a whole lot more difficult.

We limped back to Tongue and settled back into the hotel, where the landlady was surprised to see us again. It was really depressing being back there, not because of the hotel, but because it felt we had been there forever, not able to make any real progress. I had XC Weather on my laptop and kept staring at it, refreshing the page every few minutes but it really looked like we had missed the weather window. I was now pretty low. I put my head in my hands and closed my eyes wondering whether or not I'd ever be able to finish the swim. From here it seemed very unlikely.

'Hey, Bro!' I heard someone say. I recognised that voice. I looked up. There, standing in that little pub in northern Scotland, was my good friend, Dave Cornthwaite.

'Dave!' I got up and gave him a huge hug. I was good to see a friend from the real world.

'What are you doing here?'

'I just thought I'd come and say hi, you know, to show my support.'

'You're kidding!'

'Of course not, mate. Right, first things first, what are you all drinking?' Dave went to the bar and came back with a tray of drinks.

'Mate, how'd you get here?' I asked, still a bit overwhelmed to see him.

'You wouldn't believe it. A train, plane, two more trains and a taxi from Thurso. The taxi driver is waiting for me outside. I have to get a train back in a few hours.'

Dave had literally just wanted to come say hi and tell me how well I was doing. He informed me that loads of people were wishing me luck for the last bit and how I mustn't give up. It was a great boost to team morale and most of all my mental state. Dave stayed for a few hours as we chatted about all things swimming and having a bit of banter as to whose swim was harder. (Dave swam 1,000 miles down the Missouri River the year before and had Em in his crew.) When Dave left, I was feeling a whole lot more positive about completing the swim. He certainly saved me from falling deeper into a depressing downward spiral.

It was time to try and get to Thurso. The weather was just about good enough for us to potentially anchor on the east side of Strathy Point, the halfway point between here and

Thurso. I needed to make it that far, which was ten miles and almost double what I've done in the last few sessions.

We set our alarms for 3am and I was in the water at 6am. I gave it my all for about half an hour then, as luck would have it, I really needed a shit again.

'Just do it in your suit,' Em shouted from *Friday*. Getting out of the water, out of my suit and going to the loo would take at least 20 minutes, which we didn't have time for. Quite honestly, I considered shitting in my wetsuit that day but then decided against it and went aboard. Twenty minutes later, I was back in the water. My arms were burning with my higher stroke rate but I didn't care. I needed to make Strathy. It truly was winter now and with every breath I could see snow-covered mountains in the distance. Not even Scottish people swim on the north coast in November and for good reason.

Somehow I managed 10.3 miles and we made Strathy. It was time to head for anchorage. After an hour trying various spots we had no option but to head for Thurso, which was at least six hours away against tide. It would have been quicker to go back to Tongue with the tide but to get back here in the morning would have meant using all the good tide or fighting the bad tide for hours. And no one really wanted to go back to Tongue again.

We woke up at 3am and started the journey back to Strathy. Halfway there *Friday*'s engine cut out again. My heart sank. This was not the time for engine failure. We took up the floorboards and checked everywhere including the fuse we had changed earlier. Nothing seemed wrong. She was barely turning over. There was a moment of silence as we all just sat there floating aimlessly at sea. Had *Friday*'s engine finally given up this time? She had done us proud. Chugging away for the past four and a half months, she had covered the same distance as sailing from Africa to South America. Not bad for a 52-year-old boat with a 20-year-old engine.

'What now Lou?' I asked.

'Well, we'll have to call a …' Lou paused and looked towards some line running overboard. She got up and grabbed and tried to pull it but it was stuck. She leant over the side of *Friday*.

'Ah, you bastard,' she said while tugging at the rope. 'Looks like this is the problem. Line caught in the prop.'

This was what sailors call the propeller, and it was potentially a good result as we might be able to free it, or a very bad result if it was too stuck.

I was already in my suit so it made sense for me to dive down and try set it free. The prop was a good one and a half metres down and the rough waves made diving down quite tricky. I examined the prop. The line had been wrapped around the shaft about eight times and deeply imbedded. I tried to tug it but nothing came free. I came up to the surface to breathe again. I was surprisingly bad at holding my breath, I'd have thought my cardio was better by now.

I dived back down and tried counter-turning the prop, which kind of worked. I could do one half-turn before having to come back for a breath. I repeated this around

20 times, with each turn slowly tugging on the rope while trying to avoid the rudder smashing me in the face every time *Friday* moved in the wind.

After what seemed forever down there, the rope came free and I climbed back on board. My right arm was quite tired from holding on to the line for so long. I did, however, feel extremely warm from the exertion and getting back in the water wasn't as daunting as it had been.

The waves had calmed down drastically, which was a nice change from being dunked every few minutes. My route towards Thurso needed to take a detour because of a nuclear power station on the edge of the cliffs that had a two-mile exclusion zone out to sea. I did wonder what water-based deformities I'd get if I swam through some radiation water? Maybe I'd finally grow gills and become Kevin Costner in *Waterworld*. At least then maybe I'd be able to swim faster.

After a few hours, Thurso was finally in sight, I was there. I felt a huge weight off my shoulders and started to feel suddenly emotional. I immediately vomited in the water, my body giving up slightly, much like those who collapse on the finish line of a marathon. What was meant to be five days to get to Thurso from Cape Wrath landed up being nearly two weeks, and the last few days had certainly been taxing on all of us. I ended my session three miles from Thurso and we went back to the harbour to celebrate. Reaching Thurso surely meant the swim was nearly finished. We moored up and went to the local harbour-side café for some food.

As soon we entered the café, a fisherman recognised me.

'Oi, you're the swimmer aren't you?' he said, his mouth still full of food.

'Yes sir, it's pretty much in the bag, just arrived in Thurso this afternoon,' I said quite proudly, my head uncharacteristically high for the first time, ever.

'Amazing mate. Just the Pentland Firth now. Good luck there!'

'Pentland Firth?' I asked.

'Yes, Britain's most notorious stretch of water,' he said grinning, bits of baked beans stuck in his teeth. Luckily I had already vomited everything out my stomach otherwise I might have vomited again.

Not another one? It seems everywhere is Britain's most dangerous stretch of water.

'I'm sure you've thought about it but I've seen tankers go backwards there. The flood can be up to 16 knots.'

'Thanks but we'll do it at slack so should be fine hopefully.'

'I'm sure you will. Sterling effort so far, well done.'

We all went and sat down.

'Lou, is Pentland Firth really that bad?' I asked nervously.

'Yeah, it's bad at the wrong times but it'll be fine, especially after what we dealt with at Cape Wrath. The tidal atlas says only go when there is force three or less and wind with tide. Apparently even a two wind against tide makes the section pretty hairy.'

It's not over till it's over. We hadn't had a force two or three for weeks. There seemed to always be one more major hurdle and, according to some of the quite terrifying YouTube videos we watched about the Pentland Firth, it certainly looked like this could be the worst of the worst if we didn't plan it correctly. They say getting to the start line is the hardest part of any expedition. Yes that was true, but getting to the finish line this time was most certainly even harder.

That evening we took a taxi into Thurso to send some emails to everyone as it looked like my end date, if the Pentland Firth didn't kill us, would be Monday 11 November at midday, which gave us a few days' grace if the weather did pick up. My mum and Em and Owain's family wanted to come up, so needed some warning, as well as Jez who didn't want to miss the end. Speedo also wanted to be there, which was nice as I couldn't have even started the swim without them.

After the emails, we got the same taxi driver, who was really impressed with the swim and didn't charge us for the return trip. We then settled into the harbour-side pub until it was time for bed, anything to minimise time cramped up on *Friday*. Conditions were now only barely liveable on her with everything completely wet, mouldy and pretty disgusting as housekeeping had taken a backseat now that we were so close to the end.

An hour later our friendly taxi driver came back into the pub with a wad of cash in his hand.

'I'm so impressed with your swim I drove round all the pubs and got some donations for the charity. Here's about £100.'

We all stood there in shock. What wonderful generosity. We offered to buy him a pint but he said he needed to head off and with that disappeared, not wanting any form of recognition. It was gestures like this that made those long hard days seem worth it.

I continued to vomit repeatedly in the water all session as I swam past Thurso and around Dunnet Head, the tide getting stronger and stronger the more into the Pentland Firth I swam. At one point I was doing five knots, which was my second fastest pace after the Mull of Kintyre. The plan was to finish with enough tide so that we could get to Stroma three miles away. Lou pulled me out and we started to head for the safety of the small harbour on the island.

'Guess what, Ginge!' Em shouted as I got on board. She looked excited.

'We're only seven miles from John O'Groats. Seven miles, Ginge! Amazing!'

'No way!' I looked ahead but couldn't quite see the harbour. I'd learnt now not to celebrate too early but there were butterflies in my stomach. These last seven miles were potentially the hardest if conditions weren't perfect. If I didn't swim hard enough I'd get swept right past John O'Groats towards Norway.

We got within 500 metres of Stroma when the tide turned and within a few minutes we were going backwards.

'Shit!' Lou said. 'Pushed it too close. We're going to have to go back to Thurso.'

We turned around and all of a sudden were zooming along at six knots. This Pentland Firth really was strong.

We made it back to Thurso. It was *Friday* and I was due to finish on Monday so we decided to take Saturday off so that I could rest up. I'd then do most of the last seven miles to John O'Groats on Sunday and then the final bit on Monday. Sunday was also looking to be the best weather for the notorious Pentland Firth.

It was a strange last rest day as we all felt a little lost. There were no errands to do, no fuel to get, no food to buy, no route to plot, instead we all went off and did our own thing. I wandered the streets of Thurso aimlessly for hours trying to take in the last four and a half months. Part of me felt like it had gone quickly, but the other part of me felt like it was a lifetime ago we were all throwing up on *Friday* in Sennen Cove.

Sunday came and it was time to fight the Firth. We used a lot of the good tide to get to my last swim point and arrived a few hours before slack when the tide wasn't as strong. The weather was as good as it would ever be and I jumped back in and swam as fast as I could, my shoulders burning like they have never burned before. A mile later I could see John O'Groats ahead of me. We all cheered.

'Six miles to go, Ginge,' Em shouted.

I carried on. It was strange swimming in the Firth. The water was swirling in all directions. There were also loads of small whirlpools, only about an inch wide but would funnel down into the depths below me, like small inverted tornadoes.

'Five miles!' the crew shouted.

I pushed on not really thinking about anything other than that photo of John O'Groats Harbour I had on my laptop.

'Sean!' I heard Lou shout. 'We need to change direction!'

Apparently I wasn't swimming fast enough and on our current course I'd miss the harbour and be swept right past it.

'Follow us!' *Friday* changed course by over 90 degrees. It seemed drastic.

'Are you sure?' I asked from the water, and then felt guilty because I had no way of knowing my direction and also for questioning Lou's judgement, which was just plain ridiculous. She was a yacht master instructor.

'Swim, mate. Harder!' Owain shouted.

I was now facing in almost the opposite direction to John O'Groats, which was at my seven o'clock, behind me.

'Harder, mate,' Owain shouted again.

I was already pushing my hardest and not really sure I had much more in me. I closed my eyes for moment and gave ten hard strokes. I somehow felt better with my eyes closed but knew very well my cheese rolling shoulder was sending me off to the left again so opened them. I was right. I needed to head more to the right.

'Four miles!'

'Three miles!'

'Two miles!'

Those last few miles flew by as I reached an all-time record speed of eight knots, swimming in effect, backwards.

'One mile, Ginge. We're out of the main current. You can slow down now. It's in the bag, mate.'

I started to well up inside my goggles a bit. I had pretty much done it. I swam a further few hundred metres as I tried to compose myself before getting out to do the last section in the morning.

It was 11.45am on 11 November 2013 as I put on my cold, piss-smelling, wetsuit for the last time. I walked along the coast to get in alone without *Friday*, who was moored up in John O'Groats Harbour. I didn't need her today. She had done me proud and looked rugged and adventurous tied up along the harbour wall. I asked Em to kayak in with me. She deserved to do the final section after all her hard work.

I got in the water and Em kayaked from the harbour to meet me in the water.

'You've done it, Ginge! You've proved them all wrong,' Em said.

'Thanks Em for everything,' I said, struggling to get the words out. 'I couldn't have done it without you. Honestly!'

I was trying my best to stay strong. I had so many things running through my head. All those emails from people saying it was a publicity stunt. That it wasn't possible. It wasn't a real swim because I wore a wetsuit. That Sennen Cove café blog. All those people who doubted that this swim was possible – in your face!

I had completed the swim. Yes, it had taken 70 days longer than I had expected. Yes, it was much, much harder than I could ever have imagined, but I hadn't given up, none of us had given up.

Without the crew I would never have been able to make it.

Jez's gung-ho approach and anti-establishment philosophy certainly meant I made headway where certain skippers might have not continued.

Owain's level-headedness, mechanical skills, way with words in drumming up support, not to mention his knack for fishing, were huge assets to the swim.

Lou's ability to always find the best anchorages and elite sailing skills when conditions really were against us, and her enthusiasm for a proper adventure gave us all the comfort that we'd be safe in her hands.

And finally Em, my mum on the swim. She never wavered in her hard work or positive attitude as she looked after me for four and a half months, making sure I had food when I needed it, rinsing my pissy wetsuits, kayaking in the freezing cold water, never once complaining all the while being petrified of the water. Having her enthusiasm right by my side, always smiling, helped me when I was at my lowest.

Those last few hundred metres seemed to take forever as I made my way into the harbour to the cheers of a handful of people, most of whom lived nearby. I knew there was going to be some media there; it was live on BBC News and various other broadcasters were there too with their vans with satellite dishes on the roofs, exactly like you see in the movies.

I thought I should probably say something important, something inspiring for other people who want to do something that others say can't be done. I wanted to tell people two things.

One was that you should never let someone else's opinion (and opinion is all it is) of your ability affect the decisions you make in life. They don't know how hard you want it, what you're truly capable of. If I had listened to those opinions I wouldn't ever have got in the water 135 days ago.

I also wanted to tell people that we are all physically and mentally stronger than we think we are.

I wanted to tell people to aim a little higher, push a little harder, because I think they'd surprise themselves.

I had this speech all in my mind as I approached the slipway. And then, as soon as my foot hit land it all became too overwhelming. I burst out crying. Tears filled up my goggles, so I took them off and threw them away. I then felt my eyes burning. Someone had opened a bottle of champagne and sprayed it all over me. I was weeping and could barely talk and now couldn't see, and all I could hear were the voices of journalists shouting questions at me. It was all too much.

I didn't care about anything anymore as a huge sense of relief came over me.

No more jellyfish stings to the face, no more vomiting, no more toes that might fall off, no more cold, wet, sleepless nights and I could finally hang up my wetsuit.

I was done. I had finally achieved what many thought was impossible.

I had just become the first person in history to swim the length of Britain.

I never did manage to tell everyone what I wanted to. Instead I cried like a baby and talked about my beard a lot.

EPILOGUE

Three weeks later ...

I finally made it home. The three weeks after the swim were a whirlwind of rushing around the country doing magazine interviews, TV appearances and giving talks. It was surreal and at times I had to pinch myself to see if I was dreaming, most memorably when I sat next to Jason Donovan on *The One Show* sofa, which resulted a bombardment of Tweets from people saying, 'Wow, Kylie is looking hairy nowadays.'

I've been able to open my emails with confidence, knowing that I wasn't going to get any of the 'I told you it wasn't possible' or 'I'm sorry you didn't make it' messages like I received after my cycle ride. All the blogs, forums and critics have gone quiet, and instead been replaced with emails from people saying things like, 'I was too scared to cycle the length of Britain but seeing as you've swum it has giving me the confidence to get on my bike and do it.'

After sorting through my inbox, one email catches my attention; it's one from Jez. The subject is 'all moored up'. I knew instantly what he was talking about. At the end of the swim Jez had emailed me to ask what I was doing with *Friday*. He wanted to know if I wanted to sell her to him. It was a hard decision as *Friday* had been such a huge part of my adventure, but after much thought I realised that I didn't have the skill or knowledge to get her back to her former glory and if one person did, it was Jez. After my arrival in John O'Groats, Jez then took *Friday* round to Wick to rest up for the winter. He went on to repair everything, sand her down, paint her and then sailed her through the Caledonian Canal. I was really sad to see her go but it's nice to know she is still in the family.

After the swim, Em was offered some great opportunities working for adventure magazines and still emails me to contribute pieces about things I'm up to. That's after she wrote about being the first woman to kayak the length of Britain of course.

Owain now runs his adventure media consultancy business, which he started after the swim. He also arranges the talks I do in schools, so I can hopefully inspire kids to think big and not listen to people who try to tell them what they are capable of.

Lou went back to her business Nomad Sailing to relieve Jim, her brother, after he held the fort for a lot longer than expected! I managed to go out on her amazing yacht for a day when the *Guardian* filmed a feature about my swim. It was a little bit nicer than *Friday* ...

I also finally reached my £10,000 target for War Child, most of it coming in after the swim. It was nice to see the total jumping up every time I did an interview and certainly made the long journeys rushing around worth it.

Swimming the length of Britain was the hardest thing I'll probably ever do, but it certainly has given me the confidence that, if I work really hard, surround myself with the right people and never give up, I can achieve whatever I put my mind to.

ACKNOWLEDGEMENTS

My family. Mum Babette, dad Tony and sister Kerry for always supporting me in my adventures. I've put you through hell over the years but you've always supported my decisions in life. Thank you.

My crew. Jez, Em, Owain and Lou. You guys made this adventure what is was. We had an incredible time together. Thank you for giving me so much of your time.

Sally at Speedo. Out of the 350 companies I approached, you were the only one who believed in the swim as much as I did and were willing to take the risk. It was a pleasure working with you and thank you for replying to all of my many emails.

Crowdfunders. Without all of you I couldn't have finished the swim. I've mentioned you all in the next few pages but

I wanted to single out one person. A huge thank you to Anthony Riches. You know why.

CROWDFUNDERS

A huge thank you to the following people for helping me finish the swim. I couldn't have done it without you.

Denise Adams

Tracey Apperley

Thomas Arbs

Liz Barraclough

Karah Bausch

H J Beales

Christine Bellamy

Rebecca Bennett

Keely Beresford

Ali Berry

Mathew Bevan

David Bickerstaff

Sylvia Boker-Price

Adam Boon

Joe Boyce

Stuart Bradburn

Neil Bridgstock

Jo Bridle

Heather Bright

Adam Bristowe

Poul Brix

Debbie Brown

Malcolm Burns

David Butler

Will Carnegie

Tracy Chapman

Jackie Cobell

Tristan Cochrane

Adam Colburn

Colin Constance

Annie Cooper

John Corvesor

John Coxon

Gabrielle Cross

Amy-Catherine Cunningham

Alan Curr

Sean Curran

H S R Davenport

Sadie Davies

David & Samantha Dewar

Dizmon

Tracy Doyle

Nelson Edwards

Verla Edwards

Mark Everard

Sean Fane

Steven Feeney

Philippe Flamand

Jonathan Ford

Alex Gaskell

Gary Gibbons

Izi Glover

Nicola Goodchild

Simon Griffiths

Georgie Guernsey

Rachel Hall

Robert Hall-McNair

Linus Halton

Monica Hardwick

Lesley Hargrave

Susan Harper

Philip Harris

Mrs A Harrison

Bee Heller

Darren Henwood

F Hickie

Desmond Hodgkiss

Gary Hurr

Tony Ingles

Katherine Irvine

Chris Jackson

Daniel Jarman

D Jones

Michael Jones

David Kay

Rupert Kelton

Leila Ken

Mark Kleanthous

Gwendolen A Lansley

Adam Latcham

Sarah Learoyd

Bruce Loxley

Martin MacGilp

James MacKeddie

Rob Macleod

George Mahood

Idai Makaya

Rich Manning

Alison Mason

Kevin Massey

Tim Matthews

Thomas Mcguire

Trev McKerlich

Ben Mckillop

Miss T McLean

Patrick McMaster

Ben Meakin

Phil Merritt

Laura Jane Millward

Tim Moss

Beth Mottart

Maxine Murray

Gordon Pare

Catherine Pickersgill

Phil Plant

Endless Pools

James Pope

David Randel

Rudd Rayns

Hilary Richardson

Anthony Riches

Steve Robarts

Sophie Roberts

Vikki Roberts

Paul Rodger

David Ross

Adrian Rotchell

John Scrooby

Derek Shipley

Susan Simpson

Bertie Smith

Ian Smith

Nathan Smith

Carolyne Somerset

Jon Stacey

Jason Stephens

Jeremy Stephenson

John Summerton

Paul Sunderland

Andrew Tee

David Thomson

Nicola Triggs

Malcolm Walker

John Warton

Caroline Watson

Chris Watts

Haydn Welch

Tom Wilde

Daniel Wilson

Pamela Wilson

John Wiltshire

Sarah Wood

Thomas Wornham